Using

the Internet with Your Mac

Using
the Internet with Your Mac

Todd Stauffer

Using the Internet with Your Mac

Library of Congress Catalog No.: 95-71431

ISBN: 0-7897-0665-2

97 96 95   6 5 4 3 2 1

Interpretation of the printing code: the rightmost double-digit number is the year of the book's printing; the rightmost single-digit number, the number of the book's printing. For example, a printing code of 95-1 shows that the first printing of the book occurred in 1995.

Screen reproductions in this book were created with Collage Complete from Inner Media, Inc., Hollis, NH.

Composed in *ITC Century*, *ITC Highlander* and *MCPdigital* by Que Corporation

Credits

President and Publisher
Roland Elgey

Associate Publisher
Stacy Hiquet

Editorial Services Director
Elizabeth Keaffaber

Managing Editor
Sandy Doell

Director of Marketing
Lynn E. Zingraf

Senior Series Editor
Chris Nelson

Publishing Manager
Jim Minatel

Acquisitions Manager
Cheryl D. Willoughby

Product Director
Oran Sands

Senior Editor
Nancy E. Sixsmith

Editor
Kelli Brooks

Assistant Product Marketing Manager
Kim Margolius

Technical Editors
Tobin Anthony
Pete Durso

Acquisitions Coordinator
Ruth Slates

Operations Coordinator
Patricia J. Brooks

Editorial Assistant
Andrea Duvall

Book Designer
Ruth Harvey

Cover Designer
Ruth Harvey

Production Team
Brian Buschkill
Jason Carr
Joan Evan
DiMonique Ford
Amy Gornik
Damon Jordan
Daryl Kessler
Bob LaRoche
Stephanie Layton
Julie Quinn
Michael Thomas
Chris Van Camp
Jody York

Indexer
Carol Sheehan

*To Katie. How long ago should I have said this?
Thanks for growing up with me. Thanks for being
such an unbending source of support, inspiration,
and enduring friendship. You are an exceptional
person…and a huge part of whatever success and
happiness I've known.*

About the Author

Todd Stauffer has been writing non-stop about computers and the computer industry since he graduated from Texas A&M University, where he studied a bizarre combination of English literature, Management Information Systems, and entirely too much golf. A die-hard fan of the Macintosh, Todd is author of *Using Your Mac, Easy America Online* and co-author of *Special Edition Using the Internet With Your Macintosh*—all Que publications.

Todd has recently finished a stint as editor of *Texas Computing Magazine* and is currently a freelance writer and author, having a heck of a time deciding whether to live in Dallas or Colorado Springs. He has worked previously as an advertising, technical, and magazine writer—all in the computer industry. Todd can be reached by Internet e-mail at **TStauffer@aol.com**.

Acknowledgments

There's got to be something clever I can say about how the word *dead*line seems so apt here, but I can't think of one because I desperately need sleep. A tilt of my official-logo Dallas Cowboys ballcap goes to Que Product Director, Oran Sands, and Senior Editor, Nancy Sixsmith, for another editing job done exceptionally good-ly.

I feel only the humblest gratitude toward Cheryl Willoughby, Que Acquisitions Manager *extraordinaire* (and a truly beautiful person). I imagine you've been biting pretty hard on your tongue as chapters rolled…slowly…in, and I thank you for your patience.

Special thanks go to my personal Macintosh expert, David Filbey. Once again, I've been taught some of the technical underpinnings directly from the smartest guy I know—saving me from actually sitting down and (gasp!) reading it somewhere. I also have to thank David for helping me get my hands on the Power Macintosh that currently makes my desk so darned useful. (David, by the way, is a very handsome man.)

Thanks to Chris Stauffer (my ruggedly good-looking father) for understanding a last-minute change in plans and putting up with my continued experimentation in long-term unemployment. Golf soon, sir.

On top of all that, I'd like to thank another group of stunningly attractive people for putting up with me, making sure I stayed warm, dry, and well-fed for the duration. I'd especially like to thank Steven Blount (charming and chistled), Katherine Mitchell (sinuous and seemly), and Amy White (comely and captivating).

Personal thanks to Kristin Doll (radiance personified) for letting me vent, helping me cope, and buying me a beer every now and again. I know I'm impossible to get along with when I'm writing…thanks for doing it anyway.

We'd Like to Hear from You!

As part of our continuing effort to produce books of the highest possible quality, Que would like to hear your comments. To stay competitive, we *really* want you, as a computer book reader and user, to let us know what you like or dislike most about this book or other Que products.

You can mail comments, ideas, or suggestions for improving future editions to the address below, or send us a fax at (317) 581-4663. For the online inclined, Macmillan Computer Publishing has a forum on CompuServe (type **GO QUEBOOKS** at any prompt) through which our staff and authors are available for questions and comments. The address of our Internet site is **http://www.mcp.com** (World Wide Web).

In addition to exploring our forum, please feel free to contact me personally to discuss your opinions of this book: I'm **osands@que.mcp.com** on the Internet.

Thanks in advance—your comments will help us to continue publishing the best books available on computer topics in today's market.

Oran Sands
Product Development Specialist
Que Corporation
201 W. 103rd Street
Indianapolis, Indiana 46290
USA

Contents at a Glance

Table of Contents

Part II: Getting and Sending E-mail

Part IV: News and Talk

Introduction

We had computers connected to the Internet when I was in college—
although, at the time, I had no idea what good that could do anybody. I knew
I could send electronic mail (e-mail) messages to people at other colleges—
or even to folks at NASA. But I didn't know anybody at NASA. It wasn't until I
realized I could download updates to my favorite games that I even gave the
Internet a second thought.

But that was before. Sure—at one point the Internet was only significant to a
select handful of academics and scientists, busily cutting things open and
sticking them to other things, and chatting about it in Latin. But not anymore.
The Internet has exploded in growth over the last few years, making it the
most significant development in computing since the personal computer
came on the scene in the late 1970s.

And what a development! As more and more folks take to the Internet, it
becomes increasingly easy to use—and more useful. Now you can send
e-mail to tens of millions of people around the world! You can chat in "live"
group forums on almost any topic imaginable. You can send and receive
messages from thousands of folks who share your hobbies or profession.
You can even access online catalogs and do your shopping from home!

But the best part is that you get to do all of this with the greatest computer
ever conceived—a Macintosh. Life couldn't be better. As the Internet has
continued to grow in popularity, so have the number of Macintosh users on
the Internet. And the number of easy Mac-based ways to get on the Internet
have increased, too.

Enter *Using the Internet with Your Mac*. In these pages, I've made every
attempt to make getting on the Internet as easy as it was to set up and learn
how to use your Macintosh. If you agree with me that the Mac is a well-
designed, intuitive computer, then hopefully you'll agree that this book was
crafted with the same, exact intentions.

Why should I use this book?

My first priority in writing this book was to *get to the point* in a friendly and enjoyable way. I hope you'll find that I haven't talked about anything that isn't of particular interest to the Mac-based Internet user. Many books try to be all things to all people—talking about boring things like UNIX commands, DOS programs, and old, outdated ways to connect to the Internet.

Not here, amigo. We're getting right to the meat of the matter—how to connect to the Internet in the most efficient and effective way with a Macintosh. I recommend *only* the best programs, *only* the easiest solutions, and *only* the most intuitive commands.

On top of that, there is no unexplained techno-babble. Whenever I noticed a word creeping into the text that you might not have found in a *Webster's* at least twenty years ago, I nixed it. Cut it right out. If I couldn't do that—if it's the only word I could use—then I yanked it out of the text and stuck it in a special box with its definition. When we're through with it, we can easily toss it on the ground and stomp on it. Real hard.

How to use this book

Using the Internet with Your Mac was designed to start out with the essentials of understanding what the Internet is and how you get connected. Then it moves on to more in-depth discussions of the various things you can *do* once you're connected to the Internet.

Throughout the text I've tried to be lighthearted and witty, making the book (hopefully) an enjoyable read from cover to cover. But I also know that no one wants to read a computer book that way. I sure don't. So, each chapter is an all-inclusive lesson, complete with a roadmap of questions at the beginning and clearly marked section heads throughout the text.

The next few paragraphs describe what's in each of the sections.

Part I: Welcome to the Internet

After a brief introduction to the Internet, I explain the best and most cost-effective ways for a typical Macintosh user to connect to the Internet. While you won't find much in these chapters about text-only accounts and outdated e-mail systems, I do talk about the exciting new developments in online services and graphical World Wide Web access.

Part II: Getting and Sending E-mail

Here, we'll take a look at the easiest ways to access Internet electronic mail—one of the most popular reasons for getting Internet access. I'll show you how to use the most useful Macintosh-based programs to send e-mail messages, read and respond to messages, and manage your e-mail.

Part III: Finding Files and Getting Them

In this section, we concentrate on finding and transferring files to and from your Macintosh. The Internet is full of interesting places to find programs, documents and even system software for your Macintosh. If you'd like to beat the Jones to the latest software, read on.

Part IV: News and Talk

If you've got a hobby that somebody else has, too, then there's a good chance that you can talk about it in UseNet discussion groups. With upwards of 10,000 different topic areas and millions of active participants, UseNet is a very popular way to exchange thoughts, ideas, research, business tips, advice…and even the occasional insult. Plus, we spend a special chapter talking about "live" chat groups on the Internet!

Part V: The World Wide Web

Day by day, the World Wide Web becomes more exciting and enticing to new users. If you want to *surf* the Internet, this is where it happens. We'll quickly get you up-and-running with the best programs for accessing the World Wide Web. Then I'll even show you how to create your own World Wide Web presence for yourself or your business—in fewer than 20 pages!

What the Internet and this book have in common

The Internet is exploding into more and more people's homes on a daily basis, just as this book is hitting the newsstands and bookstores. I've made every effort to give you only the most up-to-date and useful information for using the Internet with your Mac.

Pick up another Internet book and see if it talks about the Mac. It does? Does it talk about UNIX, too? Or DOS? Or Windows?! Wrong book! Just like the Internet, this book was designed to cover it all...from e-mail and "live" discussions, to searching on the Internet and accessing the multimedia of the World Wide Web.

But it's also been designed to work only for Mac users. Period. To use this book, you've got to have a Macintosh and a desire to learn. Again, like the Internet, we get to pick our own little corner of the world where we can chat about the things that interest us—in our own lingo. We're Mac users, so that's what we'll talk about. Let's go!

Special elements

Each chapter of *Using the Internet with your Mac* has special elements to help you move more quickly to the information you need. These elements let you decide how much or how little you want to know on a given subject. Here's a quick breakdown:

 TIP   **Tips are where you'll get shortcuts, often-overlooked ideas, or** quick ways to remember things. Even if you basically understand the concept a chapter is presenting, you might still want to scan the tips for helpful advice.

Sidebars are things you don't need to know!

Sometimes I get carried away and just can't stop typing all of these interesting Internet things that keep pouring through my head. I get paid per page, so there's no way I'm throwing that stuff out!

But if it's something you don't need to know to survive, I'll put it in a sidebar. Just read the ones that interest you and completely ignore the ones that don't. For the most part, missing every sidebar shouldn't affect your ability to access the Internet. But reading them may enhance your appreciation for it!

CAUTION **Just about everyone should read these. If there's a chance that** you'll lose data, waste time, or otherwise threaten your Internet experience, I've put it in a **caution**. The Internet can feel a little lawless at times, and I'll try to warn you when things could get messy.

 Plain English, please!

Plain English, please! notes are where I'll define computer-nerd lingo that I'm forced to use to explain something. If you already know a word, just skip the definition and keep reading.

 Q&A *What's a Q&A?*

These are questions (with the answers) I've heard often from folks trying to get connected to the Internet with their Macs. Usually these are trouble-shooting tips and other advice for getting yourself out of jams.

Screen captures in each chapter help you understand a process or example that the text describes. And if you're fooling around with the Internet while you read, you can compare what you got with what I got, as shown in a given figure.

A `special typeface` shows what you see on the screen. If you see **boldface** you know it's an Internet address, an important new term, or something you type in.

The last word

In *Using the Internet with Your Mac*, you'll learn just about everything you need to know to get a solid head start on using most of what's possible on the Internet. But I also want you to consider sending e-mail to me, Todd Stauffer, the author of this book. My most reliable e-mail address is **TStauffer@aol.com.** *Do not hesitate* to send me any questions, concerns, confusions, or criticisms you have concerning the text that follows. If you happen to be thrilled about the book, I'd be thrilled to hear about that, too. The only thing I ask is that you *don't* use me just to test your e-mail program…there are other ways to test it. That said, please send me *anything* else.

Now, let's hit the Internet running with the most powerful communications tool ever conceived…your Macintosh!

1

What is the Internet?

● **In this chapter:**

● What's so interesting about the Internet?

● Why would I want to use the Internet?

● How the Internet got its start

● How do I use menus in Windows?

● What's a computer network?

● Why it isn't important to know how the Internet works

The Internet is both the single most amazing information tool in history—and an even bigger waste of time than television! . . . . ▶

What is the Internet? There are many ways to answer that question. I'll pick two answers for now, although it will take us the rest of the book to explore this issue entirely. Let's start with a philosophical answer, then follow with a technical one.

The Internet is clearly the most important development in the world of computers since the laser printer revolutionized publishing in the 1980s. It's literally a revolutionary way to communicate with people all around the world, and share information in a way more rich and informative than ever before. And, above all, the Internet is interactive and fun—it's mass media that allows you to get involved. And that interactivity, for the most part, is what makes it interesting.

But *what* is it, exactly? **Internet** is the word most often used to describe a huge collection of computers around the world, connected to each other by cables or phone lines that allow them to communicate. Generally, computers are connected in smaller regional groups, then are given a common connection to a global infrastructure that allows them to communicate with other computers around the world. In essence, the Internet is a planetary version of a computer network, not completely unlike the network that may connect computers in an office or school building to one another.

 Plain English, please!

You have a computer **network** when you connect two or more computers by cables or phone lines that let them share information. The Internet is a huge computer network, allowing you to share digital information with computers around the world. **"**

So you've heard of the Internet...

Or, at least, I imagine you have. TV commercials, best-selling novels, sports simulcasts, and grunge-rock concerts have all included references to the Internet. Infomercials and late-night newscasts reference their e-mail addresses. Celebrities are creating places on the Internet for you to learn more about them or send them fan mail. And, in a very public move, the White House (**http://www.whitehouse.gov**) jumped on the Internet a few years ago (see fig. 1.1).

TIP **Don't let the weird bold lettering get you down. That's an address** on the Internet, written in sort of a goofy shorthand. Soon these addresses will make more sense than the instructions on a long distance calling card.

Fig. 1.1

Here's the White House base of operations on the Internet. From here, you can send electronic mail to the First Family, and check the latest White House press releases, speeches, tour information, and much more.

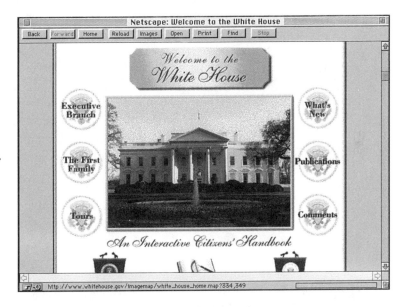

It's undeniable that the Internet is a popular phenomenon of *some sort*. In fact, the Internet's even been given that golden calf of recognition in American culture that suggests it has truly come of age…it's been in the movies. Popular cinematic thrillers have been pretty gung-ho about this technology in the last year or two, and are feeding on the curiosity that most folks seem to feel about the Internet.

But hearing about something and experiencing it are two radically different things. It's a little like that decade of my life that I spent thinking *The Manchurian Candidate* was a movie about some sort of precommunist uprising in the Far East. (What I thought Frank Sinatra was doing in it is still a mystery.) Just hearing about something is about enough to make it monolithic and completely confusing, if there isn't some explanation to go along. So let's just move straight to the tough questions.

What good is the Internet?

How about asking "What good is television?" You'll probably get as many answers about television as there are people. *No good at all. Sports only. The perfect babysitter. Global information source. The only way to watch independent foreign films on your VCR.*

Info tool or waste of time?

The Internet is both more useful than television and six times more effective for sleep deprivation. A session with the Internet can be an amazing waste of time. It can also be the single most powerful information tool on your desk. Like television, the usefulness of the Internet sort of depends on how you use it.

- See something you disagree with on the nightly newscast? You can send a comment directly to the the Cable News Network (CNN) at **cnn.feedback@cnn.com**.

- In a UFO state of mind? Even if you can't take your new furry friends home to mother, you might find some sympathetic souls at **alt.alien.visitors.**

- Looking for a new car? Most popular car companies have some sort of presence on the Internet, like Saturn's virtual showroom at **http://www.saturncars.com/** (see fig. 1.2).

- Ready to break out on your own? The Small Business Resource Center is waiting to help you at **http://www.webcom.com/~seaquest/welcome.html**.

- Are you a grade school teacher seeking colleagues around the country? Pick your specialty, then head over to the discussions in the **k12.ed.*** discussion groups (see fig. 1.3).

Fig. 1.2

The Saturn virtual showroom. Here you can get pictures and information about Saturn's cars, its history, and more...all on the Internet.

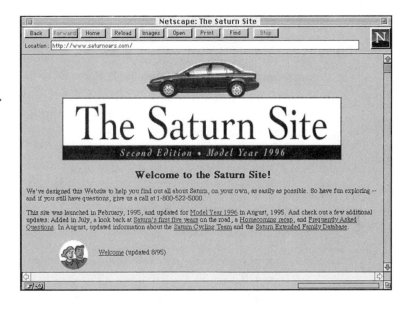

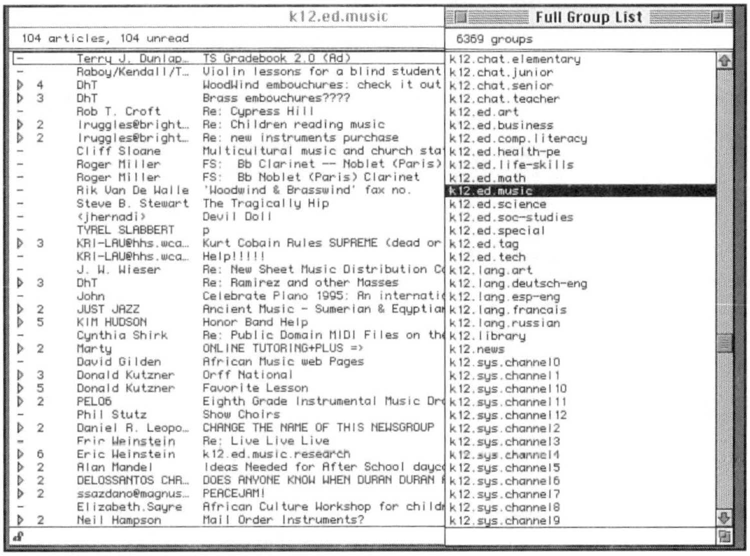

Fig. 1.3

Using a program called NewsWatcher, you have access to thousands of discussion groups on the Internet, including these groups that cover grade school education.

There's amazing variety in the things you can do, see, hear, and read about on the Internet. It's a brand-new public medium with some of the visual power of television, the informational value of reference books, and the timeliness of newspapers, magazines, and radio. You can be entertained, enlightened, taught, annoyed, and bored on the Internet. The magical part is that, unlike television, it's interactive. That means you get to entertain, enlighten, teach, annoy, and bore other people, too.

The range of things to do

Frankly, it's tough to touch on everything that's possible to do on the Internet. I'll start by hitting some of the high points, although it would take more than this chapter to be comprehensive.

- *Communicate with friends.* E-mail is easily the most popular use of the Internet. In fact, like word processing, electronic mail (see fig. 1.4) is an incredibly popular reason for purchasing a computer to begin with. Only a fax machine can occasionally rival e-mail for its speed—and e-mail doesn't use any paper.

Fig. 1.4

Using a program on your Macintosh, you can send an electronic mail message to millions of people around the world. Clearly, this capability has the power to eventually replace much of the postal correspondence of the past.

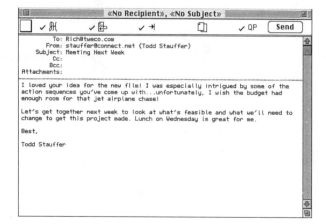

- *Participate in discussion groups.* Another very popular use of the Internet is to participate in electronic discussion groups. Using the proper computer application and an Internet connection, you can get access to over 15,000 different topic areas, where nearly anything imaginable—from pop culture to populists movements in third world countries—is discussed.

- *Conduct business.* Certain areas on the Internet allow you to advertise your product or service, take orders, or receive customer feedback. Other areas offer financial information and services, banking services, advice, consultation, industry reports, relevant news stories, and much more.

- *Research.* Universities have long been a part of the Internet, and their resources are often the most fully developed. An entire world of papers, reports, discussions, presentations, library catalogs, studies, histories, and accounts are available in nearly every science and art (see fig. 1.5).

Fig. 1.5
Accessing the University of Colorado on the Internet opens up much of that institution's learning and research.

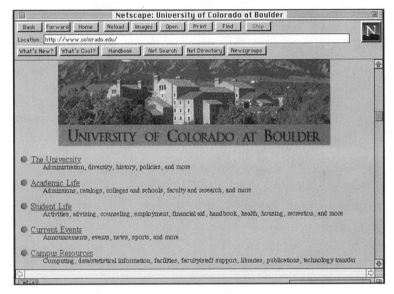

- *Shop.* The stunning interest in the Internet shown by corporate America over the last few years has resulted in tons of resources for consumer awareness online. From safety reports to online boutiques, both the wary shopper and the window shopper can find what they want.

- *Play games.* The role-playing adventurer and the strategist will be especially encouraged by what's available on the Internet. Since the Internet has long been a haunt of college students, there are many sophisticated text-based answers—and a few creative graphical solutions.

- *Be an info-junkie.* Do you follow the world news, know absolutely everything there is to know about Early Cartwrighting, or do you have some other most-of-the-time hobby? If anyone else does, too, then there's a place to discuss it and learn more about it on the Internet.

- *Get technical support.* The Internet is very computer-centric, as you may have guessed. There's a decent chance that you'll find lawnmower maintenance tips online—but you can be almost sure that someone can answer a question you have about your Mac or its components (see fig. 1.6). Even if you can't get in touch with the computer company, more than likely there's someone out there who's had your same problem.

Fig. 1.6

Here's part of Apple Computer, Inc.'s presence on the Internet. As a user, you can get answers to technical questions, shop for new products, get updated system software, and much more.

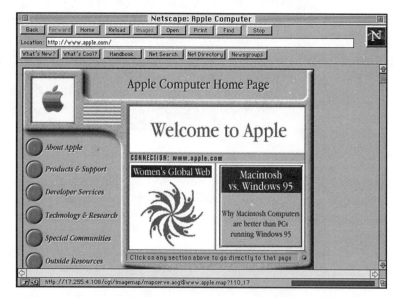

- *Transfer files.* One of the more popular uses for the Internet is the distribution of software updates and shareware programs by programmers, software companies, and other computer companies. If you've ever wanted to find a small, reliable program to perform some task on your Mac, you'll find it somewhere on the Internet.

Plain English, please!

Shareware refers to computer programs that you can try and test on your Mac before you buy them. Shareware is often written by individuals who market their own programs online. Generally, you are required to send a modest payment to the author (usually between $5 and $50) to continue using the program after a few days or weeks. **99**

Need more reasons to use the Internet? Soon you'll find them yourself. All you'll need is a little time, the right tools, and as much caffeine as your body can take.

How the Internet works...and why we don't care

You'll often hear the Internet referred to as the "Information Superhighway" and, while the highway metaphor has been overused and become clichéd, it still works.

The entire Internet is composed of tens of millions of computers connected together in order to exchange information. But, like the National Highway System, there are huge highways and there are small winding backroads.

How information moves on the Internet

Let's say you want to get from wherever you live to Houston (or, if you actually live in Houston, you want to visit some other folks who aren't lucky enough to live in such a fine metropolis). You start out in your driveway, and turn onto residential roads. These lead into local thoroughfares or larger surface streets. From there, you might move on to local highways or state highways. And finally, for the cross-country trip, you'll probably speed down an interstate highway.

Information travels on the Internet in a similar fashion. Send something from your computer to a computer in Houston and the information will start out on a relatively small connection (for example, your phone line), move on to a larger connection (your local Internet provider) and speed down the main Internet connections (the Internet's highest-speed lines, called its **backbone**) until it gets close to Houston. Then it will reverse the process to reach a particular computer.

Q&A   *How can an Internet connection be larger or smaller?*

What I really mean by larger or smaller is: *how much information can pass through a particular connection every second?* The larger the connection, the faster the transmission, since more data can get through at one time. If I'm sending you an entire page of text, I'd rather be using a page-per-second connection instead of a word-per-second connection.

Of course, on the Internet, moving around the world takes seconds…not hours or days as does driving. But time is still important, because it takes time for information to get across the Internet from one computer to another. The more information you try to transfer over the Internet, the longer it will take.

Why we don't care

Often enough, you'll hear new Internet users (called **newbies** in Internet lingo) say something along the lines of "I'm going to go use the Internet." Actually, that statement really is fairly useless. It's about as interesting as saying "I'm going to go use the International Telephone System." It's not really important how you make the call, but with whom you're going to chat (see fig. 1.7).

Fig. 1.7

In fact, you can "chat" (by typing on the keyboard) with people around the world via the Internet.

```
1: macintosh: come tease the ops..see which finger yo
     Op.       i  n  m  s  p
 screen, is there a way to lock them somewhere else, such as the left side?
<Tiger> Marathon
<DK> I want to set up my PPC 7100 as a mail machine (3 accounts or so...nothing
major). Anyone know how to do this and what software I need?
<sabi> ok fk - dhooy
*** Signoff: wuquq (Read error: 54 (Connection reset by peer))
<kidblast> doubster: How that is cheap.
<bizzy> hehe
<CPC> Win95 sucks. It was a big promotional thing.
<sabi> dk - use AIMS http://abs.apple.com/mailserver.html/
<coool> anyone know of a net mounting program?
<sabi> get rid of that trailing slash - sorry
<sabi> coool - what do you mean?
<doubting> me, too
<jrc> Anyone know how to config MacPPP for dynamic IPs?
<doubtster> Kidblast, my company site licensed the s/w
<DK> sabi: is that where I can get the software to get this going?
*** Tiger has left channel #macintosh
<doubting> My company got a site license, too
<koan> anyone wanna try homer paint ?
<sabi> jrc - you dont do it with MacPPP, just with Mactcp, use "server"
 addressing
<aristotle> apple should take a look at Windows Marketing
<CPC> What was that tomas??
*** Tiger has joined channel #macintosh
<Irving> gee, imagine that.
*** Signoff: _Chunk_ (adios)
*** Action: Irving snickers
<aristotle> apple's marketing sucks
```

The Internet itself really refers to the hardware—the computers and wiring—that transmit the data. But who really cares how? What's important on the Internet are the different **services,** or types of electronic communication available on the Internet. Electronic mail, for instance, is a type of Internet service that conforms to certain standards and protocols.

The telephone system offers many different services. You can send a fax message over phone lines. You can dial an automatic information service and use touch-tones to buy sports tickets or access weather information. Or you can call a good friend and chat about love lost. But it's all accomplished over the same phone lines.

On the Internet, you can send e-mail, join discussion groups, transfer documents or programs, watch electronic movies, or listen to digital sounds. It all happens over the same Internet connections…but in different ways. These are the services available on the Internet, and, at least to me, they're much more important than the wires and chips that make up the Internet. That's why we'll talk in depth about these services in Chapter 2 (and nearly every subsequent chapter, for that matter).

Ancient Internet history (that you can probably live without)

Late in 1969, the first four nodes of an interesting little computer network—called ARPANET—were installed in supercomputers at major research centers. Named after the Advanced Research Projects Agency of the Department of Defense, this experimental network began to thrive. In 1971, there were fifteen nodes connected over the ARPANET, and computer users around the country could share time on other computers for running programs and communicating over long distances.

Continued communications in wartime

ARPANET's original charter was to be a computer network between major centers of computing power that could survive nearly any military attack by an enemy of the United States. Based on "packet-switching" technology, the network had no central authority or standardized paths for data. Instead, information was broken up into smaller packets, and each packet was sent, independently of the others, along varying paths. So, if part of the network was taken out by an atomic bomb, natural disaster or such, the message packets could still get through—they'd just be rerouted.

As more and more computers were connected to ARPANET, however, it was discovered that this sort of network was a wonderful excuse for people to collaborate professionally, compare findings, or even chat socially. At the same time, everybody's computers were becoming more powerful, and it was less important to access supercomputers over ARPANET. The need to share programs and computer power shifted to the need to share information.

Over time, the network became increasingly decentralized and increasingly useful as more people and computers were connected. In the early 1980s, anarchy reigned supreme enough that the military spun off its own more "secure" network and handed the ARPANET to academics and others.

Next step—the NSFNET

In 1984, the National Science Foundation (NSF) decided to revamp the concept of the ARPANET by connecting the most amazing supercomputers of the time through very high-speed connections, using the same protocols as ARPANET. This updated structure formed a high-speed "backbone" called the NSFNET. This backbone was the main skeleton for expansion of the Internet, as smaller networks connected to the NSFNET to communicate with others around the world.

In subsequent years, the NSFNET was upgraded to higher and higher speeds, as more and more people connected computers to it. Throughout the late 1980s, the Internet grew as a popular way to communicate from universities and government entities. In the early 1990s, it began to explode with users from the corporate world and other organizations.

Eventually, as the backbone became too unwieldy for the NSF to manage, it awarded maintenance of the NSFNET to computing and telecommunications companies. At the same time, more commercial entities started building their own high-speed connections to the Internet, allowing them to sell access through private channels—through local Internet providers in cities around the U.S.

The Internet as it stands

The mid-1990s have seen the commercialization of the Internet that was desperately feared by Internet users and advocates fewer than five years ago. But the anarchy and freedom of the Internet continues, in spite of calls to arms for government control of encryption, legislation against "adult" themes on the Internet, highly-publicized "hacking," and other complaints.

And it seems likely that the Internet will continue to grow and thrive in some form or another. Even as alternative, more proprietary networks are being kicked around by telephone giants and cable television conglomerates, it appears that even these solutions will only build on the current theories behind the Internet. Just as most major online services (like America Online and eWorld) have eventually provided Internet access, so, it seems, will other newcomers provide such access as new communications tools emerge.

You get that for which you pay

Even just a few years ago it was difficult, if not impossible, to get an Internet connection to a typical household. As modems and Local Area Networks were getting off the ground, the technology for Internet connections was more or less the domain of large universities and government institutions.

Is the Internet the "Information Superhighway?"

This can get pretty confusing, for two reasons. First, the popular media and national leaders tend to throw around catch-phrases like "the Information Superhighway" long after any meaning they may have once had has been obliterated by misuse and repetition. Second, the metaphor of a highway system is useful in describing the Internet and it's difficult to get away from.

As I understand it, the Internet is not the "Information Superhighway" pictured by Vice President Al Gore and others, although the Internet may be a good model and testbed for this concept. The Information Superhighway concept concentrates more on the idea of a national digital infrastructure...hardware that would replace or build upon the wires that currently run their way into most people's homes.

With this infrastructure, various new methods for distributing information digitally would become infinitely more practical. The idea is that soon you'll have a high-speed digital phone line coming into your house, or perhaps your cable box will become more of a computer than a descrambler.

In any case, the bulk of the Information Superhighway discussion seems to concentrate on merging existing technologies—like computer networks, televisions, and telephones—so that tangible benefits are seen by the bulk of the population.

These benefits will range from practical teleconferencing ("video phones") to movies-on-demand systems and interactive television. Who knows, maybe one day you'll be able to participate in your favorite game show, or dial up Grandma and *show* her newborn grandchild to her.

While these things are possible or will be possible in the near future across the Internet, some sort of initiative is necessary if it's going to be a widespread phenomenon; even the currently robust Internet backbone can't handle the traffic required for TV-quality video and a national telephone system.

The mere existence of this book shows that this is no longer the case. Private, profit-oriented Internet Service Provider (ISP) companies have sprung up around the country, ready to give you a simple solution to hooking your personal computer into the Internet. And help for doing that is exactly what's coming up next in these pages, too.

 Plain English, please!

An **Internet Service Provider (ISP)** is a company or organization that establishes a high-speed link to the Internet, then sets up the appropriate computers and phone lines to allow individuals to access the Internet. Some local government agencies and universities act as ISPs, but many are for-profit companies.

Understanding how the Internet came to be will help you understand some of its nuances, frustrations, and traditions. It will also explain why there seems to be an overwhelming amount of some types of information, but less of others. Finally, it makes it clear why the Internet is such an explosive topic in popular media and culture. It may be nearly 30 years old—but, at least to the person on the street, it's still the "latest thing."

Everything You Need to Know About the Internet in 10 Pages!

● **In this chapter:**

- **The seven services of the Internet**

- **Understanding Internet addresses**

- **What is a host computer on the Internet?**

- **What's TCP/IP?**

- **How will my Mac work on the Internet?**

There are seven basic Internet services to play with. Understand these and you're on your way to "Internaut" status! . . . . ▸

With a completely decked-out entertainment system at home, you can watch cable, watch broadcast TV, watch videotapes, listen to the radio, listen to CDs, or listen to cassettes. If you're like me, you probably have at least four universal remote controls, none of which manage to drive more than two components. That's a lot like a computer connected to the Internet.

It's difficult to choose a word that perfectly describes the different aspects of the Internet. For lack of something better, I'll call them "services." The Internet has seven basic services, and each uses slightly different computer protocols and techniques for disseminating information. But don't let the word "service" confuse you…I could just as easily say something like "medium" or "aspect." Try to keep in mind that the difference between Internet services are similar to the differences between television and radio.

The seven services of the Internet

We've actually discussed these already in the first chapter, but without their proper names. Now let's put the names to each service. And, don't worry if the distinctions seem a bit fuzzy—the bulk of this book discusses the differences between the Internet services.

- **Internet e-mail.** Electronic mail is the staple of the Internet revolution. Tying into this service allows you to send an electronic message to most anyone with a computer and a modem or network connection. Internet e-mail is primarily text-based, so you won't come across many digital photos or sounds in an e-mail message.

- **UseNet newsgroups.** These are the "discussion groups" on the Internet. There are currently over 15,000 topics in UseNet's groups, and most of them are available to Macintosh users with a typical Internet connection. It's here, more than anywhere else, where lively and interactive discussion takes place with the many folks on the Internet.

- **FTP.** Named for the File Transfer Protocol that it uses, FTP service is the method by which documents and programs are transferred on the Internet. If you've ever downloaded a program from an online service like eWorld or America Online, then you're familiar with the idea behind FTP.

❝ *Plain English, please!*

When you **download** a file, you bring that file across a modem or network connection to your computer, where it is saved to your hard drive. You can download a file from your work to your house, for instance, or from any distant computer—like a computer on the Internet—to yours. **Uploading** is the reverse: sending a file from your computer across a modem or network connection to another computer. ❞

- **Gopher.** Gopher is a menu-based system for information retrieval. Even the name suggests that you're "digging" for information through a series of tunnels. The main idea is, you start with a menu, like the one in figure 2.1. From there, you decide which menu item to choose next to get the information you want. It's like the system that works your bank's ATM machine. Each choice you make brings you closer to your goal.

Fig. 2.1
Gopher is used primarily by universities and other organizations to present text-based documents like scientific papers, press releases, news articles, policies, and similar items.

In the resulting menu, you can dig even deeper.

Choosing an item in this menu narrows the choice.

- **The World Wide Web.** Easily the most visual and popular service on the Internet, the World Wide Web (WWW, W3, or Web, for short) is what most people talk about when they mention the Internet. Incorporating many of the other services mentioned previously, the Web also allows for the transmission of graphics, sounds, animations, and even digital movies (see fig. 2.2). Its basic role is similar to Gopher; it is used primarily for "electronic publishing," but its presentation and capabilities have caused it to grow in popularity, while Gopher seems steadily to decline in use.

Text is still the basic communicator.

But the Web also allows graphics.

Fig. 2.2
The Web is the fastest-growing service on the Internet, basically due to its strengths as a medium for corporate advertising and customer service. Aside from e-mail, the Web is the most compelling reason that many people seek Internet access.

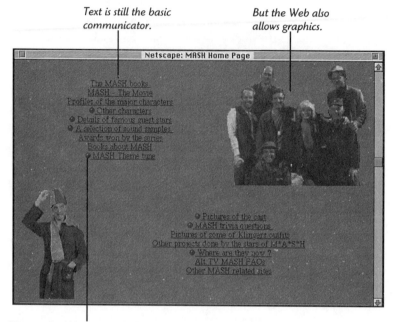

Plus sounds, video, and other more exciting ways to communicate.

- **Internet Relay Chat (IRC).** For all intents and purposes, IRC is like a keyboard-based CB-radio. The IRC service lets people around the world get together to "chat" back and forth as quickly as they can type their messages. If the Internet were a physical town, then IRC would be the coffee shop.

- **Telnet.** Although difficult to classify as a "service," Telnet is the standard by which the Internet allows one computer to run programs on another computer. It's through a Telnet program that your Mac can "log on" and run a database search at the downtown library, for instance.

Some Internet basics

So, how do we take advantage of all of these different services? First, we need to understand some basic concepts. For the most part, computers and people on the Internet are identified by "addresses," not completely unlike your home address.

The Internet e-mail address

For sending an e-mail message, an Internet address is absolutely essential. An address makes logical sense, fortunately, and sometimes it can even tell you something about a person or a computer. All addresses on the Internet follow a system called the **Domain Name System**. Let's look at a sample address—mine:

tstauffer@aol.com

 TIP When you read an Internet address aloud, say "at" for the @ symbol and "dot" for each period. My address would read "t-stauffer-at-a-o-l-dot-com."

I actually have a couple of different Internet e-mail addresses, based on the different ways I connect to the Internet. This one happens to be my America Online account, where I check my e-mail most often. So how does the address break down?

From the left, the address starts with my user name on America Online followed by the at symbol (**@**). To the right of the symbol is **aol**, which is the **subdomain name** for America Online. That is followed by a **.** and the **first level domain, com** which means that America Online is considered a commercial entity on the Internet.

 Plain English, please!

Whenever a company, organization, school, or network provider creates a presence on the Internet, it is given a **domain name**. This consists of both the subdomain and first level domain names. Actually, the Internet uses numbers to identify computers, but this name system makes it easier for people to remember addresses. **"**

Depending on how many computers are at a particular location, and how those computers are organized for the Internet, the address can be longer than mine. In general, Internet e-mail addresses look something like this:

username@host.subdomain.first-level-domain

TIP **You can identify Internet addresses by their first level domain** names: **.com** for commercial, **.edu** for education, **.mil** for military, **.gov** for government, **.org** for organization, and two letters, which generally denote a country other than the U.S. (like **.fr** for France).

Notice that my address didn't have a "host" section, since America Online's Internet mail system doesn't require one. I used to have an address at Texas A&M University, my alma mater and a previous employer, which was something like this:

stau3976@isc.tamu.edu

Notice that the format is similar: username, then the at symbol (@), followed by something new…the host name **isc** happens to stand for the Institute of Scientific Computation, a department at Texas A&M University. Since the university has tons of different computers and networks on campus—and people can often have more than one Internet account—it's important to specify the host machine where an individual is located.

 Plain English, please!

What's a **host**? For now, a host is simply any computer that you can directly access on the Internet. This includes a computer that supports users, like the host **aol.com** or **isc.tamu.edu.**

Generally you won't be forced to decide whether or not to include a host name—in fact, it's a little like an apartment number. If you need to use it, then it's part of the address. If it's not part of the address, don't worry about it.

Who's hosting this party?

Let's look at the idea of an Internet host more carefully. A host is not only a computer that lets its users access the Internet, it's also any computer that you, as a user, can get information *from*. Host computers can be both jumping-off points for some Internet users and destinations for others.

Here's an example:

support.apple.com

On the Internet, Apple Computer, Inc., has a host computer named **support.apple.com**. Since I don't have an account there, I'm not sure whether that computer is used to allow Apple employees access to the Internet. I do know, however, that that particular host is available for me to access information on Apple products (see fig. 2.3).

Fig. 2.3
support.apple.com is the host name for one of Apple Computer's main information sources on the Internet.

Notice the host name.

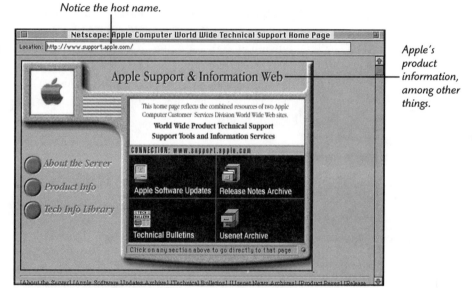

Apple's product information, among other things.

Okay, one more quick distinction. Just because a host has a single domain name, like **support.apple.com**, it doesn't necessarily mean there is only one computer associated with that name. Notice again in figure 2.2 that the full Internet address we accessed is **www.support.apple.com**, which is the complete name for one of Apple's server computers for its World Wide Web presence. More than likely, this address finally represents a particular server computer within a group of computers that all fall in the host domain of **support.apple.com**.

Plain English, please!

A **server** is a computer that provides information on a network or on the Internet. Different "server" applications are required to present different types of information on the Internet. These might include Web servers, FTP servers, and e-mail servers. **"**

TCP/IP: the language of the Internet

One thing that developed early in the growth of the Internet was a need for a common language that would allow computers from different companies to communicate with one another. If you've ever worked in an office with both Macintosh and IBM-compatible (PC) computers, you know this can be difficult—and Macs and PCs are relatively similar. On the Internet, Macs, PCs, UNIX workstations, minicomputers, and mainframes all need to be able to talk to one another.

When is a host a server?

Ever been to a really swarmy cocktail party? At almost any party, you'll probably have a "host" and you'll have "servers." Depending on the size of the party (and the snootiness factor of the guest list), your host may also be the server, or the host may hire a catering service or use the house's staff as "servers." Host and waitstaff may be one and the same, or they may be many different people, coordinated by the host.

Well, in the computer world, servers are computers designed to send and receive information on a network. If you work in a fairly high-tech office, you probably have an office network with a "server" in the backroom, where all of your shared electronic files are stored. The Internet works in a similar way.

At a *small* Internet site, the host and the server computer may be the same. If the computer is relatively sophisticated, it can actually serve many different types of information. It can act as a Web server, FTP server, Gopher server, mail server, and more...simultaneously.

But, in our example with Apple Computer, that company handles so many requests for information on the Internet that they more than likely have a dedicated computer for each type of server. And in some cases, they may have more than one server for each type of information. Since they throw relatively large "parties" on the Internet, Apple has both a host computer and number of server computers to which the host delegates requests.

Where did TCP/IP come from?

Part of the ARPANET experiment in the 1970s was figuring out how to get all of these different computers to talk to each other. What resulted was the **Transfer Control Protocol/Internet Protocol (TCP/IP)** networking standard. It's the standard by which all computers on the Internet communicate with one another. And, when you connect your Mac to the Internet, it'll need to speak in TCP/IP, too.

IP addresses: it's in the numbers

Remember when we were discussing Internet addresses, I mentioned briefly that the Internet actually uses numbers to identify computers? Those are called **IP addresses.** In our earlier example, the domain name of Apple's support host was **support.apple.com**. That computer is actually found at an IP address that follows the format: XXX.XXX.XXX.XXX. Luckily, your computer figures that number out for you...all you need to know is the domain name.

How does my Mac fit in?

On the Disk

Like any other computer, your Macintosh will need to speak TCP/IP before it can accomplish much on the Internet. This is accomplished through a System Control Panel called MacTCP (see fig. 2.4). Fortunately, if you own System 7.5 of the Mac OS, MacTCP is already included—and may already be on your system. If not, you're still in luck, because MacTCP is included on the disk that came with this book!

Fig. 2.4
The MacTCP control panel is included with System 7.5 and on this book's companion diskette.

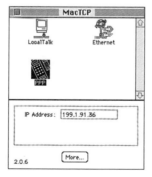

We'll discuss setting up MacTCP in Chapter 5 and Chapter 6. For now, just make sure you've got your hands on a copy of it, and understand that it's the key to getting your Mac to communicate with other computers on the Internet. Once you understand that, and you're familiar with Internet addresses and other Internet basics, you're ready to choose your Internet provider!

Q&A *Is there some way to tell if MacTCP is already installed?*

Yep. In System 7.5, just pull down the Apple menu in the top left corner of your Mac's screen, and hold down the mouse button while the pointer is on Control Panels. If MacTCP is installed, it should appear in your list of Control Panels, somewhere around "Macintosh Easy Open" and "Map." See it? If not, you'll probably need to install it yourself.

How Do I Connect to the Internet?

● **In this chapter:**

- **How much should I spend to connect to the Internet?**

- **The different ways to connect to the Internet**

- **What kind of modem should I get?**

- **I want to choose the best Internet connection**

*The best connection to the Internet does everything you want
it to for less than $50 per month* . . . . ➤

Ever stop to think about all the options available for getting signals sent to your television screen? It's actually pretty astounding. If you're happy with just the networks and local stations, you can use the TV's built-in antenna or an outside antenna. You can get basic cable, expanded cable, and pay stations. You can even get a huge satellite dish or one of those new digital satellites. And I'm sure there are more solutions on the way.

There are just as many ways to hook your computer up to the Internet. And in the end, it's the same basic trade-off for both television and the Internet: cost versus access.

Types of Internet accounts

Because you should never pay more than $50 per month for full access to the Internet, "low cost" is a relative term here. We'll start with some of the least expensive services, and move up to the more expensive—and more common—ways to connect.

E-mail and shell accounts

At one point, **e-mail** and **shell accounts** were the most common ones, but they've recently fallen by the wayside. With these accounts, your Mac isn't really connected to the Internet. Instead, you dial up a central computer using your modem and use programs on that computer to access the various services on the Internet. Your Mac only runs one program: a **terminal emulator**. All the e-mail, Gopher, UseNet, and other programs actually run on the central computer (see fig. 3.1).

 Plain English, please!

In computing lingo, a **terminal** is a computer that does no processing (or "thinking") on its own. Instead it's just a screen and a keyboard for accessing another very powerful computer. A **terminal emulator**, then, is a program that can run on a Mac that makes your Mac act like a "dumb" terminal when calling another computer by modem.

Fig. 3.1

Using a terminal emulator, your Mac can dial up a central computer to access the Internet. You'll have to learn some UNIX, though.

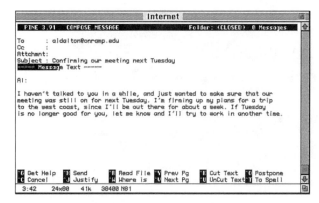

This is actually a fairly typical arrangement at many universities, where students have access to the Internet through powerful UNIX and VMS-based workstations and mainframes. For the typical home user, however, this is a cryptic, text-based solution that doesn't take much advantage of the Mac's unique features.

National online services

You may already be familiar with eWorld, America Online, CompuServe, and others. If not, let me explain briefly. There are a number of different companies that have established **online services** that let you dial in with your modem and—for an hourly fee—you can access information, play games, send e-mail, and chat with others.

Until recently, however, many of these services didn't offer much in the way of access to the Internet. Even though they offered services that are similar to what you can do on the Internet—send e-mail, do research, watch stocks, etc.—you were limited to what that company provided and who its users were.

That's changed over the past year, though, now that the big three for Mac— eWorld, America Online, and CompuServe—have added full Internet access to their list of perks (see fig. 3.2). All three have easy-to-use interfaces that make working on the Internet just like working in any other Macintosh program...although some are easier than others. The drawback? At between $3 and $5 per hour for access, using an online service to access the Internet can easily cross our $50 limit after a couple of late-night sessions.

Fig. 3.2
eWorld provides access
to nearly all of the
Internet services we've
discussed so far, while
maintaining a very
Mac-friendly "look and
feel."

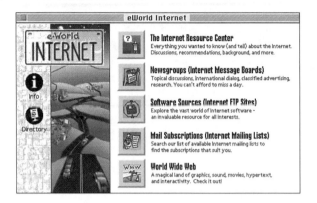

We'll take a serious look at online services in Chapter 7. For now, just realize
that online services are a great way to get your feet wet on the Internet, but
they can get expensive with heavy use.

Dial-up direct accounts (PPP and SLIP)

Now we're getting serious about our Internet connection. This is where the
MacTCP discussed in Chapter 2 comes into play. With a dial-up direct
account using **PPP** or **SLIP**, your Mac's modem will dial the Internet provider company whenever you feel like using an Internet program.

 Plain English, please!

PPP and SLIP are standard ways to get your computer to make a
TCP/IP connection using your modem. (We discuss how this works
in Chapter 4.)

Your Mac will be talking in TCP/IP—it will actually be on the Internet! This
allows you to choose your own programs to access Internet services. Pick
your favorite program for e-mail, Gopher, UseNet discussions, and the World
Wide Web.

The best part is, a dial-up account really shouldn't cost you more than $25-
$40 per month for unlimited access, depending on where you live. Of course,
some folks may need to call long distance or an 800 number to find a provider, and that may push them over our $50/month limit (long-distance toll
charges can mount quickly, and Internet providers generally charge you more
for access to an 800 number). We take a serious look at choosing an Internet
provider in the next chapter.

A dedicated Internet account

Very few individual users need dedicated Internet accounts. These are very high-speed connections designed for companies and organizations that want to have a dedicated host computer in their own building enabling multiple users to access the Internet over the company's local area network (LAN).

If you're concerned with accessing the Internet through your company, you'll want to ask your System Administrator if your company has this sort of access. Then, turn to Chapter 6, where we discuss LAN access in detail.

Dedicated Internet lines range in speed from 56Kbps (kilobits per second) up to 45Mbps (megabits per second). They range in price from around $50 per month to $10,000 per month or more. That may sound ridiculously expensive, but a typical 45Mbps line (also called a **T-3 line**) can handle hundreds or even thousands of Internet users at once.

What type of modem do I need?

A high-speed modem isn't *absolutely* necessary, but you'll probably want one, anyway. For nearly any type of Internet access, a 2400bps modem is annoyingly slow. A 9600bps modem is okay for terminal and online accounts, although a 14.4Kbps modem is ideal for these. As online services and Internet providers upgrade their service to 28.8Kbps, you should consider doing the same—especially if they don't charge extra. The faster your modem, the less money you spend.

 Q&A **My Mac came with a 2400bps modem. Should I throw it away?**

Well...you don't *have* to. It's still possible to get around on the Internet with a slow modem, especially when you're using a shell account or an online service. At the very least, use the modem a couple of times to decide if you enjoy the Internet. Realize, however, that 2400bps is too slow for anything graphical on the Internet. I wouldn't suggest even trying the World Wide Web until you get a new modem.

For a PPP or SLIP account, your best bet is at least a 14.4Kbps modem, or preferably a 28.8Kbps modem. While e-mail and other text services really don't show much of a speed increase, many other services do. In fact, the most popular Internet service, the World Wide Web, is also the most demanding for your modem.

Which Internet connection is best for me?

Remember the tradeoff: cost versus services. For the most part, the best Internet connection depends on how much you plan to use it. You may need to experiment first to figure this out—perhaps starting with Internet access through an online service. Then, as you discover what sort of user you are, you can move on to a different type of connection.

- *I only want to try it out.* Choose an online service like eWorld or America Online. Once your monthly bills get over $50, you'll know it's time to move on to a dial-up PPP or SLIP account.

- *I just want e-mail.* Choose an e-mail account or an online service. An e-mail account may be the least expensive, but it will also force you to use a cryptic interface through a terminal emulator.

- *I already have an account.* This is the only real reason to use a terminal-emulator account, especially if you work for a university or company that offers the account free of charge. The only other reason would be that you're keen on UNIX commands and text-based interfaces. And if you are, why do you own a Macintosh?

Bits and bytes: speed on the Internet

Computers "think" in binary code made up of 1s and 0s. In computerese, a **bit** represents a single instance of a 1 or 0. Eight bits make a **byte**, and it takes an entire byte to represent a character in our alphabet, like "j".

The speed of most Internet connections is measured in **bits per second** (bps). If a connection is over a thousand bits per second, it's represented as **Kbps**; over a million is **Mbps**.

So how fast is *fast*? In the real world, a typical 14.4Kbps modem (the standard $75 modem in today's computer store) transfers a full page of text across the Internet in five to ten seconds.

With a high-speed dedicated line (and no other users), that same page would theoretically take a small fraction of a second. In fact, over a 45Mbps dedicated line, you could transfer the entire contents of a typical Mac's hard drive in less than a minute.

- *I'm an Internet nut-case.* Get a PPP or SLIP connection and a high-speed modem now! The same goes for telecommuting professionals, journalists, teachers, and the bulk of other folks who need to use the Internet for education or business.

- *I'm a mega-corporate giant with money to burn.* Go ahead and spend tens of thousands of dollars a month to connect your thousands of employees to the Internet. While you're at it, pay some computer whiz a couple of grand to keep those employees from spending half the day in **alt.tv.melrose-place**.

Choosing an Internet Service Provider

● **In this chapter:**

● **What's an Internet Service Provider?**

● **Should I use a local or national company?**

● **What is this really going to cost me?**

● **What you shouldn't pay for**

● **How to figure out if you've got a bad provider**

As with any growing industry, Internet providers will either honestly try their best...or seriously try your patience!.... ⊙

I n this chapter, I'm assuming you've decided that the best way to get to the Internet is through a PPP/SLIP account (the kind that lets you connect directly to the Internet with your modem). You want relatively unlimited access to Internet services, you want to use Mac-based applications, and you don't want to spend the hourly fees associated with the online services. Good for you. This is the most cost-effective way to get serious about the Internet.

What is an Internet Service Provider (ISP)?

An **ISP** is an organization that maintains modem connections for you to call with your personal computer. These modem connections tie in to a host computer, which provides you pass-through access to the Internet. From there, your Mac is a **node** on the Internet, capable of accessing anything to which you have rights and privileges.

 Plain English, please!

A **node** is just a shorthand way of referring to any computer directly connected to the Internet (or any other computer network). **""**

How does ISP access work?

Remember that the key to Internet access is speaking the TCP/IP networking language with your Mac. You can do that easily with the MacTCP control panel. You just install it in the System Folder and restart your Mac so that it gets recognized. The problem is, once your Mac has the ability to speak TCP/IP, it still needs to find another computer to talk to. How do you connect to something that lets your Mac exercise its newly discovered language skills?

That's what PPP (see fig. 4.1) and SLIP are for. Both are Mac control panels that manage to let your Mac speak TCP/IP over a phone line. That's the reason they're there. And, to use a phone line for your connection, you've got to have someone to call. That's your ISP.

Fig. 4.1
The Config PPP control panel. This is where I tell my Mac to dial the modem and open a MacTCP network connection over the phone line.

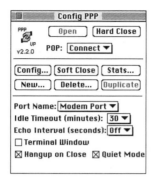

 TIP PPP is generally pronounced "pea-pea-pea," while SLIP is almost always said as it's spelled, "slip"—like what you do on a vaudeville banana peel.

Understanding PPP and SLIP

PPP and SLIP are generally accepted protocols, or little mini-computer languages, that let your Mac establish a TCP/IP connection over a phone line. **PPP** stands for **Point-to-Point Protocol**; and **SLIP** stands for **Serial Line Internet Protocol**. SLIP is the older and less efficient of the two. PPP is more advanced and much more common for Mac users.

 CAUTION An ISP that only offers SLIP connections should make you think twice. They're probably not terribly Mac-literate, and they're behind the times. Unless they're your only choice, shop around.

Both MacPPP and SLIP control panels for the Mac are available as freeware on the Internet. And, to help you make the right choice, MacPPP is included on the disk that accompanies this book.

What else does my ISP do for me?

Your ISP also maintains all appropriate servers for full access to the Internet. For instance, in order to receive mail, you have to have a mail server, which acts like a local post office. As messages come in from around the country, they are actually stored on your ISP's mail server. Then, when you log in and ask for new mail, that mail is downloaded from the server, across your phone line, to your Mac. Now you can read it and reply, as necessary.

Your ISP maintains similar servers for other Internet services like UseNet newsgroups, Domain Name Service, and others. In essence, you're paying for this "big brother" to help you find your way around the Internet and act as a go-between you and all of its scary, untamed cabling.

Q&A   ***Do I have to use an ISP to get direct access?***

Yes, for the most part. Large corporations occasionally act as their own ISPs, but only in rare instances. Universities often do, but they generally service tens of thousands of potential users. In order to access the Internet without an ISP, you'll need to know a whole lot about UNIX, workstations, networking, cabling, and programming. And you'd need something on the order of tens of thousands of dollars in startup capital. I sure couldn't do it!

National providers versus local folks

Although Internet providers come in many different flavors, there are basically two categories that are most important to consider first: national ISPs and local ISPs. The type that's best for you depends entirely on how you plan to use the Internet.

Local Internet providers

Depending on the size of the city or town you live in, you may have many competing-for-profit ISPs, a single municipal or university provider, or none at all. In all cases but the last, your local area is probably the first place you should look...unless you expect to do a lot of traveling on the Internet. From home base, local Internet providers (see fig. 4.2) tend to be more responsive, more in tune with the local community, and able to offer more hands-on advice when you run into trouble. You can also go slap somebody in his actual, physical face if you have a problem with him. (Although you should probably discuss it first.)

There are two basic problems with local providers, however. They can be much less reliable than national providers, and they don't offer access in other cities in the U.S. or around the world (national providers generally do).

On the upside, local providers often offer much better deals than national providers. There's a little buyer-beware here, but a careful selection can save you a lot of money.

Fig. 4.2
Here's a partial list of
Internet providers in
Washington state.
Ironically, at least for
the first-time user,
you'd need Internet
access to see this list
yourself.

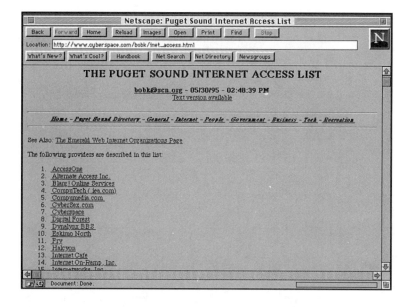

National Internet providers

There is only one advantage to using national providers…convenience. Many national providers have local access numbers in larger cities or 800 numbers you can call for access anywhere in the country. If you find yourself traveling the country and needing to connect to the Internet for full access, this may be the right way to go. This sort of service can tend to be pretty expensive, though.

Honestly, if you really do need access all around the country, you might be better off using a national online service like eWorld or America Online as your base of operations. These services almost guarantee access from most parts of the United States, and are better organized to help you find a local number. And now that they offer what's generally considered as "full access" to the Internet, they are both a convenient and a complete choice.

What your provider should do for you

That there are really good providers and really bad providers seems to conform to some law of capitalism. The worst-case situation is a mediocre provider. With providers, it's sometimes the little things that count; attention to details is often what it comes down to when powerful computing is involved.

Of paramount importance is that a provider will take care of its Mac-based clientele. While it's unlikely that you'll come across a provider that caters *only* to Mac customers (it might be tough to stay in business that way), finding a provider who knows how to get Macs connected and can help you troubleshoot your connection shouldn't be that tough.

Chalk it up to personal bias, but I believe a Macintosh-saavy provider is the only way to go. I look for providers who have professionally written and formatted instructions for establishing a connection with a Macintosh. If they can't fax their instructions to you easily, and if they don't at least offer some way to download Macintosh software to your computer, you might look elsewhere.

What you should and shouldn't pay for

I'll assume for a moment that you don't have extenuating circumstances (you live twelve miles from the nearest fire hydrant or you'd like an Internet connection for blow-by-blow advice for putting out fires on sea-going oil rigs). Let's pretend you live in a town big enough that your daughter doesn't have to date the sheriff's *only* deputy.

What you should expect to pay

For a SLIP/PPP account, a typical Internet provider will charge you a reasonable setup fee, a basic monthly fee, and, depending on the type of service you want, an hourly fee. Many providers offer flat rates for unlimited monthly connections—it'll be up to you to decide if this is a better deal than an hourly rate, depending on how much you use the service. Table 4.1 shows a couple of pretend scenarios that outline potential costs for someone who uses the Internet like I do. (Note: For AOL, I've adjusted the monthly usage to account for AOL's five "free" hours.)

Table 4.1   The amazing Internet cost differential

Provider #1		Provider #2		America Online	
Setup	$35.00	Setup	$10.00	Setup	$ 0.00
Monthly	$32.00	Monthly	$ 5.00	Monthly	$ 9.95

Provider #1		Provider #2		America Online	
Hourly	$ 0.00	Hourly	$ 1.50	Hourly	$ 2.95
x 35 hrs per month	$ 0.00	x 35 hrs per month	$52.50	x 35 hrs per month	$88.50
Total Cost over 6 months	$227.00	Total Cost over 6 months	$345.00	Total Cost over 6 months	$590.70

According to the table, it's in my best interest to find a flat-fee monthly service (like Provider #1, even if I am forced to pay a higher setup fee and a fairly substantial monthly charge. This is, in fact, about what I pay to my current ISP. And, believe it or not, I probably spend more than 35 hours per month connected to the Internet.

 CAUTION **When you choose an Internet service plan, try not to tie yourself** up for too long in a multi-month deal if you have no idea how much you'll use the Internet. Like cellular phone service, six- and 12-month plans are very popular in the Internet world—and are very expensive if you lose interest.

The figures in the table do reflect some actual, current plans for Internet service in my area. Notice that, for as much as I use the Internet, the only plan that doesn't violate our $50/month rule is plan #1.

If you only use the Internet 15 hours a month, though, then a little extra math shows that plan #2 is a better deal (about $27.50 a month) and (assuming five "free" hours) even AOL access would be reasonable ($39.45). Plan #1, a flat-fee plan, would remain $32.00 a month.

What you shouldn't pay for

Again, we'll assume a SLIP/PPP account. Other than a reasonable startup charge and a monthly/hourly fee, you shouldn't pay anything else. Especially to be avoided are accounts that require you to pay any sort of download fee or bandwidth charge. It's not terribly often that you'll come across something like this, but if you do, it's a sure sign that your provider isn't keeping up with the times.

Plain English, please!

In Net talk, **bandwidth** refers to the size of a connection between computers. A 14.4Kbps connection has less bandwidth than does a 56Kbps connection. In a sort of slang, then, using "a lot of bandwidth" means you're transferring large files or graphics across the Internet. Some providers charge you extra if you transfer more than a set number of megabytes of files in a month.

You should also avoid any "per" charges: *per* download, *per* e-mail message, *per* UseNet group, etc. Again, these charges suggest either that the provider is trying to rack up small charges, or that it's trying to hedge against the limits of its computers. It's no hard and fast rule, but these surcharges are often signs of a provider trying to support too many customers with lesser equipment.

The quality Internet provider test

How about a quick checklist to help you find the perfect provider? If you find an ISP that can answer the bulk of these questions correctly, you've probably got smooth sailing ahead.

- *Does the provider have technical experience with Mac SLIP/PPP connections and MacTCP configuration?* The ideal Mac connection isn't that tough to figure out, but technical experience and straightforward, printed instructions for MacTCP and MacPPP will help greatly.

- *What speed and type of modems are used?* If you've got a 28.8Kbps modem, then you'll definitely want a provider who boasts high-speed modems. Also, be aware of any known incompatibilities between your modem and the ISPs. Your best bet is a provider that uses modems manufactured by the same company as yours.

- *How many modem lines are available, and what is the ratio of users to lines?* The worst thing is to hear a busy signal when you want to get on the Internet. If you can get the provider's phone number for its modems, try dialing it a couple of times when you'd want to use the service. If it's often busy, look elsewhere.

- *Does the ISP provide Macintosh PPP/SLIP software and archives for Mac Internet programs?* This is another indication that the provider is serious about supporting the Mac.

- *Does the provider offer any trial programs, month-by-month service, or other "get-acquainted" deals?* Run quickly away from an ISP that is unwilling to offer you service for anything less than a six-month commitment, billed in advance. There's no law that says an ISP has to stay in business. And you'll need about a month to make sure the service is right for you.

- *Is there a back-up plan?* Find out if the ISP has additional phone numbers or is associated with another service, in case the system goes down. If all the high-speed connections are in use, can you at least get on at a lower speed?

- *Are additional services provided at reasonable cost?* Find out whether the ISP has additional services—like e-mail forwarding, file storage, and users' Web pages—at reasonable prices.

Above all, don't forget a little common sense. The best place to get the low-down on Internet providers is probably through local Mac user groups. Head down to a meeting and eavesdrop on more experienced users' Internet trials and headaches. And, as with any growing industry, keep your eyes wide open for shady deals and front-weighted payment plans.

Connecting to the Internet with a Modem and Your Mac

● In this chapter:

If you've got a Mac, a modem, an ISP, and a few minutes to spare, you're ready to get connected to the Internet. . . . . ❯

So you've found an Internet provider who taught Sam Walton the basics of customer service and Volvo the tenets of reliability. You've already figured out that you plug your modem into the little hole with a picture of a telephone handset on the back of your Mac. And you're armed with the amazingly convenient little disk in the back of this amazingly thorough (and entertaining) little book. Ready to Net?

Stuff you need to know before you start

Once you've talked a provider into giving you an account, you should have an account name and a password. If you've gotten instructions from your provider for setting up MacTCP and MacPPP, you're in even better shape.

Installing and configuring MacTCP

We've talked a little about MacTCP before, but let's go through it again. **MacTCP** is the Control Panel that allows your Mac to speak in TCP/IP—the language of the Internet. If you've got System 7.5 of the Mac OS, then you may already have the MacTCP Control Panel installed. If you don't, you'll need to install it from your System disks (or CD-ROM). You can also install it from the disk included with this book.

 CAUTION **You can't correctly configure PPP or SLIP software unless MacTCP is installed.**

 To install MacTCP, put the MacNet disk in your Mac's floppy drive. Open the disk by double-clicking the disk's icon, then drag MacTCP to your Mac's **On the Disk** active System Folder (see fig. 5.1). Now you can access the Control Panel through the Control Panels on your Apple menu.

 TIP **It'll save a little confusion if you go ahead and drag the MacPPP** and Config PPP icons to the System Folder at this time. Then, restart your Mac and continue.

Fig. 5.1
MacTCP is just a
Control Panel like any
other, easily accessed
through the Apple
menu.

*From the MacNet
disk, drag MacTCP.*

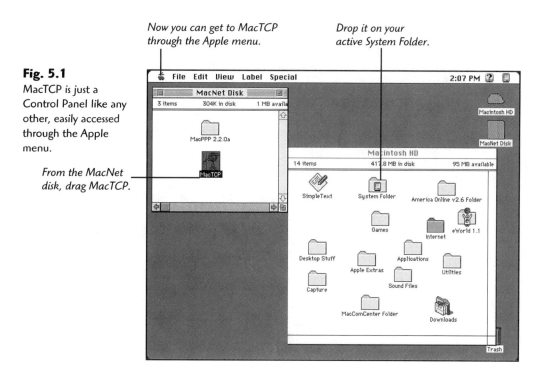

Now you'll need to configure MacTCP according to your Internet provider's
instructions. Open the Control Panel by selecting it from Control Panels in
the Apple menu (for System 7.5 and above), or double-click it in the Control
Panels folder. You should see something like figure 5.2.

Fig. 5.2
The MacTCP control
panel. If your ISP gave
you a manually
assigned IP address,
enter it here.

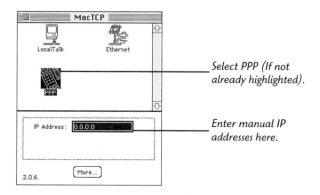

More than likely you won't have to enter anything in MacTCP's main window, although you'll want to make sure you've selected PPP (unless you ignored the previous *tip*). Then, with your configuration information in hand, click More.

Here's where we get serious (see fig. 5.3). Actually, you won't have to touch most of this stuff—it's just there to look intimidating. But you do need to be sure of a few things.

First of all, make sure that under the Obtain Address section you have the correct radio button selected. For most folks, it should be set to Server, unless you were given a manual IP address, in which case you'd choose Manually. It's generally not set to Dynamically unless your ISP specifically tells you to choose that.

Fig. 5.3
The technical under-side of the MacTCP Control Panel. I think they just put this stuff here to confuse us.

Click the Obtain Address radio button to change the setting.

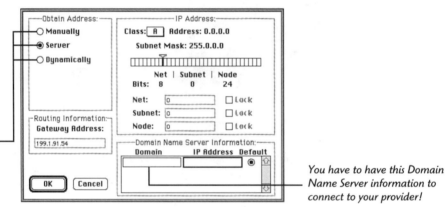

You have to have this Domain Name Server information to connect to your provider!

The only other thing you really need to worry about is the Domain Name Server Information at the bottom of the Control Panel. In the first blank field under Domain you should type in the domain name of your provider gave you. Just to the right of that you enter the IP address, then click the Default radio button.

TIP   **Look familar? The domain name and IP address are the addresses** for your ISP's name server (see Chapter 2).

You're almost done. Unless your provider gives you an alternate server name and IP address, then all you have to do is enter a single period (.) in the Domain field directly below your first entry. In the IP field, type the same IP address you used in the field above it (see fig. 5.4).

CAUTION **Before you close MacTCP, make sure the Class pop-up menu**
shows C (it's in the top right corner of the MacTCP setup dialog box).
Sometimes this will change as you toy with other settings. If it doesn't show
C, change it.

Fig. 5.4
If you've got every-
thing entered correctly,
click OK to get out.

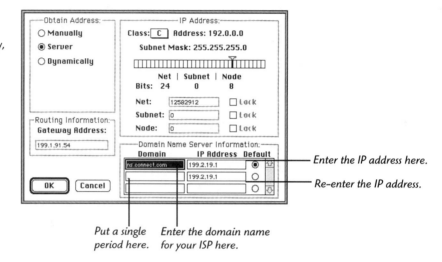

Enter the IP address here.

Re-enter the IP address.

Put a single   Enter the domain name
period here.   for your ISP here.

Now you're done. If everything looks right to you, it probably is. If it doesn't,
well, who can blame you? You're no expert, right? Click OK to close the
dialog box, and you're back at the MacTCP Control Panel. Restart your Mac,
but you can wait until you've configured MacPPP first if you want.

Dealing with the Config PPP Control Panel

If you followed my tip in the last section, you've already copied MacPPP and
Config PPP over to the System Folder. If not, then you'll want to do that now
(they're on the MacNet disk), and then restart. Reopen the MacTCP Control
Panel, and select PPP. Now you're ready to configure PPP.

Configuring PPP

Remember, PPP is what is going to make the modem connection to your
provider. That's when MacTCP will take over for communicating on the
Internet.

To configure your modem, pull down the Apple menu and choose Config PPP from the Control Panels (for System 7.5 and above), or double-click the Config PPP icon in the Control Panels window (before System 7.5). This gives you a Control Panel like the one shown in figure 5.5.

Fig. 5.5
The Config PPP
Control Panel. This is
home base for your
Internet connection.

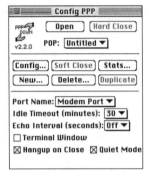

The only thing you need to worry about here is the Port Name. Use the pop-up menu to change it if your modem isn't connected to the Modem Port. (It probably is.) Then, click New to configure PPP to dial your provider.

You start by entering a name for your PPP connection. Then, click once on Config and you'll see a screen like that shown in figure 5.6. Next to Port Speed, use the pop-up menu to choose the highest speed (in bps) that your modem supports. If your phone line requires pulse-dialing, click that radio button. Finally, enter the telephone number for your Internet provider.

 TIP   **If you need to dial any special numbers before the phone number,** like a 9 for an outside line or *70 to cancel call-waiting, enter them before the number, then type a comma, as in **9,555–4567**. (The comma makes the modem pause for a second before it resumes dialing.)

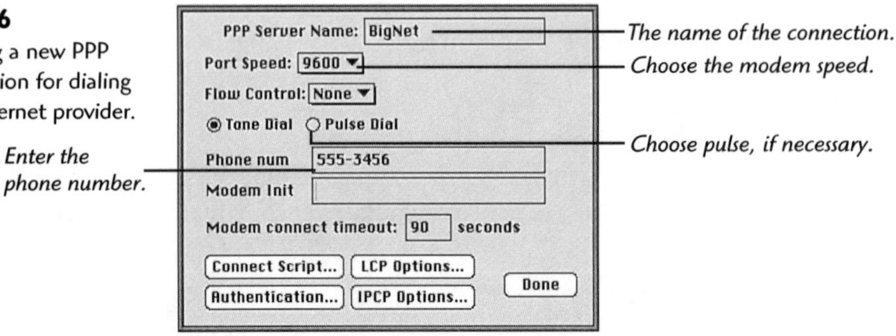

Fig. 5.6
Creating a new PPP
connection for dialing
your Internet provider.

*Enter the
phone number.*

The name of the connection.

Choose the modem speed.

Choose pulse, if necessary.

Notice that we skipped a couple of boxes? If your modem supports flow control, and your ISP suggests it, you may want to choose the recommended flow control from the Flow Control pop-up menu. This is important for high-speed (14.4Kbps and up) connections. Also, you may want to enter an **initialization string** for your modem in the Modem Init field. Consult your modem's documentation, if you're not sure what this should be.

 Plain English, please!

> An **initialization** string is a series of letters, numbers, and symbols that tell your modem how it's supposed to act for this connection. Most of the modems I've used have a "default" string that looks something like **AT&F** or **AT&F1**. If you come across something like this in your modem's manual, you're on the right track.

Setting up the log-in procedure

If you're lucky, your Internet account supports something called PAP (Password Authentication Protocol), and you can enter your ID and password every time your computer dials into the provider. If that's the case, you can click Done and move on to the "Opening the Internet Connection" section, later in this chapter. Otherwise, you'll need to create a connection script.

 TIP **Here's one place where an Internet-savvy ISP can be a big help.** A good ISP will include instructions for the connection script in its documentation.

What is this **script** thing? It's a series of commands that MacPPP sends to your ISP as it is connecting to the service. It sends your user ID and password, and then sends a command that tells the ISP's computer that this is a PPP connection. The script automates the log-in process that you would normally have to go through to gain access to a remote computer.

To create your script, click once on the Connect Script button. You are presented with the script-building dialog box displayed in figure 5.7.

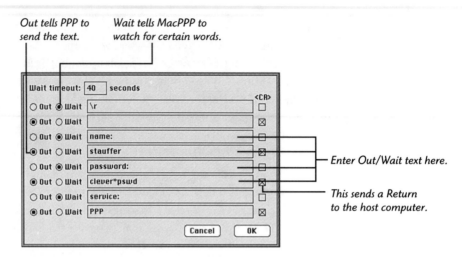

Out tells PPP to send the text.

Wait tells MacPPP to watch for certain words.

Fig. 5.7
To build a PPP connection script, you need to know exactly how the ISP's host expects you to log in.

Enter Out/Wait text here.

This sends a Return to the host computer.

I can't tell you exactly how to go about this because it's different for every ISP. But we can look at a sample script and get a feel for how this works. If your ISP isn't particularly helpful or Mac-savvy, you may still be able to come up with the proper script on your own.

A typical script starts out by waiting for the host computer to acknowledge the new connection by asking for a login name. So our script starts out with a Wait command, followed by the text login: (see fig. 5.8). When PPP detects that the host computer has sent the text login: it will go on to the next part of the script.

Fig. 5.8
The connection script is a back-and-forth process, alternately waiting for cues from the host, sending predetermined text, and returning.

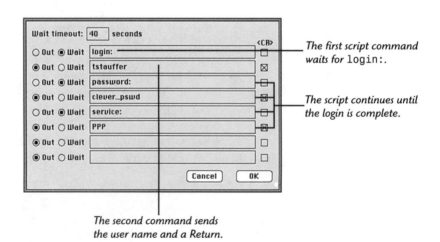

The first script command waits for login:.

The script continues until the login is complete.

The second command sends the user name and a Return.

The script continues, offering your password and any other commands that are required by your provider. Once you have the script entered appropriately, you can click OK to exit this dialog box.

CAUTION **When you enter script elements, use the Tab key to move from** field to field, and avoid stray spaces and other characters. Most hosts are picky about upper- and lowercase and extra characters in your script.

Opening the Internet connection

Once you have everything properly configured and ready to go, there are two different ways you can open the connection to your provider. The first is using the Config PPP Control Panel (see fig. 5.9). With the Control Panel on the screen, click the Open button at the top of the window.

Fig. 5.9
The best way to test your PPP connection is simply to click Open in the Config PPP Control Panel.

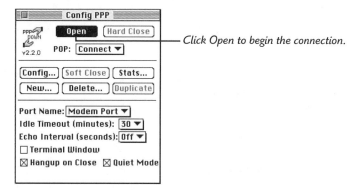

Click Open to begin the connection.

Now the Control Panel takes over, dialing your Internet provider and making the modem connection. If your provider supports PAP, you'll be prompted to enter your user name and password. If your PPP connection uses a script, you'll see your connection being negotiated in the MacPPP Status alert box. If all goes well, you'll be up and running on the Internet. How can you tell? From the firm little PPP handshake, of course (see fig. 5.10)!

Fig. 5.10
PPP up! The connection is complete, and you're ready to run some Internet applications.

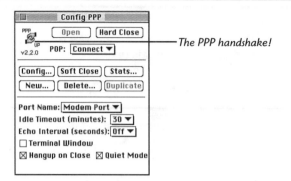

The PPP handshake!

What to do if you can't connect

Q&A *My PPP connection didn't seem to work. What do I do?*

To edit your Config PPP setup, click Config in the Config PPP Control Panel window (not New, as you did earlier). Then, use the following list to figure out why it didn't connect.

- *The Open button won't work.* You haven't correctly selected PPP in the MacTCP control panel. Do this, then restart your Mac.

- *The modem didn't dial.* If the MacPPP Status dialog box appears but your modem doesn't dial, then your problem is either that your modem isn't configured properly (for example, the modem initialization string needs to be added or your modem isn't connected). If your modem is plugged in and turned on (and you've had success with it in the past), then you may need to check your modem's manual again for an initialization string.

- *The modem dials, but doesn't connect.* If you hear those obnoxious modem tones, but you eventually get a PPP Timeout error, you may have incorrectly set your modem's Port Speed in the Config PPP Control Panel. Check your modem's speed again, and set it accordingly. Also, make sure you've set Flow Control according to your ISP's instructions.

- *The connection hangs (just stops working and sits there) while talking to the host.* If your connection script is wrong, you'll get part of the way through your login, then get a PPP Timeout error. Watch closely and see what the last successful command was. Did it accept your user name, but not your password? Then that's where your problem is. Go back to the Config PPP Control Panel, click the Config button, then click Connect Script. Compare your script to the one your ISP suggests, and correct any errors. Don't forget to check upper- and lowercase, and make sure you've used the correct user name and password.

- *It got all the way to Network, then quit.* This might still be your connect script, but it could also be a problem with the ISP. Your best bet is to call the provider's tech support folks.

The other way to open a connection

I said there were two ways to open the connection, then I just left you hanging there, wondering. Curiosity peaked, you may have even sworn under your breath in frustrated anticipation, "Tell me, tell me! What is the other way?"

Just open up your favorite Internet application. Double-click on Eudora e-mail, Netscape WWW Browser, or most other Internet applications, and it will automatically look for a MacTCP connection. If it doesn't find one, it will ask MacTCP to open one for you, and MacTCP will tell PPP to call your provider. All behind-the-scenes, with no additional effort from you.

You gotta love that thoughtful little Mac of yours.

How to end the connection

Those of you who read English and are particularly observant may be way ahead of me on this one. In the Config PPP Control Panel (see fig. 5.11), you've got two choices for closing the connection.

Fig. 5.11
To close a connection, click one of the two Close buttons.

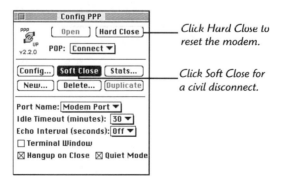

Click Hard Close to reset the modem.

Click Soft Close for a civil disconnect.

Clicking the Soft Close button will send software codes to the ISP, requesting a civil break in the modem connection. A Hard Close is reserved for times when more drastic measures are needed—like when one of your Internet applications has crashed. Clicking Hard Close will cause the modem to reset, clearing the connection without so much as a "goodbye." Do this often, and you may upset your ISP.

Connecting to the Internet with Your Mac on a LAN

● **In this chapter:**

● **How do I know if my office is connected to the Internet?**

● **I have to set up MacTCP myself. What should I ask my System Administrator?**

● **The specifics of setting up MacTCP in the office**

● **Turning the Internet connection on and off**

The best way to get an Internet connection in the office? Take your System Administrator out for an expensive lunch . . . ⊳

We've discussed previously that the Internet is basically a computer network that happens to be global in scale. So, for Internet access in the workplace, how does the Internet relate to your office's Local Area Network (LAN)? If your Mac is already busy talking to other Macs, PCs, and/or printers and modems, is it still possible to connect to the Internet?

If your system administrator has provided for Internet access, then getting your Mac up and running is easy. With the right hardware setup, it's only a question of configuring MacTCP correctly.

Is my office Mac connected to the Internet?

In most cases, if your company is connected to the Internet, someone will have already set up access for you. At the very least, all you'll need to do is properly install and configure MacTCP. We'll work under the assumption that somebody told you your LAN has access to the Internet, and all you need to do is correctly configure MacTCP. If that isn't the case, your best bet may be to take one of the folks from your Information Systems department out to lunch.

 Q&A *I asked around, and my LAN isn't connected to the Internet. I need access! What can I do?*

If your company *is* willing to give you a modem, you can connect using a PPP account as described in Chapter 5. MacTCP won't conflict with any other network activities because you're only using it over a MacPPP connection. Be aware, though, that many companies are wary of this method because it's possible that an enterprising computer hacker could get access to your corporate network over this connection. So, ask first.

If your company does have access, it will probably have a high-speed line that comes into the building, serving everyone in the company who requires Internet acccess. TCP/IP information is "routed" by your existing network to a computer that handles traffic on this line. While most companies still need help from an Internet provider of some sort, many have their own domain names (for example, **bigcorp.com**) and many maintain servers on-site for mail, UseNet discussion groups, and domain name services.

What should I ask my System Administrator?

If you've already asked her if you have Internet access, and she said "yes" or something similarly positive, then you'll want to make sure you get answers to the following questions...especially if you'll be setting up or trouble-shooting your Internet connection on your own. They are (in no particular order):

- *What is our company's domain name?* It's probably something along the lines of **bigcorp.com**.

- *What's the name of our Domain Name Server and what is its IP address?* That's for setting up MacTCP.

- *Do I need a permanent IP address (set "Manually"), or will the server assign it (set "Server") every time I initiate a connection?* Again, this is for MacTCP. If you need to set your IP address manually, you'll also need to find out if you need to set the gateway's IP address.

- *Can I have an e-mail account, and what is my e-mail address?* Hopefully it'll be ***yourname*@bigcorp.com**, but remember that you might need a host name if there are a number of different mail servers in your company.

- *What's the name of our mail server?* You'll need this later, for configuring many of your Internet applications, including your e-mail program.

- *Do we have a news server? What's it called?* To read UseNet discussion groups, you'll need the name of your news server, probably along the lines of **news.bigcorp.com**.

- *Do we have an FTP server? If so, is there any way for others to upload files to me?* Often, companies will provide an anonymous FTP site so that electronic documents can be uploaded to employees by folks outside the company. If your IS group is particularly savvy, they may have already created directories on the FTP site for your department, or they might give you your own directory.

- *Do we have a World Wide Web site?* You may want to use your company's WWW site as your own home page once you get your Web browser up and running. If your company does have a site, get the address.

Clearly, you'll also want to discuss any policies your company has regarding Internet use, and you'll want to strictly adhere to any cautions or concerns they have about security.

Configuring MacTCP for your LAN

If you haven't already, check your Control Panels and make sure MacTCP isn't already installed. (For System 7.5, pull down the Apple Menu, highlight Control Panels with the mouse pointer, and look for MacTCP in the resulting list.) If it is, chances are that your connection is up and running. If you flip through the rest of this chapter and everything seems in order, then skip ahead to Chapter 7, and install your e-mail program—you might get lucky.

 CAUTION You shouldn't (and won't be able to) install MacTCP and follow these instructions if your company has implemented Apple's new Open Transport protocols for network connections. Consult your System Administrator concerning Internet access.

Installing MacTCP

If you can't find MacTCP, it's a good idea to make sure your System Administrator knows you're going to install it yourself. She may suggest using the MacTCP that's included with System 7.5 instead of the MacTCP on the MacNet disk.

 CAUTION Let me be clear about this. I'm not trying to show you how to subvert the hierarchy of your company's organizational chart. Make sure you have the go-ahead from your System Administrator before hot-wiring your own Internet connection. Okay?

 Otherwise, it's fine to use the MacTCP provided on the MacNet disk. Just drag MacTCP from the disk to your System Folder icon. It will automatically be placed in the Control Panels folder. Now you should be able to access it through the Apple menu (see fig. 6.1).

Fig. 6.1
Here's MacTCP in the Control Panels. Select it to open the control panel for configuration.

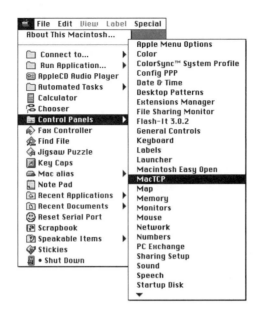

Configuring MacTCP for a LAN

Once you have the MacTCP control panel open, click More on the front to get at its settings. This is where you'll need that list of answers you got from that IS person!

In the dialog box that appears, tell MacTCP how to obtain its IP address in the Obtain Address section, as shown in figure 6.2. Chances are this is obtained either Manually or by the Server, depending on what you learned from your System Administrator. Click once on the appropriate radio button to set this.

Fig. 6.2
Here, in the guts of the MacTCP control panel, you need to tell MacTCP how it will obtain its IP address.

Click here to choose Manually.

Or click here for Server.

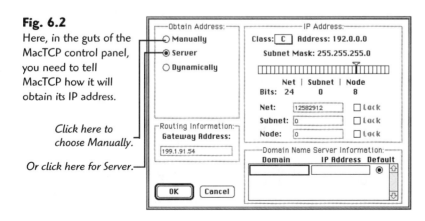

CAUTION **In the MacTCP control panel, Dynamically is very rarely used. If your administrator tells you that addresses are assigned Dynamically, that really corresponds to Server in the MacTCP control panel. Only choose Dynamically under the advice of a MacTCP expert.**

Our next step is to tell MacTCP where to find your domain name server. That's done in the bottom right corner of the dialog box. In the first field under Domain, enter the address of your name server. In the field to its immediate right, enter the IP address of that name server. Then click the radio button under Default to establish this as your default domain name server (see fig. 6.3).

Fig. 6.3
Our next step is to tell MacTCP what domain name server it will use.

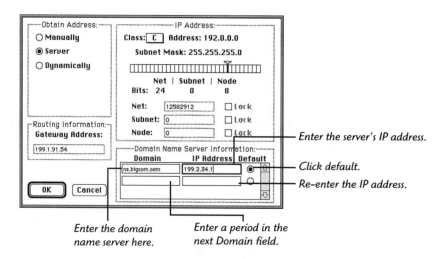

Enter the server's IP address.
Click default.
Re-enter the IP address.

Enter the domain name server here.
Enter a period in the next Domain field.

In the second Domain field, you should enter a single period (.). This tells MacTCP to use that same domain name server for obtaining IP addresses outside of the current domain. Next, enter the same IP address in the field to the right of your period.

Everything else in the dialog box should be fine, unless you chose Manually for Obtain Address. In that case, you may need to edit the Gateway Address—click once in the field, then edit away.

Now click OK to close the dialog box. If you set MacTCP to obtain your IP address manually, click once in the IP address field and enter your IP address. Finally, you'll need to select the type of network cabling your Mac uses…generally either LocalTalk or Ethernet. Click once on the appropriate icon, then click the close box to close the control panel.

Last step: restart your Mac.

TIP **Chances are, your office is using Ethernet, not Localtalk, as its** networking standard. LocalTalk is slow and usually only found in an all-Mac environment. Also, if you have a different icon in the MacTCP window (for example, TokenRing) then that's probably the one you should choose.

Starting the Internet connection

Network protocols are generally always **active**, that is, they don't take any special effort to initiate. They simply wait until a program asks them to find something over the network, then go about their business.

The same holds true for MacTCP. You don't have to do anything out of the ordinary to start the connection. Whenever you double-click an Internet application (like your e-mail or Web program), it will start out by looking for MacTCP. If it finds it, and is able to find all of the appropriate servers it needs on the Internet, then you're in business. If not, it's troubleshooting time.

Q&A *MacTCP is configured right, but doesn't seem to be working on my company's LAN. What's wrong?*

I don't know. No kidding...there are as many different ways to set up a LAN as there are sticks you could pick out to shake at one. You'll need to consult your Administrator, preferably getting her to sit at your station and check your configuration. If you're lucky, the problem will be that your Administrator forgot to tell you something.

How do I end the connection?

Turn off your Mac. Unlike PPP connections, MacTCP connections over a LAN don't need to be turned off and on. Remember, all PPP does is help your Mac use a phone line to "pretend" that it has a network connection. If you're running MacTCP over a LAN, it doesn't need to pretend to have a network connection...it actually has one!

7

Connecting to the Internet through an Online Service

In this chapter:

- **Online services defined**
- **What Internet services are available through online services?**
- **Should I choose America Online? eWorld? CompuServe?**
- **What you should expect to pay**
- **When are online services better than ISPs?**

You're a world traveller? Celebrated journalist? Somebody else is paying? Then maybe you should choose an online service as your Internet connection! . . . . >

Are you the sort of person who's willing to drive an extra five miles to have your gas pumped for you in the full-service line? Ever actually called a grocery store to have them deliver something? Do you automatically snub any country club that doesn't offer valet parking? Well, an online service might be the way to go for your Internet connection.

Actually, I'm poking fun. It's true that an online service can be one of the most expensive ways to connect to the Internet…but it's also the easiest way. Online services—particularly America Online, eWorld, and CompuServe—cater to their Macintosh customers, with Mac-like front-end software and friendly instructions. If you're not interested in a PPP account, you're not sure about this whole Internet thing yet, or if somebody else is footing the bill, try an online service.

 Plain English, please!

In technobabble, **front-end** refers to a software program that's used to access a remote computer. Many online services make an effort to design their front-end software to be friendly and easy-to-learn. **"**

So what's an online service?

Before I get carried away here, I should probably explain the idea behind online services. An **online service** is a little like a "virtual city." In fact, one of them—eWorld—uses a little picture of a city as its interface (see fig. 7.1).

The idea behind an online service is that anybody with a Mac and a modem can dial in and instantly be connected to a small community of a few hundred thousand or even a few million other users. By calling a central computer in Virginia or somewhere (usually routed through a local phone call), you can connect to a whole world of e-mail, discussions, news, live events, file transfer, travel information, and much more.

What's funny is, all that stuff you can do on an online service sounds like what you can do on the Internet, right? Well…yeah, it is. But it's a little like shopping for the perfect cuff links in your local shopping mall (an online service) versus shopping for the perfect cuff links in, say, the Greater Los Angeles Area (the Internet). There's a lot more driving to do out there on the Internet. That's why online services are good for people who like full-service gas stations—they're more convenient.

Fig. 7.1
eWorld, Apple's very own online service, is designed to take the virtual town metaphor just a little further.

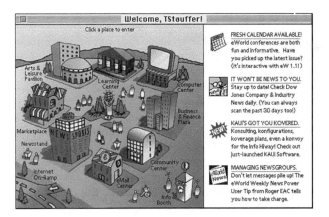

Internet services through online services

The importance of the Internet hasn't been lost on the better online services. Realizing that there were a gazillion bits of information that their users weren't privvy to, America Online (AOL), eWorld, CompuServe, and others have added software to their front-ends that lets the user take advantage of most Internet services. In fact, AOL and eWorld have pretty elegant solutions. CompuServe has some Internet solutions too, but they currently aren't terribly Mac-friendly, although that's slowly changing for the better.

If there's no objection, I'll tell you a little about the good and bad of each service as it relates to the Internet. It will be a completely dispassionate and objective discussion, based on extensive fact-finding analysis.

Believe me?

Winner by knock-out: America Online!

Why a number one rating for America Online? Because it's my favorite service. But there's good reason for that: America Online offers the most mature and complete Internet services, while taking care of their Mac customers. They're also among the largest of the services, and they offer a very straightforward rate card. If you happen to become a fan of another service, I won't hold it against you. But here's some compelling reasons to look twice at America Online's Internet services (see fig. 7.2).

Fig. 7.2
Here's AOL's Internet Center, the jumping-off point from AOL into the world of the Internet. Notice the Internet services, like FTP and UseNet.

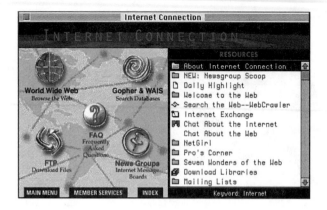

By the way, to get to the Internet Center, click on it in the AOL Main Menu (that window with all the stylized horizontal bars that shows up when you log on). Or, from anywhere on the service you can hit Command+K for the Keyword screen, then enter **Internet** and click once on Go.

Sending Internet e-mail on America Online

Internet e-mail and America Online's e-mail are relatively interchangable, and AOL has a nice interface for dealing with your electronic correspondence. All you need is an Internet address anywhere in the world and you can send that person a note with no trouble.

How do you do it? Just use America Online's standard e-mail form. From the Mail menu, choose Compose Mail. In the resulting window, you just enter an e-mail address at the top instead of an AOL screen name (see fig. 7.3).

TIP   **Want to receive Internet e-mail on AOL? Your address looks like this: *username*@aol.com.**

Mine, for instance, is **tstauffer@aol.com**. Anyone on the Internet can reach me using that address, and his or her message shows up right when I log on to AOL!

America Online's only drawback for Internet e-mail is that it can't send attached files over the Internet—like it can between AOL users. So, you can't attach a word processing document to an Internet e-mail message. And, frankly, that's not AOL's fault…the Internet e-mail protocols are pretty finicky about that sort of thing.

Fig. 7.3
With AOL, Internet
e-mail is just as easy as
regular AOL e-mail. All
you need to know is
the complete Internet
address.

*Choose Compose Mail
from the Mail menu.*

*Enter the Internet
address here.*

*And type
away!*

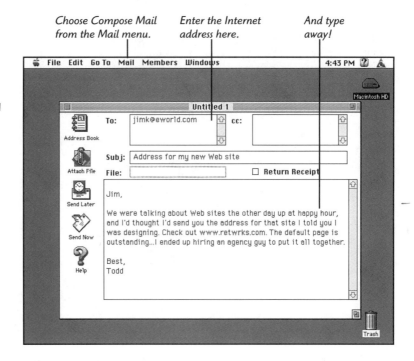

TIP   **Your AOL address book works as well for Internet addresses**
as it does for AOL screen names.

Full UseNet, Gopher, and FTP access

While you may be able to find a better newsreader or Gopher program for use
with a MacTCP connection, AOL's interface is generally solid and easy to
grasp. There's a lot of help along the way, too.

For UseNet, AOL offers access to many thousands of UseNet groups (AOL
claims upwards of 20,000), including many regional groups that you probably
wouldn't otherwise get access to through a local Internet provider. The
interface is fairly easy to figure out (see fig. 7.4) and, along the way there's a
good deal of helpful documents to keep you going.

America Online even offers a feature called FileGrabber, which helps you
pull files and documents from UseNet in the groups dedicated to the transfer
of computer files. We'll discuss this concept in more detail in Chapters 14 and
15, but for now, just realize that this is an impressive convenience.

Fig. 7.4
AOL does a good job
of making UseNet
newsgroups look like
they're just another
part of the America
Online service.

Topics in a UseNet
discussion group

Reading a
UseNet message

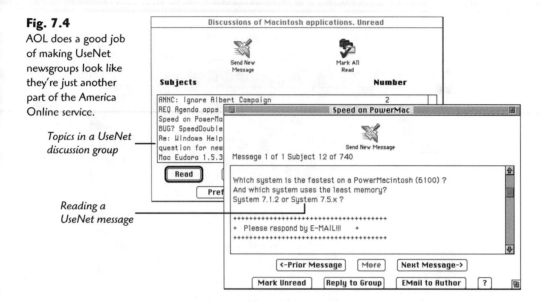

Gopher and FTP sites are just as easy to get into. AOL's FTP offers a number
of preset FTP sites that are often useful for finding good files to download.
AOL has even created its own mirrors of popular FTP sites to keep AOL users
from tying up other organizations' computers.

 Plain English, please!

> A **mirror** site is an FTP server computer that holds copies of the same files
> as another, well-known site on the Internet. The FTP directories at the
> University of Michigan and Washington University in St. Louis are popular
> sites for mirroring to other computers.

World Wide Web browser

Although nearly all of the services now have them, AOL (in version 2.6 of
their software) was first with a browser for the Macintosh. It's solid, not
terribly slow, and a good way to get acquainted with the Web. You'll definitely want to be connected to AOL at the highest speed possible, though,
or you'll be in for some waiting.

In general, Web browser programs are very similar. They all need to be able
to display standard-format documents, show you graphics, and let you move
around. But, much of the Web is based on standards set by the Netscape
Navigator—easily the most popular of Web browsers. AOL's browser isn't

able to take on everything that Netscape dishes out, so some pages can look a little weird. Overlook that, though, and this is a fine way to access the Web (see fig. 7.5).

Fig. 7.5
If you're interested in getting out on the Web and seeing what all the fuss is about, AOL's browser is a great place to start.

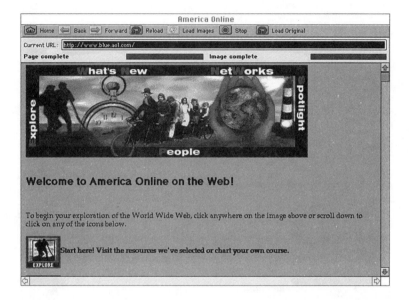

Two words of caution: *extra* and *memory*. AOL's browser is a separate program from the AOL software, and both must run at the same time—so you'll need extra computer memory. If you don't have eight megabytes already, you'll be up against the wall with AOL's software.

Lots of Mac files and support

In my opinion, AOL wins hands-down over even Apple's own service, eWorld, for support of the Mac on the Internet. It's on AOL where I'm most likely to find the latest and most diverse Internet applications. And the discussions in the Internet groups are much more lively than on eWorld.

Even if you use AOL primarily for its own content—and not just as a way to get on the Internet—you'll find it's a great place to get further acquainted with Internet thoughts and concepts. And, you'll find a lot of programs for using your PPP/SLIP connection when you finally get it up and running. Not to mention the thousands of other shareware, freeware, update, and demo programs available for Macs.

The rest of AOL

Perhaps the *most* compelling reason for using AOL for your Internet access is that the rest of the service is so useful. Not only does AOL offer gobs of interest groups, professional content, and online offers, but it's worked to integrate the Internet seamlessly into its service. You'll find links to the Internet all over the service—not just in the Internet area (see fig. 7.6).

Fig. 7.6
AOL has made an effort to roll some Internet features into the rest of its service. Among the menu and button choices for AOL content are tossed in a few links to similar services on the Internet.

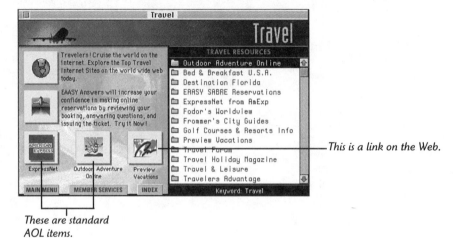

This is a link on the Web.

These are standard AOL items.

Have I justified my first-place rating yet? AOL is definitely on top of the other services for easy-to-grasp, tight integration of the Internet into its bevy of information services.

TIP   **Okay...one more reason. AOL is pioneering higher-speed access** for online services with its AOLnet network. It's the only service that I can *currently* access at 28.8Kbps, as can many other folks in major metro areas.

A close (but quiet) second: eWorld

There are two very important things to understand about eWorld before we launch into a serious discussion of its merits and shortcomings. First, eWorld is a relatively new service that caters (currently) only to Macintosh users. There is no Windows or other software for eWorld—only a Mac front end is available. Why is that significant? Because it helps explain why there aren't that many users on eWorld.

Second, eWorld licenses all of its interface technology from America Online. That's not to say that eWorld *looks* like a clone of AOL—it has a very distinct look and feel that can really only be described as "Applesque." But, if you use both services for a while, you'll realize that really only the names and fonts have changed…the interfaces are very similar.

So, for the Internauts among us, that means that Apple's Internet offers are *very* similar to AOL's, and they're usually only a few weeks or months behind AOL with any new offerings. eWorld also doesn't offer quite as many Internet services as AOL, leaving out Gopher and WAIS areas (although Gopher sites can be accessed with any Web browser, including eWorld's).

TIP　**To get to the eWorld Internet Center (see fig. 7.7), click once on** the picture of the highway on-ramp pictured in eWorld's city map. (Get it? Info-Highway?) You can also hit **Command+G**, type **Internet,** and hit Return.

Fig. 7.7
This is eWorld's Internet Center. Aside from Apple's characteristic art and fonts, it's not completely unlike AOL's Internet center.

There's a lot to like about eWorld's approach, including its very friendly look and feel. The Internet resources it offers are well integrated and don't require much in the way of a learning curve. My only real complaint is that I just can't get over the feeling that there aren't many other people here with me on the service.

Sending Internet e-mail with eWorld

Like America Online, eWorld rolls its Internet e-mail functions right into its normal e-mail system (see fig. 7.8). Just address a message with the appropriate Internet e-mail address and you can send it anywhere in the world. eWorld also offers some shortcut addresses (for example, ***username*@aol** does the same thing as ***username@aol.com***) but, honestly, I can't see much point in that, since it's important for us to get used to standard Internet addresses.

TIP For receiving Internet e-mail, your eWorld address follows the format: ***username@eworld.com***.

Enter an Internet
e-mail address here.

Enter the text of
your message.

Fig. 7.8
Internet e-mail on eWorld is as easy as it is on AOL. Just enter the address and send away. No file attachments, though.

Click to send it off.

```
┌──────────────── Compose New Message ─────────────────┐
│ [Address Book]    To: miker@onway.net        cc:      │
│ [Member Dir...]                                        │
│                                                        │
│ [Attach File...]  Subject: Found the file you were looking for! │
│                   File:                                │
│                   Mike,                                │
│ [Send Now]        I was just browsing around here on eWorld and I came across that │
│ [Send Later]      graphics program you were looking for. If you have an account, I'd suggest │
│ ☐ Notify when     signing on and checking out the user files in the Computer center. Just │
│   read            search using the keyword "graphics". It's a new file, so it should be right │
│ How to send via:  there at the top. │
│ [Internet]        Todd │
│ [Fax]                                                  │
└────────────────────────────────────────────────────────┘
```

Like America Online, you can't attach a file to an eWorld message and send it across the Internet. That simply doesn't work.

Other Internet services

Aside from e-mail, eWorld offers FTP, UseNet discussion groups, and Web access. There's also information for subscribing to Internet mailing lists, which are sort of interactive newsletters that get mailed to your eWorld account on a regular basis (see Chapter 10). All are well implemented, and eWorld does a good job of making it feel like you're still in eWorld—not on the big-ol' bad Internet.

For instance, to download a file via FTP, click once on the Software Sources button in the Internet Center. From there, you can choose one of eWorld's recommended FTP sites, or you can enter the address of one you like more. Then, eWorld presents you with the file directories of those sites. A double-click on a particular file name will download that file to your computer (see fig. 7.9).

Here are the file directories.

Fig. 7.9
eWorld's FTP system.
It's easy-to-grasp,
putting an attractive
face on the old
Internet stand-by. Take
that virus warning
seriously, though.

Double-click folders
to open them.

Find a file you want?
Double-click to download.

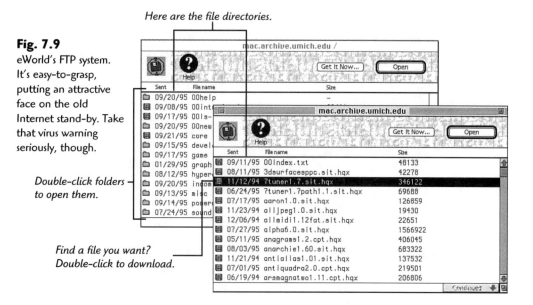

For UseNet, eWorld's got a slightly different face, but it's the same basic
technology as AOL. You choose a core group of discussion groups to follow,
and the presentation is slick enough to make it easy (see fig. 7.10). You've got
all the maintenance options you'll need—there's even some personalizing you
can do here, adding your own "signature" for appending to messages you
send on UseNet.

Fig. 7.10
UseNet on eWorld.
Capable and present-
able, there's not much
here that isn't on
America Online—
especially since AOL's
folks wrote the
program.

The newsgroup's
message list is
back here.

Here I'm reading a
particular message.

I can choose
how to reply.

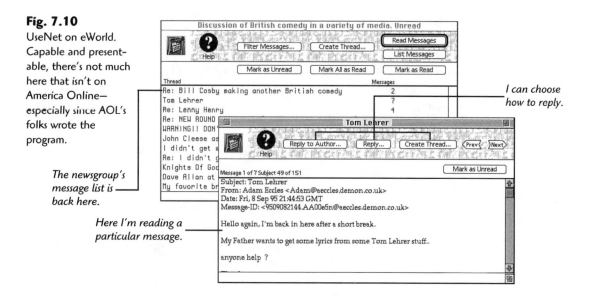

I'm not even going to show you the Web browser, which is the *same, exact* program that AOL uses for its Macintosh clients. It's no worse, although it still holds you to the same steep memory requirements. You'll need at least eight megabytes to get on eWorld and "surf" the Web.

The eWorld verdict

We can say a lot of nice stuff about eWorld. It's very Mac-centric, which makes me happy. It's Apple's own online service, so it's a great place to go for technical support…and that Apple-standard "happy people" feeling is everywhere. It has the same cost structure, the same ease-of-use and the same Web browser as AOL.

CompuServe: third, but gaining…

If I were writing this sometime late in 1996, I might not be giving the CompuServe Information Service (CIS) such a hard time—especially if it comes through with the improvements it's promised. So far, there's supposed to be a new version of the Macintosh software due at the beginning of the year: MacCIM 3.0. CompuServe has revamped its rate structure, making it a relatively low-cost alternative for Internet access. It does offer FTP, e-mail, Web services, and something the others don't offer: Telnet. That said, I'm now going to *bash* them hard.

What's wrong with CompuServe?

CompuServe's *current* Internet offerings are mediocre to pitiful (see fig. 7.11). The e-mail is okay; you still have to enter weird little commands to send an Internet mail, but at least it doesn't charge for every message any-more. The FTP is mediocre—not nearly as automatic and insightful as AOL and eWorld, but it works sometimes. The UseNet reader is the part that deserves pity—you could conceivably read discussion groups with it, but all of the fun is gone.

CompuServe doesn't offer an integrated Web browser. Instead, you call the service using MacPPP and MacTCP as if CIS were your Internet Service Provider (as discussed in Chapter 5). There are some obvious downsides to this. For one thing, you are looking to online services for ease-of-use, right? There's no advantage here. Second, there's no way that CompuServe can compete with your local provider for a high-speed connection. And, as far as I can tell, you can't access the regular CompuServe services until you quit your browser and reconnect.

Fig. 7.11
CompuServe's Internet Services screen. To get here, double-click Internet in the MacCIM's Browse window.

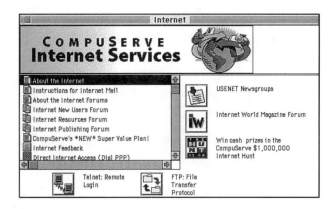

Did they do anything right?

Absolutely. The PPP connection is an interesting solution, with at least a few advantages. CompuServe is national, so you can probably figure out an easy way to use your browser all around the country. CompuServe's new rate structure lets you use the Web for 20 hours at a monthly rate of $24.95, plus $1.95 each additional hour. That's not bad, especially for light users. And, you get to use any browser you want—even Netscape Navigator—and that's a distinct advantage over AOL and eWorld.

These positives have only come about since the middle of 1995. CompuServe seems to be getting its act together—and is probably feeling the competition from other services. Frankly, CompuServe has always been the best service for breadth and depth of content, and it's always been the choice of serious business users. It used to be the perfect information service—as long as *someone else* was paying for it. And now, with the new rate structure, it can actually be cheaper to use than many of the other services.

Watch CompuServe carefully. In the next edition of this book, it may be much closer to the top.

Sending Internet e-mail on CompuServe

To send an Internet e-mail message on CompuServe, you need to remember just a tad bit more than with AOL and eWorld. From the Mail menu, choose Create Mail. That gives you the standard CompuServe mail message window (see fig. 7.12). In the Name field, just enter the given name of your recipient. In the Address field, though, you'll need to use the following format:

INTERNET: username@address

An example might be: **INTERNET: jdoe@aol.com**. The key is using the word INTERNET with a colon; otherwise, CompuServe doesn't recognize that you're trying to send a message via the Internet.

TIP **Your Internet address on CompuServe follows this pattern:**

71000.999@compuserve.com.

Make sure you substitute a period (.) for the comma in your CompuServe account number.

Here's the Out Basket.

Click Send Now.

Choose Create Mail from the Mail menu.

Fig. 7.12
Creating an Internet
e-mail message on
CompuServe is a little
different from the
other services—at least
in the addressing.

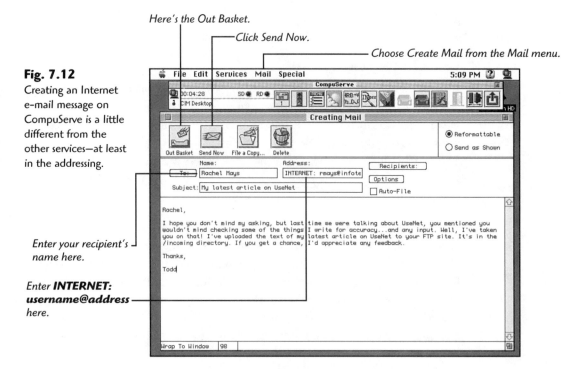

Enter your recipient's name here.

Enter **INTERNET: username@address** *here.*

To send the message, click Send Now in the Create Mail window. If you like, you can file the message in your Out Basket for sending later (or for creating mail offline).

CAUTION **As with the other services, the Send File command in the Mail**
menu won't work over the Internet because Internet e-mail handles
text *only.*

Accessing UseNet newsgroups with CompuServe

From the Internet Services window, click once on the UseNet newsgroups icon, then double-click the UseNet Reader (CIM) menu item. After you read a few messages concerning disclaimers and netiquette, you're ready to subscribe to a newgroup. That should bring up something like figure 7.13. From there, you can browse for a group that interests you in the window on the left or enter a particular group on the right. After you've subscribed to a group or two, you can start reading messages.

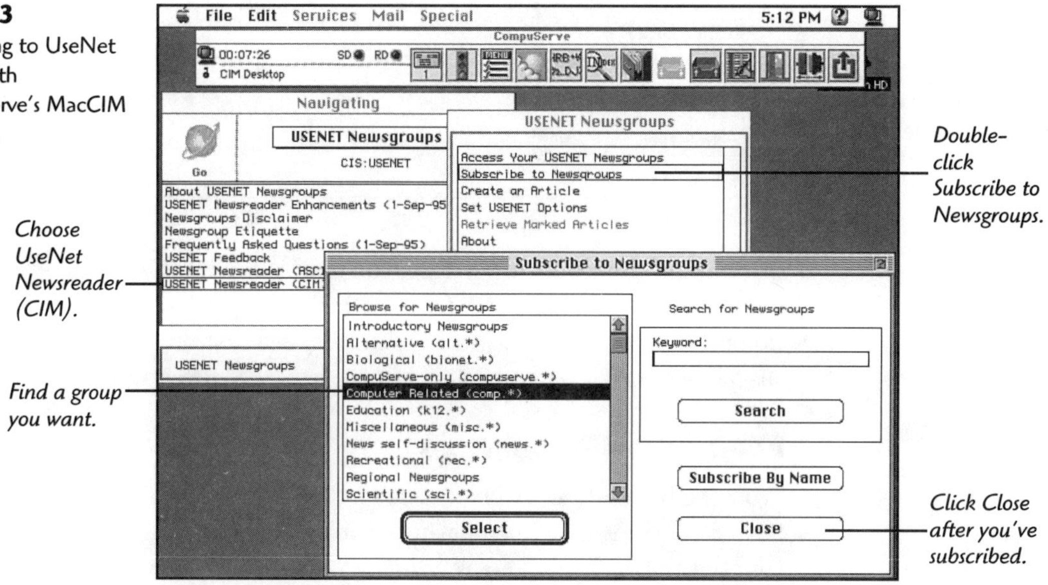

Fig. 7.13
Subscribing to UseNet groups with CompuServe's MacCIM interface.

*Choose
UseNet
Newsreader
(CIM).*

*Find a group
you want.*

*Double-
click
Subscribe to
Newsgroups.*

*Click Close
after you've
subscribed.*

Once you've used the Cancel button in each window to get back to the UseNet Newsgroups menu, you'll notice that you can now select Access Your Newsgroups. From here, choose which of your newsgroups to browse by highlighting the group (click once with the mouse) then clicking Browse. In the browsing window, click once to put an X next to the articles you'd like to read (see fig. 7.14), and then click Get. The messages you choose will show up in a new window for you to read.

Fig. 7.14
Here, deeper into
CompuServe's news-
reader, you can select
the articles you'd like
to read and respond
to.

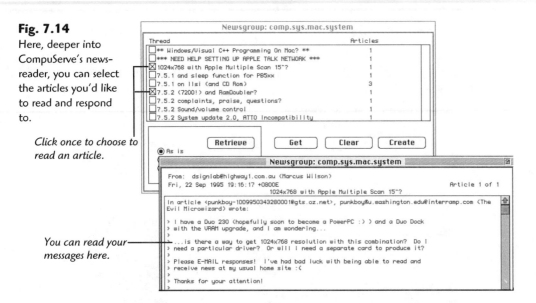

*Click once to choose to
read an article.*

*You can read your
messages here.*

(As with the other online services, you'll probably want to spend some time reading Chapters 14 and 15 before getting too involved with UseNet.) CompuServe also offers some helpful advice in text files called Newsgroups Disclaimer and Newsgroup Etiquette in the UseNet Newsgroups menu.

FTP and other services

From the Internet menu, click once on the FTP button. This brings up the File Transfer Protocol menu, where you can choose to access popular sites, choose from a listing of many sites, or enter an FTP address directly. Figure 7.15 shows a list of sites. Double-click on the site you wish to access.

From there, CompuServe shows a sign-on dialog box, and clicking OK will attempt to sign on to the remote FTP site. If everything goes well, a directory listing of files available at that site appears. To dig deeper into a directory, just double-click that directory's name. To download a file, click once to put an X next to its name, and then click Retrieve.

 TIP   **Unlike many FTP interfaces, CompuServe will allow you to down-**
load more than one file at a time, as long as they're all in the current directory. Just put an X next to every file you want, then click Retrieve when you're done. (Or, to download the entire directory, don't mark any files with an X.)

Done accessing a site? Just click Leave to get back to the List of FTP Sites.

Fig. 7.15
You have a couple of different ways to access FTP sites on CompuServe. If you need some help finding a good site, these menus are the right place to start.

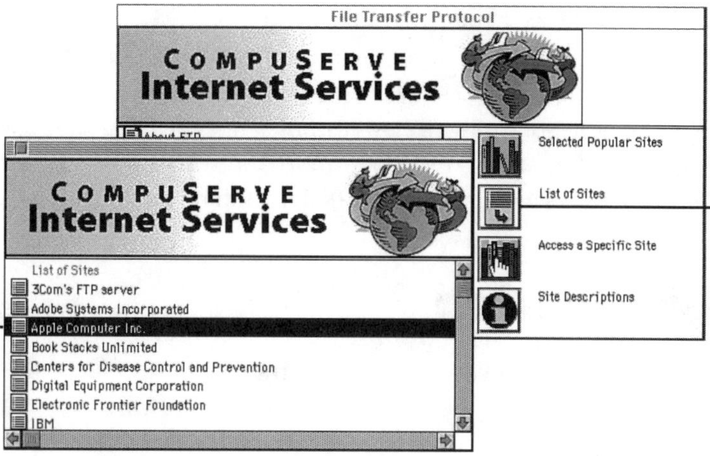

Double-click Apple Computer and you're on your way to Apple's FTP site.

In the File Transport Protocol menu, choose List of Sites.

Other Internet services

CompuServe also allows you to initiate Telnet sessions, which connect you to remote computers through a terminal emulator. To begin a Telnet session, simply click once on the Telnet button in the Internet Services window. You can then decide whether to enter your own address or select from one of the popular spots CompuServe provides.

For World Wide Web access, as described above, you'll need to initiate a MacPPP session through CompuServe. (For additional instructions, see Chapter 5.) CompuServe includes specific configuration instructions online from the Internet Services menu.

Is there anything wrong with using an online service?

At the beginning of this chapter, I mentioned that using an online service for your Internet connection can be something of a trade-off. But what exactly are you missing out on? Most of the online services offer a decent array of services, but, CompuServe aside, you're generally stuck with the interface that the online service provides. (And CompuServe really only lets you select a Web browser.) On top of that, none of the services offer access to Internet Relay Chat and only CompuServe offers Telnet access.

The biggest complaint I hear from folks who use an online service is the loss of freedom to choose their interface. With a PPP account and Eudora e-mail, for instance, you have many more options for saving and filing e-mail, automating e-mail answers, and managing your time spent communicating. Online services tend to be more "bare bones" about these services, with none of the extras that the full-fledged Internet applications offer.

The best decision

For most folks, especially Internet "newbies," deciding for or against an online service boils down to a question of cost. For America Online and eWorld, that comes to $9.95 a month for the first five hours, and $2.95 per hour after that. For CompuServe, you can get 20 hours for $24.95, with each additional hour costing $1.95.

If you're a business traveller, or you have trouble coming across a local Internet provider, then the convenience of an online service is hard to beat. Plus, it's a great way to get started on the Internet. In fact, you might even find the online service itself is pretty useful, which may make the whole experience even more worthwhile.

For more information, call:

America Online
800-827-6364

CompuServe
800-848-8990

eWorld
800-775-4556

8

The 21st Century Post Office: Internet E-mail

● In this chapter:

- ● Why e-mail is so popular

- ● How to find someone's Internet address

- ● What can I send in an e-mail message?

- ● Are there any rules for sending e-mail messages?

A telegraph on every desk? Well, if it makes you happy…but in this day and age, we call it e-mail . . . . ●

Have you noticed that it's become more and more impossible to actually reach someone on the phone? The more technology we have for getting in touch with one another, the less we actually do. Voice mail, pagers, cellular phones, computerized answering systems, digital secretaries, and personal phone numbers all abound. And, all too often, you still can't get through.

Is e-mail different? I think it is. For the first time in history you can communicate almost instantly—in writing. Why is that important? Well, we've had telephones for a century and letter writing still seems to be fairly popular. Written communication can sometimes be better for getting our point across—especially if we feel the need to do so without interruption. It's also more polite than a telephone. An e-mail message just sits in your electronic in-box, patiently waiting until you have a few minutes to sip your afternoon fruit juice and stare at the computer screen.

The death (and rebirth) of the personal letter

Until recently, the drawback to written communication was that it took too long to transmit to your audience. A postal letter takes three to five days; an overnight delivery is at least twelve hours away. Not since the telegraph— with apologies to the fax machine—has written communication been able to speed up. And convenience hasn't really improved since ZIP codes were implemented.

But, with a computer connected to the Internet, you can potentially send a written message to anyone in the world (who has access to a computer) in a matter of minutes (see fig. 8.1). That means the only reason to buy first-class stamps is to send checks to your utility company—if you don't already pay most of your bills by modem. For personal correspondence, there doesn't seem to be any reason not to use your computer (except, maybe, the perfume on the envelope thing).

The key to Internet e-mail, of course, is knowing the address of the person with whom you wish to correspond. And that's the biggest *problem* with e-mail, too. It's nearly impossible to find an address you don't know. There's no phonebook to speak of...and, considering the tens of millions of Internet users, finding a particular one is a daunting prospect.

Fig. 8.1
My brother (a student at Washington State U.) and I frequently exchange notes over the Internet. Getting him to write a normal letter on paper is like pulling teeth with a tennis racquet.

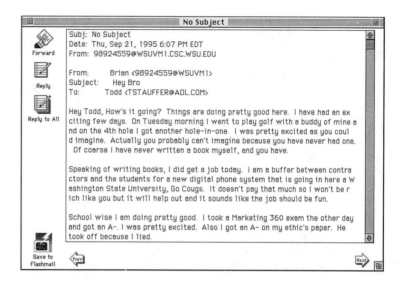

How do you find an Internet address?

Let me say this before we get carried away in this discussion: the best way to get someone's e-mail address is to ask him. Many people are giving of their addresses freely—especially in the corporate world. In fact, if you haven't already, it's a good idea to put your e-mail address on your business card. Once you get used to the concept of e-mail, you'll see that an e-mail address is at least as important as a phone number for business communications.

 TIP While we're talking business cards, it's also a good idea to put the address for your (or your company's) World Wide Web site on your card. (We'll talk more about personal Web sites in Chapter 20.)

They've actually printed some directories!

With no guarantee expressed or implied, I might suggest you spend some time in your local bookstore. A number of different publishers have made the effort to create an Internet equivalent of your local phone book that holds addresses of thousands of users. Obviously, finding a single individual will be tough—although you could get lucky. If nothing else, one of these guides might help narrow the search. An e-mail or Web site address for the company where your recipient works, for instance, might get you closer to your goal.

InterNIC: Internet directory services

For about five percent of the Internet population, there *is* a way to look up Internet addresses. InterNIC, a service provided by AT&T Corporation, is an organization responsible for developing directory services for the Internet.

InterNIC (see fig. 8.2) is doing a good job, but the anarchic nature of the Internet tends to preclude such things as universal documentation. Not only do addresses tend to change too quickly, but there are generally-held cultural qualms against such efforts as well. If you think unlisted phone numbers are inconvenient, you haven't begun to search for someone on the Internet.

Fig. 8.2
InterNIC on the World Wide Web. There are other ways to access these databases, but I suggest the Web for ease-of-use.

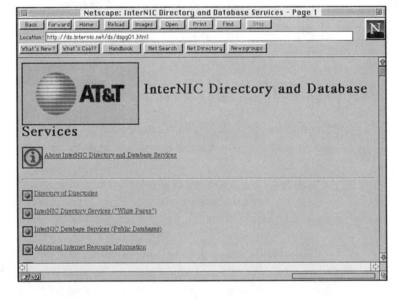

I know we haven't discussed using your Web browser yet, but it's the best way to access InterNIC. (You might want to refer to Chapters 17 and 18). For now, I'll just show you the searching process on InterNIC's Web site.

To get to InterNIC, point to the following Web address (**URL**) with your browser: **http://ds.internic.net/ds/dspg01.html**. You'll come up with the page you just saw in figure 8.2, which is a jumping-off point into a number of Internet directory databases. Then, click once on the link called InterNIC Directory Services ("White Pages"). This is where most of the searching for individual addresses is done.

Plain English, please!

> A **Universal Resource Locator (URL)** is a very silly way of saying "Internet address, Plus". Used almost exclusively by Web browsers, a URL gives not only an Internet address, but the type of service (for example, **gopher://host.domain.net**). (We'll talk a lot about them in Chapter 17.)

InterNIC offers three different ways to search: X.500, NetFind, and WHOIS. Depending on what you know about a person, some are more successful than others.

Using the X.500 when you know the company name

Actually, this works well if you also know the organization or university. Realize, though, that the X.500 system only includes about 2,800 organizations world-wide, at the time of this writing. This ain't bad, but it means there are a lot of folks left out. An organization has to agree to participate, and, at least according to InterNIC, many companies and organizations are unwilling to provide access to their user databases.

From the Internet White Pages screen, click once on the World-wide X.500 Directory link. On the next screen, click Access the U.S. pilot.(Note that this link may change when it's no longer a pilot program.) What results is the top level of the X.500 directory (see fig. 8.3).

Fig. 8.3
Like many things on the Web, the X.500 directory looks and works like an interactive table of contents. Just click whatever describes what you're looking for.

Click one of these links to dig into the directory.

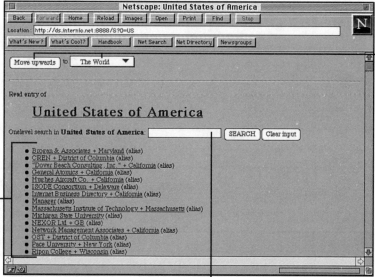

This button and pop-up menu are for moving up and down in the directory.

Enter a search word to search this level.

You see now why you need to know where your missing friend works. Let's say you are going to search for someone who attends the University of Texas. From this menu, you can click either Texas or University of Texas (which appears when you scroll the window down in figure 8.3). Let's pick the University link. Click that, and you get the screen shown in figure 8.4.

Fig. 8.4
Once you get down to this level in the directory, you can search for actual people. Try a last name and click Search.

Enter a name in the box.

Then click the button to search for it.

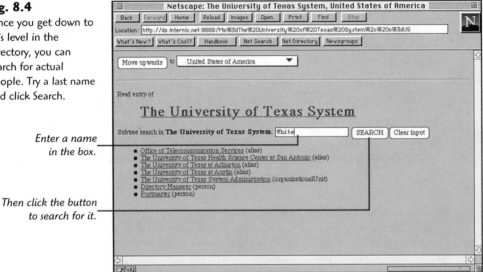

On this page you can search for an actual person. Enter the last name— **White**, for instance—and see what happens (see fig. 8.5).

Fig. 8.5
Look at this list! Click one of these names and you've hit paydirt.

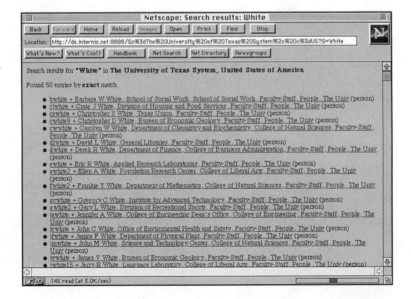

The resulting list shows the names of people that matched your search parameter in the University of Texas system. Your last step would be to click an actual name, which would give you the Internet address of (and probably additional information concerning) the person you are seeking. Pretty cool, huh?

Use NetFind if you know location

The second InterNIC service is called **NetFind**, and it's a little less complicated than X.500. NetFind doesn't actually search its own database. Instead, it sends out requests to other Internet directories and attempts to narrow the search based on the search "keys" you give it.

From the Internet White Pages screen, choose the entry for NetFind. Then click on Search NetFind for E-mail Addresses. That brings us to the screen shown in figure 8.6.

TIP **Notice that in figure 8.6 we're actually accessing a Gopher server** with a Web browser (see Chapter 13 for more on Gopher). It's important to remember that this is possible, especially if you use an online service for your Internet activities.

Fig. 8.6
The NetFind search screen. Make sure you use the right format for your search, or you won't find anything at all.

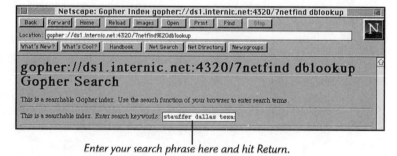

Enter your search phrase here and hit Return.

Your NetFind search phrase (the stuff you enter in the Search field on the screen) should adhere to the following format:

name keyword keyword ... ...

In this format, *name* is the last name of the person you're searching for, and each *keyword* is either an organization's name or a regional name. You should use at least two keywords, but more are possible. For instance, to find my Internet address, use my city, state, and the name of my Internet provider as keywords:

stauffer dallas texas connect

This is a great way to search for me, and, frankly, it's the only successful search I've ever witnessed on NetFind! (See fig. 8.7.) You really need to have a good idea of who you're looking for, and hope that her company or organization releases information on employees or members. Knowing the city or state and an Internet provider's name (**connect** is the domain name of my current Internet provider) is a great way to find someone with NetFind.

Fig. 8.7
You've got a promising lead. This seems to be my Internet provider.

Now that you've got a good-looking lead, you need to choose it to start the search for the actual name. Notice that NetFind is working backward through your search phrase here—using the keywords to narrow the search. Now that you're selecting a specific site, it will try to find the name (see fig. 8.8).

Fig. 8.8
Success! It may be hard to tell, but NetFind is giving you my actual Internet address there at the bottom.

Bingo!

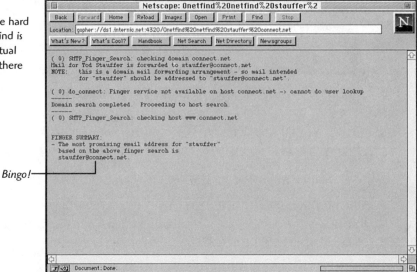

Finally, if the stars are aligned and the gods are smiling, you may just end up with an Internet address. This time NetFind found mine…it's the last line there in figure 8.8, **stauffer@connect.net**. That's my PPP account's mail address.

Do you at least have a name? Try WHOIS.

The last search engine is called WHOIS (said "who is"). In this one, all you need to know is the name of the person for whom you're searching. WHOIS is all about syntax, so you'll need to follow the rules carefully.

You start from the Internet White Pages screen by clicking once on WHOIS Person/Organization. Then, on the next screen, click Query InterNIC WHOIS server to get to the screen in figure 8.9.

Fig. 8.9
Here's the WHOIS search screen. Just enter the name you want to search for in the field and hit Return.

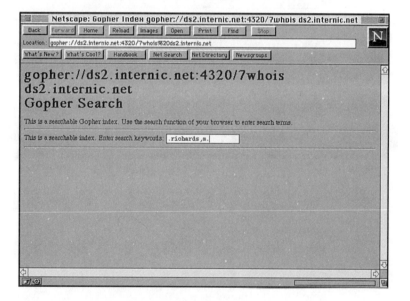

In the search field, there are a couple of rules to follow. For a person's name, enter the name with a period (.) at the beginning of the query. If you have a first and last name, enter it like this: **.doe,john** with a period, a comma, and no spaces. Just a last name can be: **.doe** or **.do.**, where the trailing period means "last names that start with 'do' and end with whatever." If you enter a query with no period at the beginning, WHOIS will assume you're looking for an organization, not a person.

There are more complete instructions available in the document Search Instructions found on the same screen where Query InterNIC WHOIS server is. But that's the general idea. Good luck.

What you can send by e-mail

As a general rule, the only thing you can send by e-mail is text because Internet e-mail protocols are only designed to transfer ASCII text. **ASCII** stands for **American Standard Code for Information Interchange**, and it's a very basic level of text that doesn't allow for special fonts, formatting, and sizes. It's also the standard that lets different computers—like IBM PCs or UNIX workstations—read e-mail messages you create on your Mac. When you create an e-mail message in an e-mail program, it sends that letter in ASCII.

Since Internet e-mail can only handle ASCII, it's impossible to *directly* send binary files to someone else. Now, that's not to say that there aren't ways around this.

 Plain English, please!

Basically, a **binary** file is any program or document that isn't just basic text. Even word processing documents (which contain information on font size, centering, margins, and so forth) are binary files—as are spreadsheets, games, graphics files, and most anything else you can use or create with your Mac. **99**

You only get what you ASCII...

So, if you can't transfer binary documents and programs, how can you send them through the Internet e-mail system? You need to *translate* them into ASCII, send them as an e-mail message, then *translate* them back. It's like a secret decoder system—you change the binary information into text, send it, then it's changed back into a program or document on the other side. How? In most cases, you use a process called BinHex (see fig. 8.10).

I know this looks pretty weird, but, luckily, Eudora can handle this BinHex issue automatically—especially when you're sending documents and pro-grams to other Mac and Eudora users. If you're lucky, you'll never have to worry about this. If you regularly send files back and forth to folks who use other computer platforms (like PCs or UNIX machines), then you'll need to know more about binary to ASCII translation.

Fig. 8.10
Here's a word processing document that's been "binhexed" into ASCII text. Looks like gibberish, but it can be turned back into a document by your recipient.

TIP **Use a compression program (like Compact Pro or StuffIt! Lite)** before sending files over the Internet. This makes them smaller, so they take less time to transfer. (If compression programs are Greek to you, check out Chapter 11.)

Internet etiquette: please read this!

Okay now, where's that soapbox when I need it?

When you start to get a lot of e-mail in your mailbox every day, you'll begin to appreciate these suggestions. But even if you're just getting started with e-mail, you might want to look these over to make sure you're not unintentionally upsetting someone. Some of these may surprise you.

- **Don't send files without a prior agreement.** We've just finished discussing that it's possible to send files through Internet mail, but it can be pretty darned annoying if you don't want the file. Documents and programs tend to be large, and it's no fun to sit and watch your computer for five or ten minutes while it downloads a PageMaker brochure that you didn't care to see. Make sure your recipient *wants* the file, first.

- **Never type in all caps**. On the Internet, TYPING IN ALL CAPS IS YELLING! Since there aren't many ways to express emotion in ASCII text, all caps is to be reserved for making an exceptional point. Did you HEAR ME? It's usually better to emphasize words by putting single astericks on either side of a word, but not *everything* you write. If you're that emphatic about something or someone, maybe you should go ahead and give them a phone call.

- **Make your subject meaningful and your message brief.** All e-mail messages have a subject line, and it's usually the first thing that your recipient sees in his e-mail In box. Subject lines like I was thinking... or Hi! can be really annoying when you're trying to figure out whether or not you have time to read. Keep it to the point. We Need to Discuss the Book Proposal or Re: I'm Leaving You For Another Man are much better attention grabbers.

- **Quote relevant text when you reply.** Most e-mail programs have a feature that allows you to quote the text of a previous message in the reply. Even if your e-mail program doesn't, you can use cut and paste to quote the important stuff (see fig. 8.11). Don't quote the whole message, just the key points. It helps your recipient remember what he said, and keeps him from puzzling over a message that says I agree completely! when he doesn't remember what he asked.

Greater-than brackets mean a quote is starting.

Fig. 8.11
Here's a properly quoted message. It's also typical to see every line of quoted text begin with a bracket— different e-mail programs handle quotes differently.

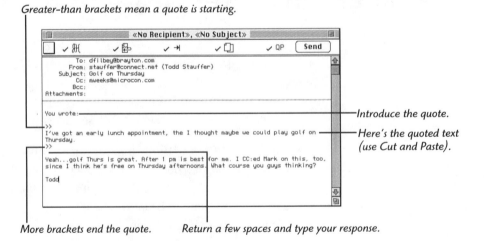

Introduce the quote.

Here's the quoted text (use Cut and Paste).

More brackets end the quote.

Return a few spaces and type your response.

- **Forward messages sparingly.** It's especially important to stay away from chain letters and e-mail advertisements—nothing makes an Internet guru angry quicker. When you do forward a message, make sure it's something your recipient can use and will definitely appreciate.

Sending and Receiving Internet E-mail with Eudora Light

● **In this chapter:**

- **Where to get Eudora Light**

- **What do I need to know to set up Eudora?**

- **Creating your own e-mail messages**

- **How do I read and reply to messages?**

- **Where can I get more info on Eudora Light?**

Easily, the most popular Macintosh e-mail program is Eudora Light. And, just our luck, it's free, too! . . . . ▶

Now that we've covered the basics of Internet e-mail in Chapter 8, we can move on to one of the more popular e-mail programs for the Macintosh, Eudora Light. If you've got a MacPPP account, this is probably the e-mail program you'll want to start out with—it's free, for one thing, and able to handle most people's e-mail needs. If you find you need another program, Qualcomm, the company responsible for Eudora Light, offers more robust e-mail solutions.

At this point, let's just get Eudora Light installed and operational on your machine. In just a few minutes, we should be sending and reading Internet e-mail like crazy.

Starting out with Eudora Light

First things first...you'll need a copy of Eudora. There's a convenient copy on the MacNet disk included with this book. This version is designed for Mac System 7 or above. It's *not* the version written in native Power Macintosh code, so, if you've got a Power Mac, you'll eventually want the "fat" version, which is available from the FTP sites (the included version will work for now, just not at Power Mac speeds).

If you already know how to access FTP, or you can get at FTP through an online service, then you can download the latest version of Eudora Light from **ftp.qualcomm.com** in the directory /quest/mac/eudora/. Or point your Web browser to **http://www.qualcomm.com/quest/freeware.html**.

Otherwise, simply insert the MacNet disk in your Mac's floppy drive and double-click its icon. In the resulting window, drag the Eudora1.5.3 icon to your Mac's hard drive or desktop. When it's done copying, double-click the new icon and choose a folder on your Mac to store the program in.

To start Eudora Light, double-click the Eudora Light icon.

Setting up Eudora Light

The first time you start Eudora Light, you'll be presented with the Settings dialog box (see fig. 9.1). Although this box offers a lot of different choices, all you need to worry about at this point is the Getting Started choices you're presented with when you launch the program.

TIP **You'll need to know at least your e-mail address to configure** Eudora. You should also know the address of your ISP's mail server.

Fig. 9.1
The Settings dialog box can seem a little intimidating, but all you really need to know is your Internet address.

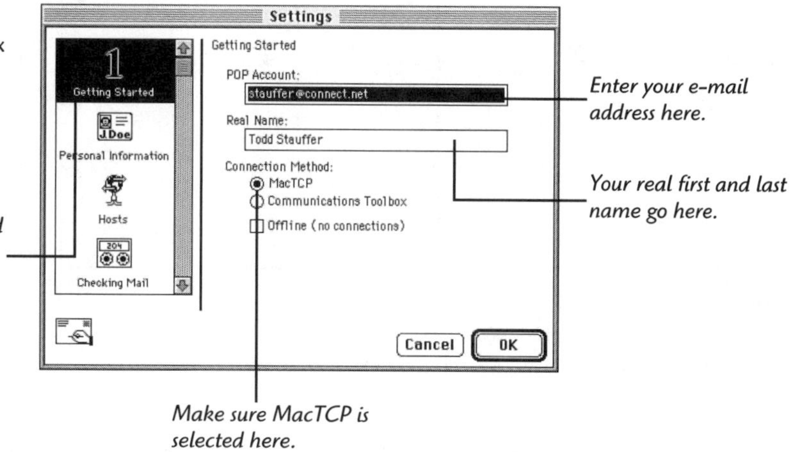

Getting Started should be highlighted.

> **Settings**
>
> Getting Started
>
> POP Account:
> stauffer@connect.net
>
> Real Name:
> Todd Stauffer
>
> Connection Method:
> ⦿ MacTCP
> ○ Communications Toolbox
> ☐ Offline (no connections)
>
> Getting Started
> Personal Information
> Hosts
> Checking Mail
>
> [Cancel] [OK]

Enter your e-mail address here.

Your real first and last name go here.

Make sure MacTCP is selected here.

After you enter the information as pictured in figure 9.1, click OK in the Settings box. Eudora has all the information it needs to send and receive messages for you...the rest of the settings are basic preference issues.

Sending a mail message

Most e-mail messages look the same as typical office memos. They're structured that way to make communications between different computer types and programs easier. All the parts of the memo are there—To, From, Subject, and even a space for carbon copies (see fig. 9.2). In an office memo, these spots can be filled with a number of different things. In an e-mail message, though, we need to conform to the standards to ensure that the message is sent correctly.

The To, From, Cc and Bcc spaces all require valid Internet addresses to send the e-mail correctly. The To and From spaces must always be filled in for any e-mail message, but the Cc and Bcc spaces may be left blank when not needed. You may notice that the From field is automatically filled in with the Internet address you gave Eudora in Settings. You'll need to fill in the other fields yourself (hit Tab once to move from field to field).

Fig. 9.2
The Eudora Light New Message window. It's here where you do all of your creative e-mail writing.

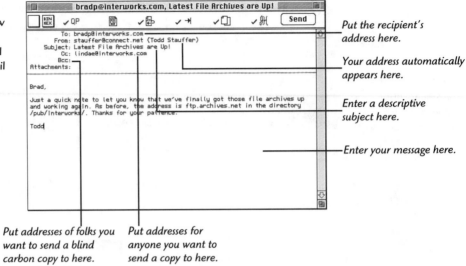

Put the recipient's address here.

Your address automatically appears here.

Enter a descriptive subject here.

Enter your message here.

Put addresses of folks you want to send a blind carbon copy to here.

Put addresses for anyone you want to send a copy to here.

TIP **Bcc stands for blind carbon copy. Put an Internet address in this** field and that person will get a copy—but none of your other recipients will know.

Also, remember to enter a meaningful subject. An important part of e-mail etiquette is making your subject line descriptive; aside from your e-mail address and name, your recipients won't see anything about your e-mail except the subject. So make sure they know whether it's important or it's something they can wait to read.

Finally, the message area awaits your creativity. Type your message any way you choose, remembering that the text will wrap itself at the edge of the window—you only need to hit Return at the end of a paragraph.

When you're done typing, click once on Send. Eudora Light will call your mail server, connect, and send the message. It's out over the Internet!

TIP **Want to test Eudora to make sure it's sending mail? If you don't** have a good friend for this, check with your ISP. He may have a special address where you can send test messages. (*Please* don't send "test" messages to me! Of course, praise, criticism, or questions are always welcome.)

Eudora Lights's interface for new messages

Sending a new mail message really isn't that tough, but we should probably cover all eventualities by looking quickly at that New Message window again. What are all of those little icons up there? Figure 9.3 shows them. For the most part, they're there for convenience. But it's a good idea to know what they are, since they can drastically change the way your e-mail will appear to the outside world.

Fig. 9.3
The four right-most icons in the New Message window let you decide how the message will look to your recipient and whether or not you'll keep a copy for yourself.

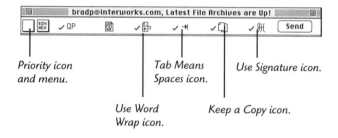

Priority icon and menu.
Tab Means Spaces icon.
Use Signature icon.
Use Word Wrap icon.
Keep a Copy icon.

A "check" next to any one of these icons means it's on; to turn it off, click it once and the check will disappear. In a nutshell, here's what they mean:

- **Use Word Wrap**. When this feature is on, Eudora will automatically enter ASCII returns at the end of each line of text before sending the message. That way (as long as your window is less than 80 characters wide), e-mail messages will look the same to your recipient as they do to you.

- **Tab Means Spaces**. There are no tabs in ASCII text files, but selecting this feature will cause Eudora to enter about eight spaces when you hit the Tab key in the message area.

- **Keep a Copy**. With this selected, Eudora will automatically save a copy of this message when you send it. You can access these copies by pulling down the Mailbox menu and selecting Out.

- **Use Signature**. With this feature selected, your e-mail message will be automatically "signed" with your signature file.

- **Priority.** In the top left corner of your New Message window is the priority menu. Click and hold your mouse button on the empty box; up pops a little menu. Move the mouse up or down to select the "priority" level of this message. Actually, this is for your reader's information only—it won't get across the Internet any faster or slower, no matter what priority you set.

Putting your unique signature on it

One of the trademarks of an Internet veteran is a good signature file. It's not enough to simply sign your e-mail messages with your name—you'll need something more creative. To edit your signature file, pull down the Window menu and select Signature (see fig. 9.4).

Fig. 9.4
The Signature file window. Put your best stuff here, but please don't overdo it!

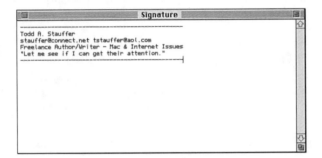

The key to a good signature is brevity and cleverness. The typical signature file is four or five lines long, and includes your name, your job, and your company (if pertinent). It also includes all relevant Internet information (e-mail address, Web site, and so on) and your favorite quote or joke. Often people will use a line of asterisks (*) or dashes (--) at the top of their signature to set it apart from the rest of the message.

CAUTION **If you use an Internet address through your company, it may be** important to add My views do not represent those of my company or some similar disclaimer to your signature if you're not acting as an official representative of the company.

Attaching files to Eudora messages

In Chapter 8, I pointed out that you can't send documents and programs through Internet e-mail in their binary form, but it is possible to send them if you first translate them into ASCII text, then send. Eudora Light will let you do exactly that without too much effort.

To send an attachment, you start by creating a New Message, as described previously. After you've entered the text of your message (you can actually do this at any time), pull down the Message menu and choose Attach Document. You'll be presented with a File Open dialog box, where you can find the document or program you want to attach to the message (see fig. 9.5). Click once on Open and the file is attached to the message. (Notice that the file name appears in the Attachments field of the e-mail message.)

Fig. 9.5
It's complicated to send files through Internet e-mail, but Eudora Light does its best to help.

Choose Attach Document from the Message menu.

Find the file in this dialog box and click Open.

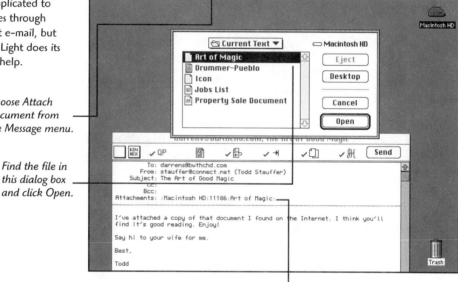

The file name appears in the Attachments field.

 TIP **Don't forget that it's a good idea to compress files with Compact** Pro or StuffIt before sending them over the Internet. For more on compression utilities, see Chapter 12.

Now, this file can easily be extracted and returned to its original state by someone who has Eudora Light or a compatible e-mail program. It's a little tougher for someone who doesn't have one of these programs, but it can be done. Extracting a file manually is covered in Chapter 16.

CAUTION **Currently, none of the major online services can send or receive** attachments to e-mail messages.

Receiving and reading e-mail messages

Eudora Light's interface works a little like your desk at the office. Under the Mailbox menu are a couple of standard items, including an In Box, Out Box and Trash. These are the basic windows for managing your e-mail. If it's not already showing, you can see your In Box by selecting it in the Mailbox menu (see fig. 9.6).

Fig. 9.6
Eudora Light's In Box revealed. To read a message, just double-click its row with your mouse.

Eudora's status of the message.

Priority level (if any).

Sender's name and/ or e-mail address.

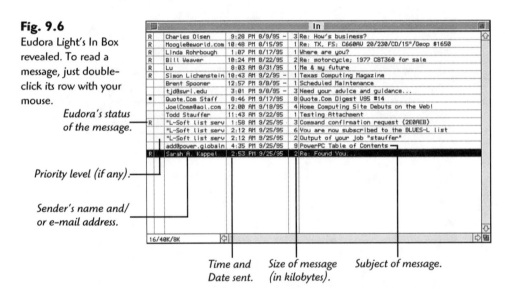

Time and Date sent.

Size of message (in kilobytes).

Subject of message.

The In Box gives you some vital statistics concerning the e-mail messages you've received and, when more come in, this is where they'll show up. Especially important is the message status in the first column. A dot means the message is new, an R means that you've sent a reply, and an F means that you've forwarded the message.

It's from the In Box window that you can read a message as well. Just double-click the row that the message is in, and you get a window like that shown in figure 9.7. Now you can read away!

Fig. 9.7
A typical e-mail message, as read in Eudora Light.

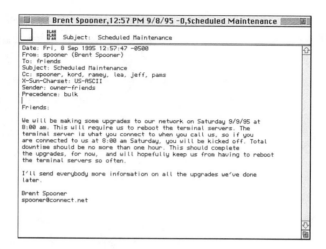

```
▓▓▓▓▓    Brent Spooner,12:57 PM 9/8/95 -0,Scheduled Maintenance    ▓▓▓▓▓

  [ ]   BLAH   Subject:  Scheduled Maintenance
        BLAH
        BLAH
Date: Fri, 8 Sep 1995 12:57:47 -0500
From: spooner (Brent Spooner)
To: friends
Subject: Scheduled Maintenance
Cc: spooner, kord, ramey, lea, jeff, pams
X-Sun-Charset: US-ASCII
Sender: owner-friends
Precedence: bulk

Friends:

We will be making some upgrades to our network on Saturday 9/9/95 at
8:00 am. This will require us to reboot the terminal servers. The
terminal server is what you connect to when you call us, so if you
are connected to us at 8:00 am Saturday, you will be kicked off. Total
downtime should be no more than one hour. This should complete
the upgrades, for now,  and will hopefully keep us from having to reboot
the terminal servers so often.

I'll send everybody more information on all the upgrades we've done
later.

Brent Spooner
spooner@connect.net
```

That's all there is to it, really. When you're done reading, just click the window's close box in the top left corner.

TIP See the "Blah, Blah, Blah" in the top corner? Cute, huh? Click it once and Eudora will show you all of the Internet routing information for this message. Interesting, if you go for that sort of thing.

Receiving attached files

Every once in awhile, you may receive a mail message that includes an attached file. Again, as long as the file was attached by a program compatible with Eudora, you shouldn't have any trouble—it should happen automatically. If you receive an attachment, Eudora Light will extract it for you, and put it in a special folder. Where? We start in the System Folder (see fig. 9.8).

In the System Folder window, you should see a folder called Eudora Folder. Double-click that and you're getting really warm. See a folder called Attachments Folder? Double-click that and (*voilà!*) there's your attachment. Double-click the attachment's icon to launch the application with which it's associated.

Q&A   *I don't want my attachments saved in the System Folder. Is there some way to save them in another folder?*

Sure, by selecting Settings in the Special menu. In the resulting dialog box, choose the Attachments icon. On the right side of the screen is a field called Attachments Folder. Click once in the field, then choose a new folder for your attachments in the dialog box. Click Use Folder to choose the folder you've pointed to, then click OK in the Settings dialog box. Your attachments will now be saved in the folder of your choice.

Fig 9.8
Eudora automatically receives attachments and puts them in a special folder on your Mac's hard drive.

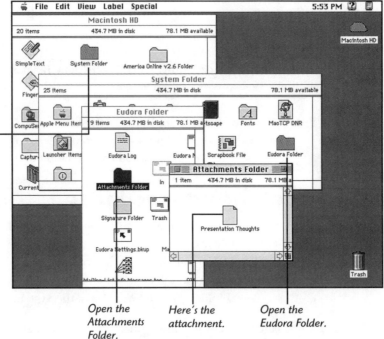

Open the System Folder.

Open the Attachments Folder.

Here's the attachment.

Open the Eudora Folder.

Replying to and forwarding messages

Once you've received a few e-mail messages, you'll be ready to start replying to what you're reading. Two important things to remember: be careful that you reply to the right people and quote messages properly.

Generally when you reply to a message you'll be sending that message back to the author of the original message. What you need to be careful of are names in the Cc: line. Depending on how Eudora Light is set up, you may or not be responding to all those folks, too.

Replying in kind

By default, your replies will only be sent to the person who originated the message and not to others in the Cc: field. To create a reply, select the window with the original message, then pull down the Message menu and choose Reply. You'll be presented with the Reply window, where you can type your return message (see fig. 9.9).

Fig. 9.9

Replying to an e-mail message. Everything is ready and waiting for your responses.

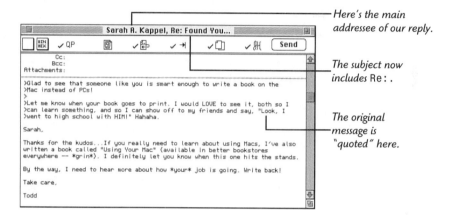

Here's the main addressee of our reply.

The subject now includes Re: .

The original message is "quoted" here.

Notice the quoted text in the message? (It's the text with the > symbol in front of each line.) Take care now to edit it down to the essentials of the message. There's no point in quoting everything—so delete any lines that aren't relevant to your response. Then type what you've gotta say, and click Send. That message is headed back from whence it came.

TIP **To send your reply to *everyone* mentioned in the original message** (all Cc: and Bcc: folks), hold down the Option key while you select Reply.

Being a bit forward?

If you get an interesting message you'd like someone else to see or maybe a question to which you don't know the answer, you might want to forward that message to another Internet user.

Easily done. With the original message open and selected, pull down the Message menu and choose Forward. In the resulting window (see fig. 9.10), the original message will be quoted, and you can enter the e-mail address for the person to whom you want to forward the message.

Fig. 9.10
Passing the buck? Go
ahead and forward that
message to someone
who has more time on
their hands.

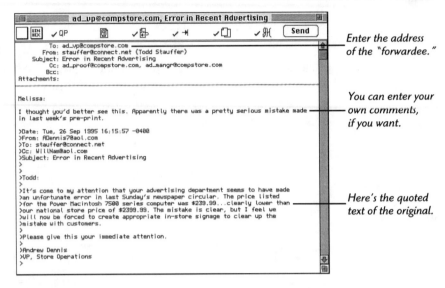

Enter the address
of the "forwardee."

You can enter your
own comments,
if you want.

Here's the quoted
text of the original.

You can also edit the quoted text of the original message (no fair doctoring the message, now) and enter your own comments. Hit Send when you're done, and now you've included someone else in the loop.

Do enough forwarding, and pretty soon you can convene a committee to discuss the e-mail, elect a board of directors, create a few special task forces, and never again get another thing accomplished!

Managing your e-mail

Get enough mail and eventually you may decide that just an In and Out box aren't enough to really keep this e-mail thing under control. Want to create more mailboxes to keep messages in? Not a problem. Pull down the Transfer menu and select New. In the resulting dialog box, you can create a new mailbox for organizing your messages (see fig. 9.11).

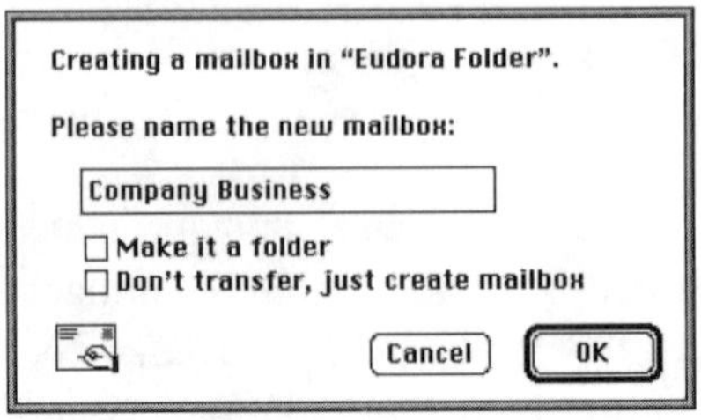

Fig. 9.11
Creating a new
mailbox. Do this over
and over again until
you've got everything
covered and you'll be
Mr. or Ms. Organized
E-Mail Person.

Creating a mailbox in "Eudora Folder".

Please name the new mailbox:

Company Business

☐ Make it a folder
☐ Don't transfer, just create mailbox

Cancel   OK

In the dialog box, type the title for the new mailbox in the field, then put an X in the appropriate box, depending on whether or not you want to transfer the currently selected message when the box is created. Click OK and you've got a new mailbox.

To see a listing of that mailbox's contents, select it from the mailbox window. To transfer other messages to that box, select the message's row in your In box, then select the new mailbox from the Transfer window. Now the message is in the new mailbox, where you can completely forget about it until it's too late to do whatever you were supposed to do about it. Perfect!

TIP **If you have an e-mail message's subject highlighted in the In box** window when you select the New command, you can also transfer that message to your new mailbox. Sorta makes sense—it is, after all, under the Transfer menu.

Deleting e-mail messages

Two ways to do this one. First way: highlight the e-mail message in your In box (or whatever mailbox it's in), and press the Delete key. It will be moved to your Trash mailbox. You can also highlight the message and choose Trash from the Transfer menu. The message will be "transferred" to the Trash mailbox.

Want to check the trash? Pull down the Mailbox menu and select Trash. The resulting window will include all the messages you've deleted since you last emptied Eudora's trash.

Speaking of which, to empty the trash, pull down the Special menu and select Empty Trash. Any e-mail messages you've previously deleted are now gone for good.

Q&A **What's with all these trash cans? Is the Eudora trash the same as my Mac's Trash icon?**

No. The writers of Eudora Light decided to use an internal trash "mailbox" for deleting e-mail messages. Don't confuse *this* trash with your Mac's Trash can in the Finder. When you Empty Trash in Eudora Light, all you're really doing is getting rid of e-mail messages, not anything else. And selecting Empty Trash in the Finder works like it always did, but it doesn't affect e-mail messages in Eudora Light.

Getting more information on Eudora Light

You may have noticed that there aren't any documentation files for Eudora Light included with the program. They're distributed separately. Once you've figured out your Web browser, though, you can download the documentation to your computer if you'd like more information on using Eudora Light. Just point your browser to **http://www.qualcomm.com/quest/freeware.html**. Or use FTP to download the documentation from **ftp.qualcomm.com**.

10

Internet Mailing Lists: E-mail Newsletters

● **In this chapter:**

● **What is a mailing list?**

● **How to find the interesting ones**

● **What are the rules for sending messages?**

● **I've got a thousand e-mail messages now! Help!**

● **Mailing-list maintenance tips**

With an e-mail account, you can communicate with friends and colleagues. But what about folks you don't know—with your same interests? If they're out there, they've probably started mailing lists . . . . ▶

With an e-mail account up and working correctly, you're open to a whole new world of near-instant communications. It's useful and fun; a great new way to get something said. But is there anything else you can do with that e-mail address of yours?

Well, if you'd really like to fill your In box in a hurry, you need to subscribe to some Internet mailing lists. It's here that you can use e-mail to discuss thousands of different topics—probably anything you can imagine. And you can use Eudora Light or a similar program for the entire experience!

What's a mailing list?

A **mailing list** works a little like a (desirable) chain letter, in that everyone who reads the list tends to contribute to it. In this way, discussions are carried on within the topic of the list.

Subscribe to a mailing list, and messages will start filling your e-mail In box. These are e-mail messages, but they're not written only to you—they're broadcast to everyone who subscribes to the list. As you read the list, you'll start to get a feel for the different threads of conversation that are taking place. When you're ready to contribute, you do so by sending an e-mail message to the list's server computer. Sometimes, it is then automatically broadcast to the rest of the subscribers.

What types of things are discussed?

Mailing lists, like UseNet discussion groups, cover an incredible variety of topics. In fact, many UseNet groups start out as mailing-lists and become full-fledged UseNet groups after reaching a certain level of popularity. Not limited to just computer-related or technical issues, there's a mailing list for just about every interest, hobby, profession, or cause. Here are some examples:

- *MAZDA-LIST*. Technical and non-technical discussions concerning all Mazda and Mazda-engineered automobiles.

- *PowerPC News.* A read-only digest of news stories related to PowerPC technology (the microprocessor inside the Power Macintosh and IBM RISC computers).

- *BLUES-L.* Discussions of blues music and performers from Charley Patton to Stevie Ray Vaughn.

- *Law and Order.* Conversations concerning the popular television show *Law and Order.* Topics include plot lines, characters, actors, producers, and related real-life cases.

- *VOCALIST.* For singers and those interesting in singing. Topics include technique, practicing, voice care, auditions, concerts, records, and choir/ensemble singing.

The different types of lists

Mailing lists can actually come in many different forms. Some lists (like PowerPC News) are designed only to distribute information in one direction—they aren't pure discussion groups, and they don't encourage responses from readers. Others are for discussion, but they are **edited**, suggesting that the group has at least one human being who reads every message and decides if it is appropriate for distribution.

Some groups are **moderated**, meaning that there's at least one person responsible for keeping the discussions on topic. **Unmoderated** lists broadcast any message sent to the list and the discussion flows without the help of anyone in an official capacity.

Lists can show up in your in-box in different forms, too. **Digests** (see fig. 10.1), are compilations of all of the messages sent in a given time period. They arrive in your e-mail box at one particular time every day, week, or other interval. Or, you can receive a mailing list as an **index**, and you'll be sent a list of all recent contributions to the discussion. You can then choose what to read.

 TIP When possible, it's a good idea to subscribe to mailing lists and immediately "set" them to digest or index forms, until you're sure you want to spend your time keeping up with the list's discussions. I'll show you how later in this chapter.

Fig. 10.1
Here's a mailing list in digest form. It arrives in my In box all at once, instead of as individual messages throughout the day.

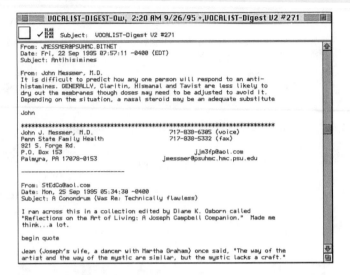

```
▣▤▤ VOCALIST-DIGEST-Ow, 2:20 AM 9/26/95 +,VOCALIST-Digest V2 #271 ▤▤▣
┌──┐ ✓ BLAH   Subject:  VOCALIST-Digest V2 #271
│  │   BLAH
└──┘   BLAH
From: JMESSMER@PSUHMC.BITNET
Date: Fri, 22 Sep 1995 07:57:11 -0400 (EDT)
Subject: Antihisimines

From: John Messmer, M.D.
It is difficult to predict how any one person will respond to an anti-
histamines. GENERALLY, Claritin, Hismanal and Tavist are less likely to
dry out the membranes though doses may need to be adjusted to avoid it.
Depending on the situation, a nasal steroid may be an adequate substitute

John

***********************************************************************
John J. Messmer, M.D.                        717-838-6305 (voice)
Penn State Family Health                     717-838-5332 (fax)
921 S. Forge Rd.
P.O. Box 153                                       jjm3fp@aol.com
Palmyra, PA 17078-0153                       jmessmer@psuhmc.hmc.psu.edu

------------------------------------

From: StEdCo@aol.com
Date: Mon, 25 Sep 1995 05:34:30 -0400
Subject: A Conondrum (Was Re: Technically flawless)

I ran across this in a collection edited by Diane K. Osborn called
"Reflections on the Art of Living: A Joseph Campbell Companion."  Made me
think...a lot.

begin quote

Jean (Joseph's wife, a dancer with Martha Graham) once said, "The way of the
artist and the way of the mystic are similar, but the mystic lacks a craft."
```

How do I get started with mailing lists?

To begin reading a mailing list, you always begin by subscribing to the list. This is accomplished in different ways, depending on how the list is managed. Generally, you'll send an e-mail message to the administrator of the list. But here's the catch: the administrator can be either a human being or a computer. Depending on which this is, your e-mail needs to be properly structured.

CAUTION **Use the correct e-mail address for sending administrative requests** to the list. Most lists have at least two e-mail addresses: one for dealing with your subscription and one for *contributing* to the list. Send your message to the wrong address and you'll either upset the administrator or the thousands of subscribers who read the list!

Finding the right mailing lists

The best way to get a list of mailing lists available is to FTP it from **rtfm.mit.edu** in the following directory:

/pub/usenet/news.answers/mail/mailing.lists/

The entire list is in a number of files; you'll probably want to download every part.

Many online services offer some kind of database for finding a mailing list that tickles your fancy. You may also find references to mailing lists in UseNet newsgroups and on the World Wide Web.

Subscribing to a computer-administered list

To subscribe to a mailing list that's administered by a computer, you need to be very careful that you follow the instructions exactly. If you don't send your request in the correct format, the computer may not be able to process the request. Generally, this follows a common format:

SUBSCRIBE LIST-NAME Recipient-Name

For our example, I'll subscribe to the Blues discussion list, BLUES-L. To do this, I send an e-mail message to **LISTSERV@brownvm.brown.edu** (see fig. 10.2). The computer doesn't care what I put in the subject line—in fact, I don't need to put anything. In the body of the message, though, I need to put a very specific command, as follows:

SUBSCRIBE BLUES-L Todd Stauffer

(Capitalization doesn't always matter, but all caps is the most common way to type mailing-list commands.) This is the appropriate command for subscribing to the list, including my name in the command. Once I start receiving the mailing list, there's a different address for sending my own contributions:

BLUES-L@brownvm.brown.edu.

Fig. 10.2

A typical subscription e-mail for a computer-administered list.

Put the "subscribing" e-mail address here.

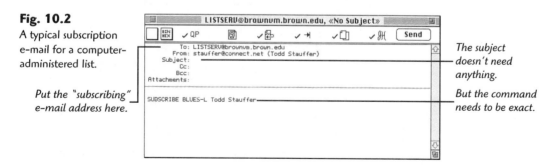

The subject doesn't need anything.

But the command needs to be exact.

Most computer administrators will ignore anything extra you put in your message—it's only looking for specific commands. There's not much point in idle chit-chat anyway, but if your e-mail program automatically adds a signature or quote to your messages, you usually don't have to turn it off just to send this command.

Subscribing to a human-administered list

The main difference here is that a person is reading your request, so it's a bit more informal. Most human administrators still want you to be fairly clear in your subscription, and many will request that you send certain keywords in your message. But that doesn't mean you're required to use the same rigidity as you are with a computer. Concise and polite should do the trick.

MAZDA-LIST seems to be a human-administered list; at least it doesn't quite conform to the standards of an automated one. So, I'll make this a bit more polite.

I send my request to **mazda-request@ms.uky.edu** (see fig. 10.3). In the subject field I'll type **SUBSCRIBE**. In the body, I'll type something along the lines of **Please SUBSCRIBE MAZDA-LIST Todd Stauffer. Thank you.** And let it go at that.

 TIP **If you're not sure how a mailing list is administered, send your** request like the MAZDA-LIST example. You'll notice that my message says SUBSCRIBE MAZDA-LIST Todd Stauffer, even though this is a human-administered list. Were it actually a computer-based list, the request might still work.

Fig. 10.3
A typical request to a human mailing list administrator.

Enter the subscribing address.

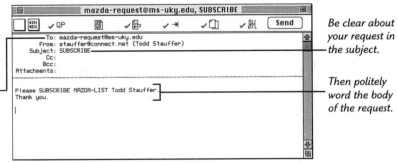

Be clear about your request in the subject.

Then politely word the body of the request.

Take special care that your message subject is clear and appropriate—many human administrators will implement your request based only on your subject and e-mail address. Also, take extra care that you *don't* send your contributions (articles for and responses to the list) to the administrative e-mail address. That just wastes the human administrator's time.

What happens after I subscribe?

If you sent your request to a computer-administered list, you can probably expect a response within a few minutes. If your list is human-administered, your request will be handled at his or her convenience, so don't be too surprised if it takes a day or more.

 CAUTION **Be patient with your human-administered list. Don't resend your** request to subscribe until a good deal of time has passed with no response. When you do resend your request, briefly and politely explain why you felt you had to resend it.

With some computer-administered lists, you may receive a confirmation notice, like the one shown in figure 10.4. The purpose of this is to make sure the list can properly send you the discussion messages.

Fig. 10.4
A confirmation notice from a computer administrator.

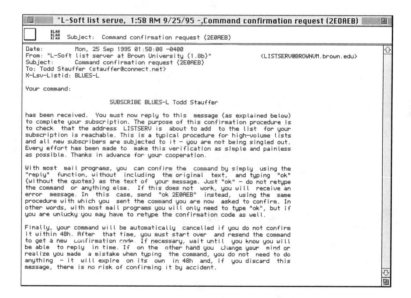

Generally, these confirmations require that you reply to the e-mail message using your e-mail program. Most of the time you should delete all quoted text and enter whatever is requested (often, you can just type **ok**); then send the reply back. You should receive a welcome e-mail in a few more minutes.

Your mailing list welcome message

If you've subscribed successfully, you'll probably receive a welcoming e-mail message from the list. It's important that you keep a copy of this message somewhere on your hard drive (or in another message box in your e-mail program) so that you can remember the correct addresses for unsubscribing, sending commands, and contributing to the list.

Most computer administrators will send you a message similar to the one in figure 10.5. Human administrators may send you something different. Either way, read it carefully and save it somewhere you'll remember.

Fig. 10.5
A typical welcome message from a computer-administered mailing list. Save it somewhere so you'll remember the list's addresses.

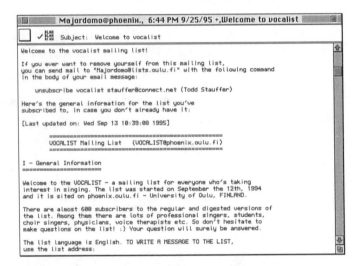

Reading and contributing to the mailing list

Once you receive confirmation on your successful subscription, you should start seeing messages appear in your In box. This can take between a few minutes and a few days, depending on how automated the mailing list server is.

To read the list, just open the messages as you would any e-mail. You may notice that some of the conversations are out of sync—occasionally, you'll read a response before you've read the original question. It will take a few days to get used to this—and get into the flow of conversation on the list—so be patient.

TIP **Sit and read the messages for a few days or weeks before sending** your own. It's called **lurking** and it's a good idea when you first join a list. Get a feel for the list's sense of community and appropriate behavior. Some lists are very tightly knit, and you'll quickly grow used to the folks who regularly respond.

Responding directly to messages

The most important rule in dealing with mailing lists is coming up really soon. You'll notice that it's really important because it is a paragraph unto itself, and the whole thing is in italics.

Make sure that your contributions to the list are appropriate for the entire group to read. Don't waste anybody's time.

What does that mean? Discussions on the list should be interesting for an entire group to read—potentially hundreds or thousands of folks. If you've got something a little more personal to talk about, there's a way to handle that, too. Send an e-mail directly to the person you want to chat with (see fig. 10.6).

Fig. 10.6
I'm discussing something that's not of general interest, so I send an e-mail directly to the individual concerned.

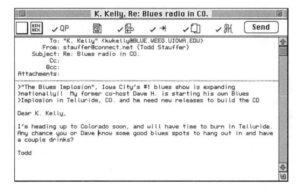

You're in the BLUES-L mailing list, reading about someone who mentions that he lives in Salt Lake City. You realize this is a great potential resource for some info on Utah skiing—another interest of yours. Send your skiing-concerned message *directly* to that person. Other blues freaks don't want to hear about skiing.

CAUTION **If you use your e-mail program to respond to an individual's** mailing list message, make sure it only includes that one person in the To field of your new e-mail message. If your program includes "all recipients" you may accidentally send that message to people who don't care.

Posting a message for the whole group

If your response or message *is* of general interest, then all you really need to do is send your message to the contributions e-mail address of the list (not the administrative address!). Type your message in your e-mail program, addressing it just to the address of the list. For our Mazda automobiles list, that address is: **MAZDA-LIST@ms.uky.edu** (as opposed to the administrative address: **mazda-request@ms.uky.edu**).

By default, you probably won't get a copy of your own e-mail contribution in your In box. But, unless the message is returned to you as "undeliverable," you'd better go ahead and assume the message made it. If you send it twice,

Netiquette lesson one: mailing lists

You may have heard discussion before concerning **netiquette**: etiquette rules for the Internet. As silly as it may seem sometimes, it really is a good idea to know as much netiquette as you can. Are you scared of nasty messages in your e-mail box? Probably not...but it can be a waste of your time.

And that's really the key to most netiquette issues...wasting time or disk space. In mailing lists, this means following a few quick and easy rules:

- Make sure your messages are appropriate for the entire group to read.

- Memorize (or come close to it) your welcome message. It should include all "local" rules for the list.

- Read the Frequently Asked Questions (FAQ) document if one is available for your mailing list.

- If you send a particularly long message (more than two pages or so), include the word long in the subject line.

- NEVER send binary files to a mailing list that doesn't generally accept them.

- Don't over-quote messages—just hit the high points. Be concise and on topic.

We hit some more rules of netiquette in the UseNet chapters. Basically, just be a good citizen. Our info-highway can sometimes feel like a crowded subway car—so be considerate and don't waste oxygen.

you'll definitely upset some of the list's subscribers. You can tell your mailing list server to send your messages back to you. (You'll see how in the table at the end of this chapter.)

Mailing-list commands and unsubscribing

Often, mailing lists are offered in both message-by-message and digest formats. If you're interested in switching between the two (or doing some other mailing-list maintenance) the process is similar to subscribing. For computer-managed lists, you'll need to send a properly formatted request.

 TIP **For human-administered lists, the appropriate way to change what** you see and receive can vary quite a bit. That's why you should keep your welcome message. Refer to it for instructions on switching to digests or changing other mailing-list attributes.

Changing to digest format

For most computer-administered lists, you send a standard-style e-mail message to the administrative address. To switch to a digest format, for instance, you'll either send a message with SET *list name* DIGEST in the body of the message—or you'll send a message like that shown in figure 10.7.

Fig. 10.7
Here's another way some computer administrators do it. I need to subscribe to the digest and unsubscribe to the normal list—otherwise, I'll get both!

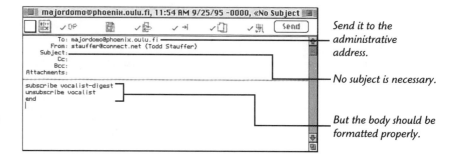

Send it to the administrative address.

No subject is necessary.

But the body should be formatted properly.

Unsubscribing a list

If you've decided that this list isn't everything you thought it was—or you just can't keep up anymore—unsubscribing is fairly straightforward.

TIP **Going on vacation? You don't have to unsubscribe to stop your** lists for a short duration. See the next section, "Other list-maintenance commands," for additional commands for dealing with short-term absences.

For human-administered lists, simply send an e-mail to the administrative address that includes `UNSUBSCRIBE` in the subject line. You might also include something polite in the body of the message that says you enjoyed their service, think they're the greatest, wonk, wonk, yada, yada....

For a computer-administered list, send the following command in the body of an e-mail message you send to the administrative address:

SIGNOFF *list-name your-full-name*

Some automated lists will require that you send `UNSUBSCRIBE` instead of `SIGNOFF`, so check your welcome message.

Other list-maintenance commands

So what else can you do to manage your mailing lists? Aside from digests and indexes, some lists will allow you to send submissions to your own In box (called "repro"-ducing), receive an acknowledgment for a successful post, temporarily stop a subscription, get help for the list's commands, and more.

Plain English, please!

In the online world, a **post** is a message you send for general consumption. When you send a message, you're "posting"—whether to mailing lists, UseNet groups, AOL discussion rooms, or something similar. Sometimes the word "post" specifically suggests that you're starting a new discussion; not just replying to another person's message. Why the word "post"? Because we used to call all these online areas computer bulletin boards—so "posting a message" just followed the metaphor.

The following table includes many of the most common commands sent to computer-based mailing lists. Make sure you check your welcome message for any differences—nine times out of ten these will work.

Table 10.1   Mailing list subscription commands

Command	Description
SUBscribe *listname your full name*	Use to subscribe to a list.
SIGNOFF *listname*	Takes you off a mailing list.
SIGNOFF *	Takes you off all lists on a server.
SIGNOFF * (NETWIDE)	Takes you off all lists in the network.
SET *listname* NOMail or SET *listname*	Command to temporarily stop or renew a subscription.
Mail	Mailing list posting and reading commands.
SET *listname* REPro or SET *listname* NOREPro	Determines whether you get a copy of your own posting to the mailing list.
SET *listname* ACK or SET *listname* NOACK	Determines whether you receive an acknowledgment for posting a message to the mailing list.
SET *listname* DIGests or SET *listname* INDex	Request to receive digests or indexes of messages rather than getting all messages.
Help	Request for a list of commands.
Query (*listname*)	Asks for an overview of your subscription options—the SET command will change them.
INDex (*listname*)	Request for a directory list of archived files for the mailing list (not all mailing lists archive their messages).

11

FTP: Find That Program!

● In this chapter:

- What is FTP and why is it useful?

- The FTP directory structure revealed

- Finding great (and often free!) files for your Mac

- How do I download files?

- Will this file will work with my Mac?

If you're the Indiana Jones of the Internet, then FTP is where you'll dig for treasure. Just take the right tools . . . . ➢

I t is sometimes called the electronic frontier...and on the Internet, files are California gold. *Somewhere, someplace, along some pathway on the Internet is that one file that you simply must have.* Maybe it's an electronic image of your dream car; the perfect utility for creating recipe-cards with your word processor; or the shareware video game that's destined to keep you up all hours of the night, effectively destroying your career.

The perfect file is out there. Waiting.

All around the world, computer centers maintain huge disk drives full of files available to anyone who has an Internet connection and the right FTP address. You've got to seek out the right file, and there are millions to choose from. Luckily, you'll probably have fun looking for it...and you'll come across some other gems along the way.

What is FTP?

The chapter title is misleading—**FTP** actually stands for **File Transfer Protocol**. What is it? (Do I really have to say this?) Why, it's the protocol for transferring files on the the Internet, of course. We've discussed before that binary files can't be transferred through e-mail or mailing lists without being translated to text first. Well, you can download files directly when you connect to an FTP site (see fig. 11.1).

Fig. 11.1

Using an FTP capable program (Anarchie, in this example) you can access a remote computer (an FTP server) to download files directly to your Mac.

File folders (directories) on the remote computer.

Program files you can download.

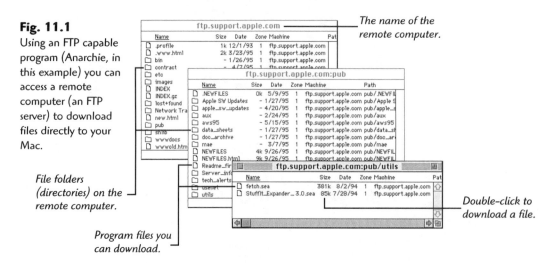

The name of the remote computer.

Double-click to download a file.

FTP can transfer both text and binary files—but it needs to be told which it is transferring at a given time. Most Mac programs do this automatically, so you probably won't have to worry about it. But you should be aware that text files and binary files (including documents, programs, pictures, and other files) are treated differently by FTP.

 Plain English, please!

> The terms **FTP**, **download**, and **upload** are relatively interchangable in the Internet world. If you say you're going to "FTP a file from" somewhere, you really mean you're going to download it from that site. Saying you'll "FTP the file to" somewhere really means you'll use FTP to upload a file to that computer.

FTP also describes the standard for making file names available for browsing on the Internet. You may have noticed that figure 11.1 looks a little like the way you handle files in Microsoft Windows and on some UNIX-based computers (or even in Mac's Finder if you look at a folder using View by Name). Files are arranged in directories, which you double-click to reveal their contents. You continue to dig through the directories until you get to a program or file that interests you.

How does this directory idea work?

Imagine the Sunday edition of your newspaper. You're looking for a story that gives the intimate details of a bank robbery that took place at your branch of the state bank.

Starting from the front page, you see from the contents listing that the Metro section is section 3C. So you open the paper to section 3C. Now you see the contents for the Metro section—the story you want is on page 12 of that section. Now you can turn to that page and look for the headline for your story. Find it, and you can "download" the story to your brain by reading it (see fig. 11.2).

Fig. 11.2

If you've ever read a newspaper or worked with one of those text-based computer operating systems (like UNIX or DOS) then you understand how FTP is organized.

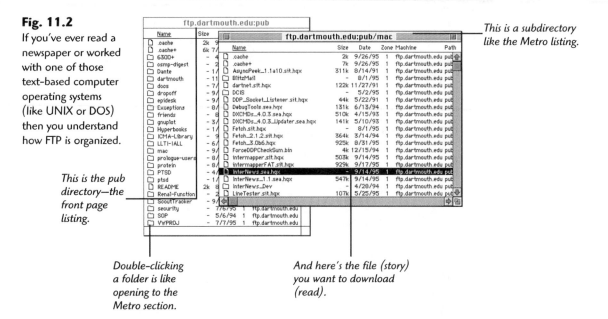

This is a subdirectory like the Metro listing.

This is the pub directory—the front page listing.

 Double-clicking a folder is like opening to the Metro section.

And here's the file (story) you want to download (read).

You start by telling your FTP software to call up an FTP server computer. This computer is running special software that allows it to communicate over the Internet using the FTP standard. When the FTP server agrees to talk to you, it sends you the main directory listing for its archive. Double-click the name of a subdirectory, and the FTP server will return all the contents information in that subdirectory. Your FTP software opens a new window to show you those contents. Finally, you get to the file you want to download. Double-click it and the FTP server will send a copy of it over the Internet to your computer.

66 *Plain English, please!*

FTP sites are often called **archives** because they work a little like a library's archives or a newspaper's morgue. Computer files are stored on the site's hard drives and directories are created to point to where on the drives those files are stored. When you find the file you want, a double-click "requests" that file, which is then found in its storage place, copied, and sent to your computer. 99

Finding interesting FTP sites

There are really two ways to use FTP effectively—you can search manually for files by browsing file directories, or you can use a search database to find the exact file you want. It's a little like using a microfiche in a library versus using the library's computer system. The fiche is for browsing information quickly; the computer system is for locating a specific title or article.

We'll talk about finding specific files in detail when we discuss Anarchie in Chapter 12. For now, let's concentrate on browsing.

FTP addresses and directory paths

FTP addresses are fairly straightforward, especially if you read the discussion of server computers in Chapter 2. An FTP address is simply a standard Internet server address that follows this form:

host.domain.domain-type.

An example would be **ftp.dartmouth.edu**, which connects you to Dartmouth College's main FTP site.

In other chapters in this book, I've sometimes told you where you could download a file using FTP. Not only did I give you an FTP address, but I'd often give you a directory path as well. A path statement might look like this:

/pub/mac/Fetch_2.1.2.sit.hqx

So what does that mean? It means that to find the file Fetch2.1.2, you should first open the pub directory. pub stands for public, and most FTP sites have one—it's where you'll be able to access their generally available files. From the pub listing, double-click the mac directory. In the mac directory listing, you'll find the entry for the file Fetch_2.1.2.sit.hqx. Double-click that entry, and the program will be downloaded to your computer (see fig. 11.3).

 TIP **See that first slash (/) in front of pub? That slash is actually what's** called the first-level directory on any FTP server. It's generally where you'll find the pub directory.

Fig. 11.3

Using a directory path to dig for the file you want. There are FTP directory paths throughout this book—and now you understand them!

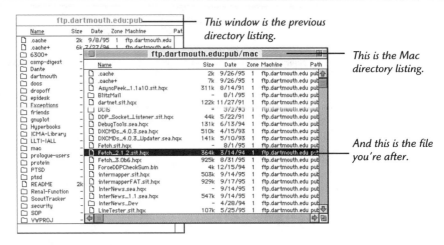

This window is the previous directory listing.

This is the Mac directory listing.

And this is the file you're after.

Which FTP site interests you?

The first thing you need to know before you browse an FTP site is what FTP site you are going to browse. Using a Macintosh makes this a little easier—you'll probably be most interested in Macintosh-related FTP sites. Here are a couple to get you started:

- **INFO-MAC FTP Sites.** INFO-MAC is a very popular archive of Macintosh files that originates at MIT and is duplicated, or "mirrored," on computers all around the world.

- **The University of Michigan Mac Archives.** Competes with the INFO-MAC archives as most popular. Also includes a number of mirror sites around the world.

- **The University of Texas Mac Archives.** Another popular Mac site, this one features a variety of shareware and freeware programs, sounds, graphics, and system software extensions.

- **University of Washington Mac/Internet Archives.** Focuses on Internet tools for Macintosh computers.

- **Apple Support Archives.** Sponsored by Apple Computer, Inc., these archives include official updates and fixes for Macintosh system software and official Apple software products.

This is just a quick sample of what's available. Table 11.1 shows you some of the different ways to access these archives.

Table 11.1 Popular Mac FTP servers and directory paths

Archive name	FTP address	Directory path
INFO-MAC	mirror.apple.com	/mirrors/Info-Mac.Archive/
	ftp.hawaii.edu	/mirrors/info-mac/
	grind.isca.uiowa.edu	/mac/infomac/
	ftp.delphi.com	/pub/mirrors/info-mac/
	wuarchive.wustl.edu	/systems/mac/info-mac/
	mirrors.aol.com	/pub/info-mac/
	ftp.uu.net	/systems/mac/info-mac/
	ftp.pht.com	/pub/mac/info-mac/
U Michigan	archive.orst.edu	/pub/mirrors/archive.umich.edu/
	grind.isca.uiowa.edu	/mac/umich/
	wuarchive.wustl.edu	/systems/mac/umich.edu/
	mirrors.aol.com	/pub/mac
	ftp.pht.com	/mirrors/umich/
U Texas	ftp.utexas.edu	/pub/mac
U Washington	ftp.uwtc.washington.edu	/pub/mac
Apple Support	ftp.support.apple.com	/pub/

Q&A *I can't seem to get through to an FTP site. Am I using the wrong FTP server?*

Most sites only allow a certain number of users at a given time; the one you chose is probably too busy. Choose FTP sites and mirror sites that are closest to you geographically. This cuts down on Internet traffic and gives you a better chance of speedy success in the transfer. Also, if you have trouble connecting to a particular site, try connecting at off-peak (late night/weekend) times.

Dealing with downloaded files

Once you've waded through an FTP site's directories and found the file you want, you download it to your machine by double-clicking its icon. Generally, your FTP application asks you where you want to save the file on your Mac's hard drive. Now you're in for a wait—depending on the size of the file and the speed of your Internet connection. Once the file arrives, your FTP application translates the file back from BinHex (if necessary) and leaves you with the file on your hard drive (see fig. 11.4). But now what do you do with it?

Fig. 11.4
Here's the file you wanted. What's that *.sit* on the end?

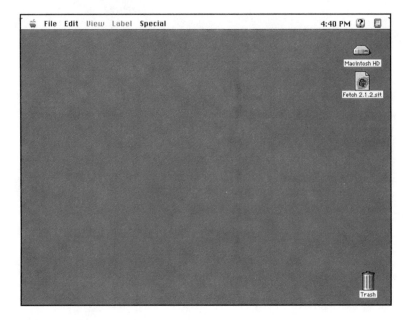

File compression

Notice the three letters on the end of the file. That's a **file extension**—an "extension" to the name of the file that tells that you need to do something else with this file before you can use it.

You may know that it's possible to take a document or program, and compress its contents so that it's smaller for transport over a phone connection or network. The key to this process is that compression renders the document or program unusable until you *decompress* it. And for that, you need a special program.

Fortunately, you have one. Distributed for free by Aladdin Systems, Inc., StuffIt Expander is a must for any Internet-connected Macintosh desktop. That's why it's included on the disk that came with this book. Just drag it from the MacNet disk's window onto your Mac's desktop and leave it somewhere convenient (see fig. 11.5).

Fig. 11.5
I like to place StuffIt Expander right where I can see it, just above the Trash can. I use it almost as much.

StuffIt Expander can actually handle a number of different translations and decompressions, including the StuffIt format, Compact Pro format, and BinHex.

Plain English, please!

StuffIt and **Compact Pro** are two popular compression and archiving utilities for the Macintosh. So popular, in fact, that they've become competing standards for Mac users. Compact Pro tends to make files a little smaller, but StuffIt seems to be more common. Generally, decompression utilities (like StuffIt Expander) will handle both. "

To decompress a downloaded file, just drag it to the StuffIt Expander icon and drop it. The file will be expanded to its original state, showing you the file's icon and eliminating the name extension. Now it's useful.

File archives: compression's Big Brother

There's not much difference between a compressed file and a compressed file archive—an archive simply contains more than one file. StuffIt and Compact Pro both have the ability to add more than one file—or even entire folders—to a compressed archive. The resulting archive is just one file: compressed, but often still huge (see fig. 11.6).

Fig. 11.6
Looking at a compressed archive with the StuffIt Lite shareware program. The archive holds many files, but the whole is smaller and easier to transfer.

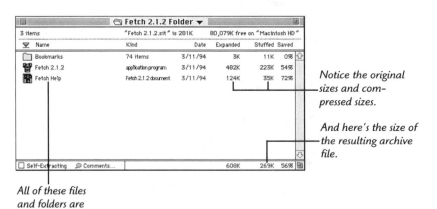

Notice the original sizes and compressed sizes.

And here's the size of the resulting archive file.

All of these files and folders are in the archive.

Understanding file extensions

On the Internet, you'll run across a bunch of files, with a bunch of different extensions. The question for you is two-fold. Will this file work with my Mac and, if so, how do I translate to a usable format? Let's look at common extensions.

- **.sit** files are StuffIt extensions. These are almost always original Mac documents and programs.

- **.sea** files are self-extracting archives.

- **.cpt** files are Compact Pro archives; almost always Mac files.

- **.zip** files are archives created by DOS- or Windows-based computers. These will occasionally be useful to you, especially if you have a DOS-compatible Mac, use SoftWindows, or use file-compatible programs like MS Word or QuarkExpress. You'll need another program (like *Zip-It* by Tommy Brown) to decompress these.

- **.hqx** is a BinHex file. Generally a native Mac file or application.

- **.uu** is a UUEncoded file, the BinHex of the DOS and UNIX world. If it's a document, it may be useful.

- **.tif**, **.jpg**, and **.gif** are graphics file formats that are generally compatible between different computer types.

- **.mpg** and **.qt** are cross-platform movie file formats. (.mpg is short for MPEG; .qt is a QuickTime file.

- **.au** is a Mac sound file; **.wav** is an MS Windows sound file. These formats are becoming more universal, and utilities are available to translate and play these on most any computer.

- **.z, .Z** and **.tar** files are UNIX-based compression and archiving formats. Most of this stuff won't be useful to the typical Mac owner.

Self-extracting compressed files and archives

The other type of compressed file you'll come across is a self-extracting archive—almost always with an .sea extension. For these archives, all you need to do is double-click the file icon. A little "extractor" program has been embedded in the archive, giving it the capability to expand and make its files useful all on its own.

It is convenient to use self-extracting archives, but the cost is the size of the file. Including the extractor program usually adds between 15 and 60 kilobytes to the archive, depending on the program that creates it and the size of the file or files that you're compressing. This often isn't too much to pay for the extra convenience—unless your modem connection is very slow.

12

Searching for Files and Using Anarchie

● **In this chapter:**

- **Searching for files on the Internet**

- **Who is this Archie character?**

- **Anarchie: the best Mac program for FTP**

- **How do I access a specific site with Anarchie?**

- **Accessing Archie databases with Anarchie**

- **Can I send files with Anarchie?**

Show your DOS, Windows, or UNIX buddies the Anarchie FTP application and you'll see some envy on their faces. How should you respond? "Welcome to Macintosh". . . . . ▶

Now that we've covered some of the basics of FTP theory, let's do two more things. First, I'll show you how searching for files works on the Internet. Then we'll take an in-depth look at using the Anarchie program for both browsing and searching.

Searching for files on the Internet

I said in the last chapter that searching for files on the Internet is a little like using your library's computer to find a particular book or article for research. Well, that's almost true. The only major difference is that the file-searching databases on the the Internet are nowhere near as complete as your library's computer system probably is.

 Plain English, please!

What's a **database**? You may be familiar with databases you create in FileMaker Pro or ClarisWorks, but a database really refers to any collection of information that's organized using indexes to the data. On a computer, these indexes are what allow you to enter keywords for your search. **"**

The Archie databases on the Internet—the databases designed for file searching—try hard, but they can only get file information from FTP sites that allow them to, and they're not always completely up-to-date. But they do cover an amazing number of files, and you will probably have a good deal of luck finding the files you want—if you know their names.

Who is Archie?

Conceived as part of a collaborative cute-fest when the Internet was infinitely smaller, the name **Archie** doesn't actually stand for anything. It is, instead, a reference to the Archie character of comic book fame.

What's important to us, though, is that Archie is a system of recording the file names of files available via FTP on server computers around the world. Archie servers log on to popular FTP sites on a regular basis, record all the file names and their directory paths, then organize that information into a database that you can search. That's all there is to it. Using the right program, like Anarchie, you send a simple request to search the database. After a few seconds, you're presented with a list of possible choices (see fig. 12.1).

Fig. 12.1
With FTP and Archie searches rolled into one, Anarchie is an elegant solution—especially if you've ever used anything else.

Enter a search phrase here.

FTP download in progress!

Anarchie lets you double-click to get that file.

After searching, Archie sends back a list.

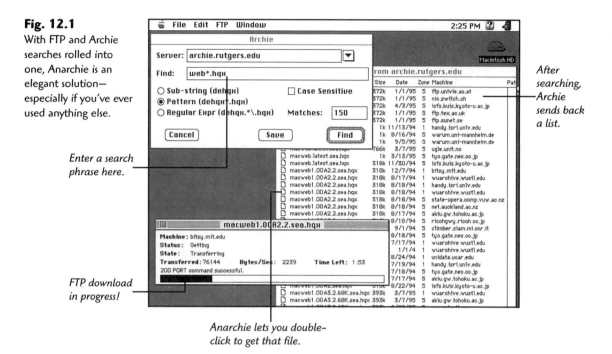

First, let's set up Anarchie to work with your Mac. Then we'll search and dig for some files.

Setting up and browsing with Anarchie

Anarchie is a graphical Macintosh solution to both searching Archie servers and accessing FTP sites. It was written by the famed and fabled Internet guru Peter Lewis, well-known for his inexpensive shareware contributions to Mac-based netting. He does ask a $10 shareware fee for Anarchie, but it'll probably be the best ten bucks you've spent in a while.

 TIP **Anarchie is shareware, so if you use it for more than a few weeks,** send your ten bucks. If you're absolutely against the idea of paying for your FTP, you can download Fetch, a limited (but free) FTP program. I show you how in Chapter 11.

You can download the latest version of Anarchie via FTP at **ftp.share.com** in the directory /pub/peterlewis/. You can also get at it by pointing your Web browser to **http://www.ese.ogi.edu/peterlewis/programs.html**. And it's available on mirror sites around the world.

On the Disk

Of course, you can't FTP without FTP software, so we've included Anarchie on the disk. Simply copy the self-extracting Anarchie archive from the disk to a convenient place on your Mac's hard drive. Then, double-click the archive to start the self-expansion process (see fig. 12.2).

Fig. 12.2
Double-clicking the archive icon creates the Anarchie folder. In the folder is the program, some documentation, text files, and data files.

Installing Internet Config

The next step is to install something called **Internet Config** that comes with Anarchie. It's actually a program designed to make configuring many of your Internet applications easier—other Internet applications developers are slowly starting to take advantage of it (see the sidebar, "What, exactly, is Internet Config?"). For now, we definitely need it for Anarchie. I'll point out when it will make our other applications easier in later chapters.

Open your Anarchie folder, then open the Internet Config folder. You'll see an icon called Internet Config. Double-click it. You are asked if you want to install the Internet Config Extension. Click Install, then click OK in the resulting confirmation box. Next, you'll see the Internet Config windows shown in figure 12.3.

Fig. 12.3
You'll want to set up at least Email and File Transfer for Anarchie to work properly.

Click here to set up e-mail settings.

Click here to set up Anarchie settings.

Enter your e-mail address here.

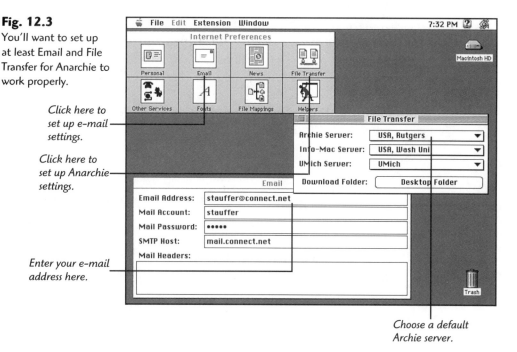

Choose a default Archie server.

What, exactly, is Internet Config?

As Anarchie matures, it increasingly becomes the Internet FTP application of choice in the Mac world. And that makes its author, Peter Lewis, powerful. Toss in the fact that he's an honest-to-goodness Internet guru, and it's not surprising that he has created and rolled some emerging Interent-related technology into new versions of his programs. But what does that mean for us?

Internet Config (IC), written jointly by Mr. Lewis and an individual who seems to be mysteriously named only "Quinn," is a system-extension and configuration program designed to give you one central program for entering Internet-related information. As we get deeper into this book, you'll notice that you have to configure each Internet application you use separately with

redundant information like e-mail address, mail server, news server, and signature file.

IC was created to overcome this by providing a universal Internet configuration system. Ideally, you only enter your information once—in the IC setup program. Then any IC-aware Internet application can consult IC when it wants to know something about your Internet connection.

The problem is, not all Internet applications support it, and only two—Anarchie and NewsWatcher—are programs that I recommend. Others are coming along, but they are still some time away. For now, you've got to have IC to run Anarchie, and it will help with NewsWatcher (for UseNet discussions, see Chapter 14. But in the future, you may never have to configure another Internet application again!

You must give Anarchie your e-mail address to send to anonymous FTP sites as your password (that's considered good netiquette). You'll also need to use the pop-up menu to choose a default Archie server in the File Transfer setup. You can choose to enter defaults for the other servers, as well.

TIP **To change the default download directory, click once on the** button next to Download Directory (in fig. 12.3, the button says Desktop Folder). In the resulting dialog box, choose the directory to which you'd like Anarchie to save downloaded files.

Now you can choose Quit from Internet Config's File menu, and start Anarchie.

Firing up Anarchie for the first time

To start Anarchie, double-click its file cabinet icon. If you didn't follow the instructions detailed in the previous section, you'll see a dialog box that asks if you want to run the Internet Config program. If you haven't already done so, go ahead and run the program according to the steps outlined in the previous section.

In the next window, you'll be asked if you want to use the Internet Version Control System. Respond either way…it's up to you.

TIP **Once you have Anarchie running, you can access Anarchie Guide,** a help system using the new Apple Guide technology in System 7.5 and above. Just pull down the ? (Help) menu and choose Anarchie Guide.

In the meantime, your Mac should be trying to make a PPP connection (if it wasn't already active). Then, you're presented with a screen that looks like figure 12.4.

Fig. 12.4
Anarchie at startup.
Notice the list of
interesting Mac-related
sites around the world.

Exploring with Anarchie

Anarchie has made browsing for interesting files easy by providing us with a
list of **bookmarks**, or references to convenient sites. Want to explore one?
Just double-click it in the Bookmark window (see fig. 12.5).

Fig. 12.5
Browsing from the
bookmarks list.

*Let's browse
this FTP site.*

*After connecting,
you get this menu.*

*Double-click
to dig further.*

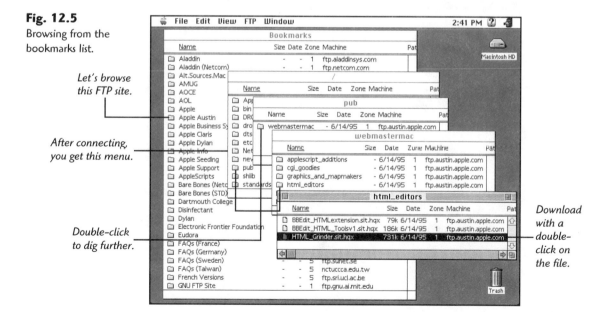

*Download
with a
double-
click on
the file.*

Double-click the directory names to bring up the listing for a directory. To download a file, double-click the file name.

 TIP   **Don't forget that the fastest and most appropriate connections** are to servers that are geographically close to you. You should especially avoid trans-oceanic connections wherever you can.

Browsing a specific (not listed) site

Want to access a site you can't find on the list? That's easy, too. Just pull down the FTP menu and select the Get menu item. You are then presented with the dialog box in figure 12.6.

 CAUTION   **That's Get, not Get Selection. Get Selection will open a connec-** tion that you've highlighted in the bookmarks list—just as if you'd double-clicked its name.

Enter the FTP address here.

The Path to the file (if you know it).

Fig. 12.6
Get via FTP dialog box.

Click the radio button for listing or file.

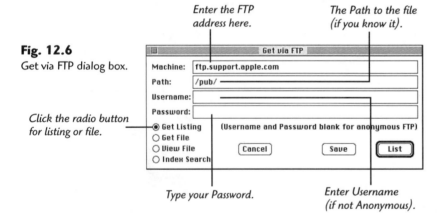

Type your Password.

Enter Username (if not Anonymous).

Until now, every time we've talked about accessing an FTP server, we've actually been signing on as anonymous users. FTP is used very often for anonymous access—that's how the general public swaps files. You'll notice in figure 12.6, though, that you can enter a name and password if you're signing onto an FTP site that requires them.

Plain English, please!

In FTP lingo, **anonymous** access is used to talk to FTP servers that allow the general public to download their files. This is in contrast to **restricted access** FTP sites that require you to have a username and password (like an FTP site at your company, for instance).

Enter the FTP server's address in the Machine: field and a directory path to the file you want (if you know it) in the Path: field. You can also enter **/PUB** if you'd just like to see that server's public directory listing. Leave the Name and Password fields blank for an anonymous connection, or enter the appropriate username and password if you're accessing a restricted site. Click List to get the directory listing from the remote site.

Now, browse away!

Downloading a specific file

Every once in a while, you may know exactly what FTP server you want to access and what file you want to download. For instance, I've given you specific addresses, directory paths, and file names throughout this book. So you can just skip all the directory listing stuff and immediately download a file (see fig. 12.7).

Fig. 12.7
Directly downloading a file with Anarchie. Don't forget to select the Get File radio button.

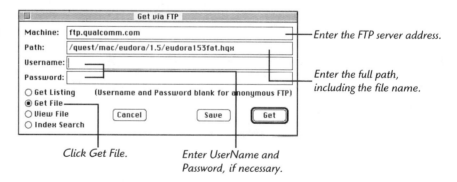

Enter the FTP server address.

Enter the full path, including the file name.

Click Get File.

Enter UserName and Password, if necessary.

There are two keys to success here. First, you need to enter the *exact* directory path, including the filename. Don't forget the inital / that indicates the root directory, and then a trailing / to indicate the directory that the file is in. Follow that with the file name. Here's an example:

/pub/mac/games/funtime.sit.hqx

You need to know all this information to properly download the file. With that entered, make sure you select the Get File radio button. Notice now that the button in the right-bottom corner of the dialog has changed to Get. Click that button, and Anarchie attempts to retrieve the file.

Q&A *I want to download a file, but all I have is the URL. How do I do it?*

Just paste the complete URL into the Machine field. Anarchie will automatically break it up into an FTP server address and directory path for you. You must use the Paste command, though. If you type the URL in the Machine field, then select the entire URL with the mouse, choose Copy from the Edit menu, then immediately choose Paste.

Using Anarchie to search for files

Here we are, finally. With those explanations out of the way, we can get down to doing what Anarchie was really designed to do—search for files using Archie servers.

Sending an Archie request

How do we start? Under Anarchie's File menu, the first command is Archie. Select that, and you get a small search dialog box like the one in figure 12.8.

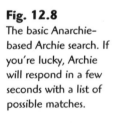

Fig. 12.8
The basic Anarchie-based Archie search. If you're lucky, Archie will respond in a few seconds with a list of possible matches.

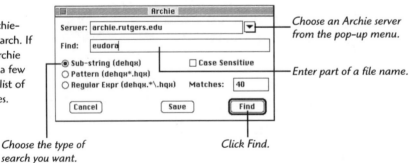

Choose an Archie server from the pop-up menu.

Enter part of a file name.

Choose the type of search you want.

Click Find.

Select the Archie server you'd like to use in the pop-up menu at the top of the dialog box. Now, enter part of a file name you want to search for in the Find field. Next, choose the type of search Archie will implement. In almost all cases, you should choose Sub-string, which will search for any file that contains the text in the Find field. You'll also probably want to change the number of matches from 40 to something considerably more, like 150. Then, click Find.

When should you use the other search types? If you happen to know most of the file name you're looking for, but just aren't sure about a couple of letters or numbers (say, the version number) you can use a Pattern search phrase. Something like **Anarchie*.sit.hqx** would return files that start with "Anarchie" then something else, followed by ".sit.hqx". Example: **Anarchie160.sit.hqx**.

If you know how to create a regular expression for an Archie search, Anarchie gives you that opportunity. Regular expressions are a little like pattern searches, but are more involved and a little more rooted in command-line UNIX. You should be able to get by without them—even the Anarchie Guide refuses to try to explain them.

Downloading files found by Archie

The result of your Archie search is a list of sites that carry files that meet your search request (see fig. 12.9). See anything that interests you? Double-click it, and Anarchie will access that FTP site. If you double-click a directory, it will retrieve that directory list. Double-click a file and Anarchie will download it to your computer.

If Archie didn't find what you're looking for, you'll need to go back to the Archie search dialog box and try again. Sometimes it takes a couple of tries to hit the right Find phrase.

 TIP Remember that Archie searches through *file names*, not descriptions or categories. If you don't have some idea what the file *might* be
called, you're better off browsing FTP sites.

Fig. 12.9
After you get Archie's
results, you can explore
them or download
them.

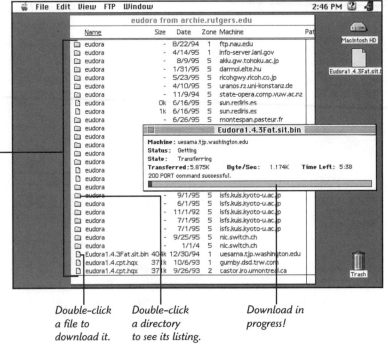

*Here's a list of files and
directories Archie found.*

*Double-click
a file to
download it.*

*Double-click
a directory
to see its listing.*

*Download in
progress!*

Uploading files with Anarchie

I know, I know. I've waited a long, long time to bring this up. Well…you don't
do much uploading on the Internet. Or, uh, at least I don't. Everybody's a
little different, though, and I'm sure you'll probably eventually find a reason
to upload a file to an FTP server.

Here's how it's done—as long as you're using System 7.5 or above and the
latest version of Anarchie.

 TIP **Older system software will work, too, if you have Apple's Drag**
Manager extension properly installed in the Extensions Folder.

Open the listing for the directory chosen for the uploaded file. You can do
this manually through the Get command, or you can just double-click one of
the Bookmark listings.

Then, in the Finder, click and hold the mouse on the upload-intended file, and drag it to the Anarchie directory listing. Now, drop it in that window. Anarchie opens a status box to let you watch the progress of the upload (see fig. 12.10).

Fig. 12.10
Uploading with Anarchie. You probably won't do it often, but it's still good to know how.

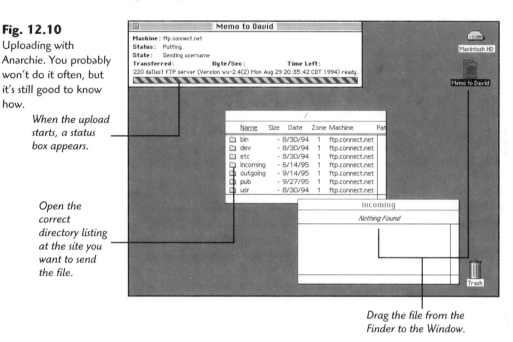

When the upload starts, a status box appears.

Open the correct directory listing at the site you want to send the file.

Drag the file from the Finder to the Window.

The status box will tell you quickly when it's done uploading and then disappear. I hope the FTP site appreciates what you're doing.

 CAUTION   In fact, be *sure* that the FTP site will appreciate your upload. Only attempt to upload files in directories that are designated to accept them, and follow any policies the FTP site (especially public FTP sites) has concerning uploads. Get permission from the System Administrator before using a public site to swap files with friends or colleagues.

13

Tunneling through Gopherspace and Using TurboGopher

● **In this chapter:**

- **Wasn't Gopher that guy on *Love Boat*??**

- **Setting up TurboGopher for your Mac**

- **Digging around (geographically) in Gopherspace.**

- **Searching made easy: Go-pher it directly!**

- **Downloading files and documents through Gopher**

Get used to Gopher and you'll be double-clicking menus with the best of them. In fact, maybe you should avoid finer restaurants . . . . ⊘

Okay, I'm prepared to be brutally honest here and offer you an option. While you should probably read this whole chapter to learn about Gopher, you don't have to use TurboGopher if you don't want to.

How can I say that? Because any World Wide Web browser worth its bytes can easily handle the most complex Gopher connection. That said, TurboGopher is a great program, and if you're serious about information retrieval on the Internet, keep a copy around.

You should definitely read the other parts of this chapter, including the introduction to Gopher, how to get around, and how to search. But, if you decide to use your Web browser to access Gopher servers, I won't hold it against you.

The key to Gopher: menus

Gopher is a menu-based information retrieval system designed for easy access to documents stored on the Internet. In fact, Gopher was designed as a *document-retrieval system*, so most of what's available for you to access is ASCII text. But, Gopher menus can also be used to access sound, graphics, video, and other files. You can even download applications using Gopher.

The "menus" that a typical Macintosh user is accustomed to are not completely unlike Gopher menus, but using the same word for both can be a bit confusing. Gopher **menus** are hierarchical listings of the contents of a site (or links to other sites). It's almost like a clickable table of contents in a book (see fig. 13.1). Want to see what's in chapter three? Just double-click its entry.

Fig. 13.1
Typical Gopher menus.
Notice how they're
like an interactive
table of contents—just
double-click a menu
item to see the next
menu or download
a file.

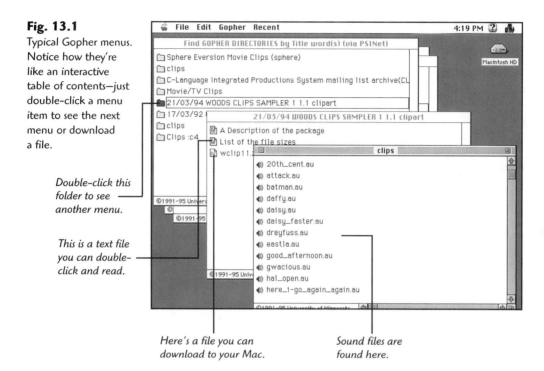

*Double-click this
folder to see
another menu.*

*This is a text file
you can double-
click and read.*

*Here's a file you can
download to your Mac.*

*Sound files are
found here.*

You can already see how easy it is to get around Gopher—it's basically just
point and click. There really is no special or advanced maneuvering to do.
Just keep tunneling through menus until you get to what you want.

Where'd they get that name?

Originally conceived and created at the University
of Minnesota, **Gopher** is named for that
university's mascot. It also happens to be a nice
little metaphor for the way information is found;
you "go-fer" it, digging deeper into menus to find
what you want. (Sadly, it really has nothing to do
with the guy from *Love Boat*.)

Notice the title of the chapter...the Gopher
metaphor even works there. Digging through
Gopher menus to find what you want is
tunneling in NetSpeak.

Installing and using TurboGopher

You need to start by downloading the latest version of TurboGopher. You can get it from **boombox.micro.umn.edu** in the directory /pub/gopher/ Macintosh-TurboGopher/. Once you've decompressed it and stored it somewhere on your Mac's hard drive, all you have to do is double-click its icon. Your PPP connection will come up, if necessary, and you'll be presented with the following screen (see fig. 13.2).

Fig. 13.2
The home of all Gophers (and your home Gopher menu, too)—the University of Minnesota. From here, you can get to nearly any Gopher in the world.

Notice the icons.

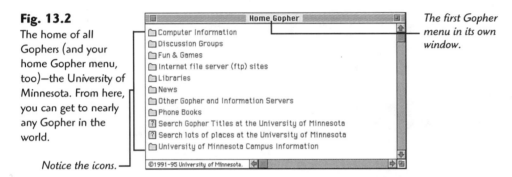

The first Gopher menu in its own window.

TurboGopher automatically opens up to the University of Minnesota: homebase for most Gopher operations. Notice, if you will, that the icons for some of the listings are different. TurboGopher, like most Gopher and Web applications, uses different icons to represent different types of documents. What do they mean?

- **Folder**. These are submenus. Double-click to see another menu.

- **Question mark**. Double-click this to search a database for specific Gopher-based information and files.

- **Document**. Double-click to read this text document.

- **Floppy disk**. Double-click to download a Macintosh file.

- **Starburst document**. Double-click to download a GIF, JPEG, or other image file.

- **Speaker symbol**. Double-click to download a sound file.

- **Terminal symbol**. Double-click to access a remote computer using Telnet protocols.

Notice how "double-click" appears in every single one of those bullet points? I'm often accused of redundancies in my writing, but this was done on purpose. There really is very little else you can do with TurboGopher. Double-clicking folders and other icons is just about all you need to know to find stuff using Gopher.

Just keep clicking. The University of Minnesota home Gopher menu provides some great leads. Explore for a while.

Tunneling with Gopher: the long way

Once things get dull at the University of Minnesota, it's time to explore **Gopherspace** the long way—geographically. Gopher servers around the world are conveniently organized by region in the University of Minnesota's Other Gopher and Information Servers menu, as shown in figure 13.3 . To see what I mean, double-click that item.

Fig. 13.3
Have a favorite continent? You can pick it here in Other Gopher and Information Servers.

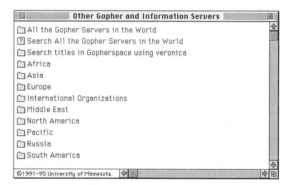

Your next step is to start narrowing your regional search. For this example, choose North America. In the next menu, choose USA. Next, double-click Georgia. That brings you to figure 13.4.

 Plain English, please!

> **Gopherspace** is just a cute way of saying "everything you can access using the Gopher system." Like **cyberspace**, it suggests that you're entering a vast realm of electronic information.

Fig. 13.4
The geographical search continues. If you know where your information is, you can get there from here.

Notice the trail of windows in the background.

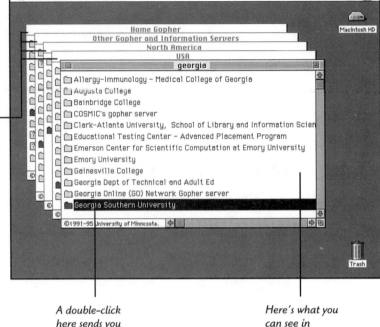

```
 🍎  File  Edit  Gopher  Recent                    4:22 PM  2  🐾

                                                          💾
                                                      Macintosh HD
              ┌─────────────────────────────────────┐
              │          Home Gopher                 │
              │   Other Gopher and Information Servers│
              │          North America               │
              │             USA                      │
              │            georgia                   │
    ┌─────────────────────────────────────────────────────────┐ ▲
    │ 📁 Allergy-immunology - Medical College of Georgia       │
    │ 📁 Augusta College                                       │
    │ 📁 Bainbridge College                                    │
    │ 📁 COSMIC's gopher server                                │
    │ 📁 Clark-Atlanta University,  School of Library and Information Scien│
    │ 📁 Educational Testing Center - Advanced Placement Program│
    │ 📁 Emerson Center for Scientific Computation at Emory University│
    │ 📁 Emory University                                      │
    │ 📁 Gainesville College                                   │
    │ 📁 Georgia Dept of Technical and Adult Ed                │
    │ 📁 Georgia Online (GO) Network Gopher server             │
    │ ■ Georgia Southern University                            │ ▼
    └─────────────────────────────────────────────────────────┘
      ©1991-95 University of Minnesota.  ◄ ▶

                                                          🗑
                                                         Trash
```

A double-click here sends you deeper.

Here's what you can see in Georgia.

The Albuquerque advantage: why use TurboGopher?

I mentioned at the beginning of this chapter that I wouldn't lose sleep if you decided to use your Web browser to access Gopher sites. But, there is an advantage to using TurboGopher.

Remember the old Bugs Bunny cartoons where Bugs would travel underground, making that funny little trail in the earth wherever he went? Then he would pop up in front of Elmer Fudd, staring down the barrel of a shotgun and say, "I musta taken a wrong turn at Albuquerque."

Take a wrong turn in TurboGopher, and you can follow your Gopher trail back. That's why all those windows stay open. They leave a trail of the menus you've been through in search of the information you wanted. Take a wrong turn, and you can just close windows until you get back to the menu that lets you make a better choice.

Of course, you can go back to early menus with your Web browser, too, but you can't see the trail you're making. Most browsers only keep a single window open at a time. It's a matter of personal preference, but I like the way TurboGopher does it.

If you have some idea *where* in the world you want to access something, then you can use this geographical search method to get straight there. Easy enough, right?

Searching for Gopher things: the short way

Sometimes you'd just rather get right on to something, wouldn't you? Perhaps you don't know *where* an item is, and it's not readily apparent from the topics in Minnesota's home menu. What can you do? Consult one of Archie's good friends.

Searching all of Gopherspace

Somebody actually came up with a (clever?) acronym to justify using the name Veronica for Gopher's search engine, although it's clearly a reference, once again, to Archie Comics. Veronica (obstensibly) stands for:

Very **E**asy **R**odent-**O**riented **N**et-wide **I**ndex to **C**omputerized **A**rchives

It's just one man's opinion, but, "yuck." Oh well, that's what it's called. What it does is something much better.

You've got to start out by accessing it. Many Gopher sites around the world offer a menu choice for entering your Veronica search phrase—but the best place for you to start is where you started your geographical search—the Minnesota home page.

Starting from the home page, select Other Gopher and Information Servers. On the next menu, double-click Search titles in Gopherspace using veronica. Menu items change often, but it should look something like figure 13.5.

Fig. 13.5
There are a number of different places and ways to search with Veronica.

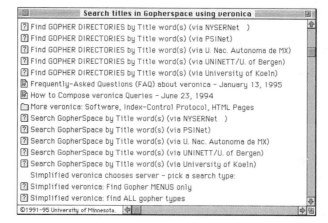

Search titles in Gopherspace using veronica

- [?] Find GOPHER DIRECTORIES by Title word(s) (via NYSERNet)
- [?] Find GOPHER DIRECTORIES by Title word(s) (via PSINet)
- [?] Find GOPHER DIRECTORIES by Title word(s) (via U. Nac. Autonoma de MX)
- [?] Find GOPHER DIRECTORIES by Title word(s) (via UNINETT/U. of Bergen)
- [?] Find GOPHER DIRECTORIES by Title word(s) (via University of Koeln)
- Frequently-Asked Questions (FAQ) about veronica - January 13, 1995
- How to Compose veronica Queries - June 23, 1994
- More veronica: Software, Index-Control Protocol, HTML Pages
- [?] Search GopherSpace by Title word(s) (via NYSERNet)
- [?] Search GopherSpace by Title word(s) (via PSINet)
- [?] Search GopherSpace by Title word(s) (via U. Nac. Autonoma de MX)
- [?] Search GopherSpace by Title word(s) (via UNINETT/U. of Bergen)
- [?] Search GopherSpace by Title word(s) (via University of Koeln)
-   Simplified veronica chooses server - pick a search type:
- [?] Simplified veronica: Find Gopher MENUS only
- [?] Simplified veronica: find ALL gopher types

©1991-95 University of Minnesota.

Realize that Veronica doesn't search the text of documents, only the titles of menu items. Enter the search word **job** and it will find a document called Job Listings, but it won't find a document called "Complaints" in which someone has written "Man, do I need a job."

You can limit your search by choosing to receive Gopher menus only when you search with Veronica. This means that your search results will only be items that lead to other menus—not documents, sound files, or downloadable files. This is useful when your search word is a very common one, like **macintosh**, **internet**, or **the**. (I'm being sarcastic. Don't search using "the" as your keyword.)

Double-click a menu item that seems to be the type of search you'd like to try. (I chose one of the Gopher title searches at the top of the menu.) The resulting search box is shown in figure 13.6.

Fig. 13.6
TurboGopher's search box.

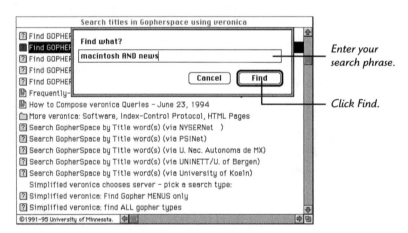

Enter your search phrase.

Click Find.

TIP **You also choose the server to use for your Veronica search. As** with nearly all other Internet searches, use the one that is closest to you geographically.

So, what should your search phrase be? Well, here are the quick rules: upper- and lowercase don't matter, and you can use logical operators—AND, OR, and NOT. Try to be as concise and specific as possible about what you're trying to find. See the following sidebar for more on Veronica searches.

Q&A *I keep getting* `Too Many Connections` *messages from Veronica. What do I do?*

Veronica is often very busy, but realize that Veronica queries really don't take much time—many, many people are jumping on and off quickly. You have two choices. Keep trying or switch servers (for example, use PSINet instead of SUNET). Actually, there's a third choice: wait awhile.

Suggestions for talking to Veronica

Veronica can be a little fickle in her responses. So, you'll need to word your queries carefully if you expect to get the right kind of feedback. These are a few of my suggestions for a successful conversation:

- Use more than one word to narrow your query. Include the AND, OR, and NOT operators.

- Use wild cards in your query. Type in **mac***, and you'll get anything that begins with the three letters m-a-c.

- Be a little creative; think about how things would be titled. If you can't find something using **Buffalo Bills** as your search phrase, try **Superbowl AND Losers**. Never know.

- Use the special -t operator. If you type the query **Football –ts**, you'll get only sound files that include the word `Football` in their titles. The query **Stats –t9** returns a list of binary files (documents, programs, etc.)

that includes `Stats` in their titles. Here are some of the letters and numbers you can follow that -t with:

0	Text file
1	Directory
4	Mac BinHex file
5	PC binary file
7	Gopher menu
8	Telnet session
9	Binary file
s	Sound
i	Image file (other than a GIF)
g	GIF image
h	HTML document (World Wide Web page)

Searching a specific Gopher site

Look out…this could turn into a riot. Just to keep the laughter at a fevered pitch, somebody decided to name the other Gopher searching system **Jughead**; once again creating a completely inane acronym that only has a cursory relationship to its actual function:

Jonzy's **U**niversal **G**opher **H**ierarchy **E**xcavation **A**nd **D**isplay

Why is Jughead different? Jughead searches only a specific Gopher server or site, as opposed to Veronica, which searches all of Gopherspace. Jughead tends to be more accurate because it's locally maintained—and thus closer to the information.

So, Jughead's not a bad idea if you happen to know *where* you want to look for something. If, for instance, you know you're searching for something at the University of Utah, you can tunnel straight there, then use its Jughead system for a local search (see fig. 13.7).

Fig. 13.7
Using Jughead to search a local Gopher site. Since it doesn't have to cover the world, Jughead is often much more accurate.

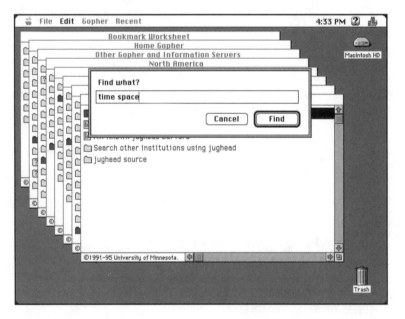

Jughead works pretty much the same way Veronica does, allowing you to use single search words and AND, OR, and NOT phrases. (More than one word without a conjunction is assumed to be an AND phrase. For example, `Ford Mustang` is assumed to mean `Ford AND Mustang`.)

TIP **Want to search for Gopher sites that offer Jughead? Use Veronica** and search for **jughead -t7**. The -t7 means you'll only get submenu listings—not documents or programs that include jughead in the name.

Downloading from Gopher sites

Gopher is great for document retrieval, but it can transfer files as well. Those files can be typical downloads—like programs or documents—or sound and video files. How do you get them? Find a site that offers them, first (see fig. 13.8). Then, just double-click.

Fig. 13.8
Downloading with Gopher is still nothing more than a double-click of the mouse.

These are downloadable files.

Here's a download in progress.

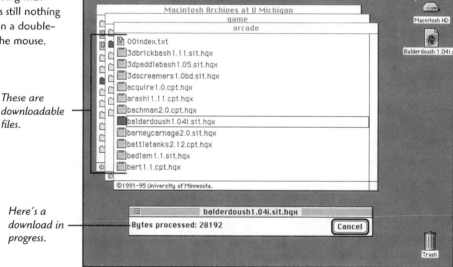

 TIP **The University of Minnesota home menu offers a submenu of FTP** sites you can explore.

When you start the download, your TurboGopher will alert you with a small progress box showing you how long it's taking to download. Other programs will tell you in different ways. Once the program has arrived, you're ready to translate it from BinHex and decompress or de-archive the file. How? Just like you did with FTP downloads in Chapter 11—drag it to StuffIt Expander!

14

Virtual Discussion Groups: UseNet

● In this chapter:

- What is UseNet and what makes it interesting?

- Why are these discussion group names so weird?

- Down and (sometimes) dirty with the "alternative" newsgroups

- How do I read these messages? How do I reply?

- UseNet netiquette: be polite, play fair, and don't hog the screen

Got something to say to the world? Millions of UseNet users participate in discussions in more than 12,000 major topic areas. Bring your brain! . . . . ➤

Depending on the sort of person you are, you may spend the bulk of your Internet time in UseNet discussion groups. It's here, more than anywhere else on the Internet (with the possible exception of mailing lists), where user interaction and participation are the key. Sure, you can get a lot of information—both formally and informally presented—in UseNet groups. But the point, ultimately, is to communicate. And to do that, you've got to take part.

There are upwards of 12,000 UseNet discussion groups available for individual Internet providers to carry. Most tend to offer between 5,000 and 8,000 groups, depending on the locality, type of service, and their restrictions.

What is UseNet?

Although its name makes it sound like a physical network (like APRANet or the Internet), **UseNet** is actually an Internet service—it describes a method for moving data over the Internet—not a physical setup of cabling and computers.

UseNet isn't completely unlike e-mail, and is even more like Internet mailing lists. Using special **newsreader** software, you download messages to your computer, read them, and respond to them. As with mailing lists, you can respond publicly or via private e-mail. The major difference between a **newsgroup** and a mailing list is that the newsgroup doesn't arrive in your In box with the text of all messages. Newsgroup messages stay on your UseNet server computer until you decide they're worth reading (see fig. 14.1).

 Plain English, please!

More than a little confusion comes from the fact that everything associated with UseNet seems to be called **news**—something or another. If this throws you off, just substitute the word **discussion** for **news**. UseNet has little to do with the type of news you see on CNN or read in a local paper. Newsgroups are, for the most part, very much like discussion groups on CompuServe or America Online.

There isn't much that's terribly formal about UseNet. Computer software on your service provider's computer is responsible for sending, retrieving, and storing messages for groups that the provider decides to make available to its users. It's up to you to find the groups that interest you, and then send your messages appropriately.

Fig. 14.1
Reading UseNet
newsgroups with
NewsWatcher for the
Macintosh.

*The number
of messages
in the group.*

*The number
of messages.*

*The person who
started the topic.*

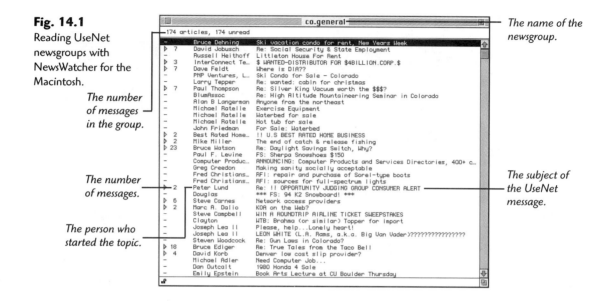

*The name of the
newsgroup.*

*The subject of
the UseNet
message.*

UseNet is a community effort with no central authority. There is also quite a bit of "netiquette" associated with UseNet, but we'll talk about it in depth later in this chapter.

Getting around UseNet newsgroups

As with most of our other Internet services, the key to UseNet is understanding the addressing scheme: specifically, UseNet newsgroup names. Again, we're reminded of the UNIX world with this crazy scheme for naming groups. It makes sense, eventually, but you might have to look at it sideways.

First-level group names

Groups are named in several levels—the first level being a generic identifier that tells you what "type" of discussion group it is. For example, notice the following address:

comp.sys.mac.advocacy

The comp in the address tells you that this group discusses computer issues. There are several standard first-level names, as shown in table 14.1.

Table 14.1   First-level UseNet newsgroup names

First-level name	What it means
biz	business issues
comp	computing topics
news	general news and topical discussions
rec	recreation (hobbies/arts) topics
sci	scientific discussions
soc	social issues
talk	debate-oriented groups
misc	other general discussions

The table is by no means exhaustive. First-level names can be local-issues groups (dfw for Dallas/Fort Worth), university-specific (mit for Massachusetts Institute of Technology), different language groups (fr for French), or newsgroups specific to a particular network (clari for the ClariNet news network).

TIP   **Okay, I lied. You *can* get current events and news information** (like CNN or the newspaper) on UseNet. That's what the ClariNet newsgroups are. ClariNet is a commercial part of the UseNet that offers newswire stories and commentary.

The "alternative" newsgroups

There is one more first-level name we haven't touched on: alt (for "alternative"), which includes newsgroups your mother never told you about. Actually, alt groups aren't *all* weird. But the alt groups do allow more freedom with the language and variation in topics than do most of the other types of newsgroups. And they are never moderated or controlled. In fact, alt groups don't even have to go through the same creation process that other groups do—if you want an alt group, you've got it.

CAUTION If you've heard any of the debate concerning the anarchy of the Internet—welcome to the alt groups. This is where a lot of it happens. Yes, there are groups that distribute pornography. Yes, there are explicit discussions, egotistical accounts of misdeeds, and bad poetry. That's not everything alt groups are about, but it's an obvious subset. What can I say? Parental discretion advised.

Some System Administrators don't download the alternative newsgroups for their university or business Internet users. Maybe that's not such a bad idea. There's a lot of good in the alt groups—but most of it is for entertainment and diversion.

What (else) is in a name?

After the first-level name, the rest of a newsgroup's name is a hierarchy that gets more and more specific. In **comp.sys.mac.advocacy**, the next level, sys, encompasses discussions concerning different computer systems. Then, getting more specific, the mac means we're discussing issues related to the Macintosh.

TIP When you say these names out loud, you usually read each part of the name as a word whenever possible (say "Mac," not "M-A-C"). And you say "dot" when you see a period ("."), if you're trying to tell someone how to find the group. If you're just chatting about it, you could easily say, "I was on mac advocacy the other day...".

Finally, we get to this specific group advocacy, which is where people discuss whether or not the Macintosh is better or more powerful than a Cray supercomputer or the collective subconscience of humanity.

There is also a group called **comp.sys.mac.apps** that discusses Macintosh applications; another, **comp.sys.ibm.pc.misc** (see fig. 14.2), lets people chat up their miscellaneous concerns about those *other* computers. (You'll probably see lots of messages that say My PC is broken again! or Can anybody figure out how to make this thing print?.)

Fig. 14.2
The Full Group List in
Newswatcher shows
you a few of the
computer newsgroups
available.

Reading newsgroups

You'll want to start with UseNet by browsing some newsgroups that seem to
follow your interests. In Newswatcher and other programs, you begin by
subscribing (see Chapter 15) to the group…a little like a mailing list. Then,
you get a listing of the messages in that group, and choose what you want to
read and what you want to ignore (see fig. 14.3).

Fig. 14.3
Browse through the
newsgroups and read
what interests you.

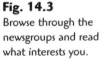
The message listing
for this group.

The group
name.

Read the
message here.

On the Mac, browsing and reading newsgroups is generally only a matter of moving the mouse around and clicking on things. What is more important is how to possibly read everything that's available. You can't—even if you devote yourself to it full time. NewsWatcher and other newsreaders help you a little, but it's ultimately up to you to manage your time.

Following discussion threads

One of the ways your newsreader can help is by recognizing discussion **threads** and presenting newsgroups so that the continuing discussions in the group are clear. To jump into a pit of thousands of unorganized messages and get up to speed in the newsgroup can be nearly impossible. Fortunately, newsreaders have the capability to present discussion threads.

 Plain English, please!

> When a newsreader recognizes message **threads**, it organizes the responses to a particular message and it makes it clear that they're linked. Generally, any message with the same subject is placed in a thread, which allows you to follow the discussion from the original message through all of its responses.

If you've subscribed to any mailing lists, as described in Chapter 10, you'll notice that the idea of reading threaded discussions is in direct contrast to the way mailing lists work. With a mailing list, all messages appear in whatever order they are posted by other subscribers. Using your newsreader, however, presents the messages in a UseNet newsgroup more logically—according to the discussion topics (see fig. 14.4).

Fig. 14.4
Using a threaded newsreader, UseNet is organized into logical topic-oriented discussions.

This is a single message—no responses yet.

The number of messages in this thread.

Here's the subject of a thread.

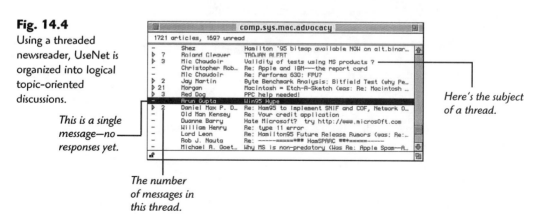

As you look for interesting discussions, then, you can read all of the original posts and responses in a particular topic without hunting through the entire listing. Very convenient.

Q&A **I'm reading a response in a UseNet newsgroup, but I can't find the original post. Why?**

UseNet message groups take up an absurd amount of hard drive space on your Internet provider's computers. For that reason, most UseNet news servers are programmed to delete *any* messages that are over a week or two old. So, it's possible that weeks have elapsed since the original message was posted, and you are only able to read the more recent responses.

Posting to newsgroups: UseNet netiquette

Because of discussion threads, it's important for you to decide whether or not to send an original message or a response when you contribute your wisdom to a UseNet discussion. Because you may be sending responses to messages fairly quickly, you'll want to be well prepared before you post an original message. Why? Because you need to make sure you're very clear on UseNet etiquette before creating an original message.

Reponding in newsgroup discussions

In order to maintain the threads discussed previously, responses force you to use the same subject as the original message in the thread (see fig. 14.5). You should, too. The idea of a response is to further the discussion within that particular topic—not talk about something completely different.

Netiquette for original posting

Eventually, you'll be ready to post an original message. Post incorrectly in a UseNet discussion, though, and you're likely to get **flamed**. Why? Because there are certain norms that you must conform to in UseNet discussions. There are no rules, but there is a sense of community. UseNet is important to a lot of participants, and you'll want to take extra care that you don't offend them.

Fig. 14.5
When responding, it's important to stay on topic. New topics require original messages.

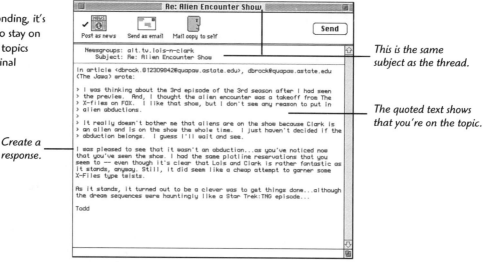

This is the same subject as the thread.

The quoted text shows that you're on the topic.

Create a response.

66 *Plain English, please!*

Flamed is a picturesque way of saying "sent mean messages." On UseNet, a breach of netiquette usually results in public humiliation by an irate subscriber. But flames aren't just reserved for new users. When these electronic insults are traded back and forth by members of the group, it's called a **flame war.** 99

We've been over the golden rule of Internet netiquette. Remember? *Waste not.* Here's how that applies to UseNet.

- **Make sure your thought justifies a public message.** It may be a better idea to send a private e-mail message to someone you come across on a UseNet newsgroup. Consider this before posting a public message that's not of general interest to the group.

- **Be concise.** Don't get carried away with wordiness. Your message should be complete; if you don't have much to say, maybe you shouldn't say it. Don't waste space with your life story or idle chatter.

- **Have a good subject.** In a response, of course, you have to use the topic at hand as your subject. But in an original post, make the purpose of your message clear. Also, remember to add **(long)** to any message that ends up over a page or two in length.

- **Format your messages well.** Try to keep your line lengths around 60–65 characters. Many UseNet users are using newsreaders that are less sophisticated than Newswatcher, and poorly formatted messages will drive them crazy.

- **Watch grammar and spelling.** No one will fault you for an occasional typo, but make sure your grammar and spelling don't affect the usefulness of your post.

- **Send your message to the appropriate group.** Make sure your topic is pertinent to the purpose of the discussion group. Don't send a message about how much you hate Windows 95 to **rec.autos**, no matter how venomous your loathing.

TIP   **Want to send a test message to make sure you've got this whole** posting thing down? Send it to **misc.test** or **alt.test**. Do NOT send it to a regular newsgroup!

- **Keep your signature reasonable.** We talked about signatures in our discussion about e-mail. You can use them on UseNet, too. And they need to be just as brief and useful—no more than four lines long, if you can help it.

- **Avoid crossposting.** Although many newsreaders make crossposting fairly simple, it's something you should do only after a lot of consideration. Crossposting is often considered rude, especially if all groups are not appropriate for the message.

 Plain English, please!

> **Crossposting** is sending the same exact message to two or more newsgroups. It's a common tool for folks who send out unscrupulous messages trying to attract business. 🎵🎵

- **Only discuss your business or product if it's truly informative to the appropriate group.** And keep any business-oriented messages low-key. No `FIRE SALE TODAY` messages are appropriate, although a message like this is okay: `In fact, I own a company that offers just a service. If you'd like, call. . .`

The FAQ: frequently asked questions

I've saved the most important UseNet netiquette issue for last. *Read the Frequently Asked Questions (FAQ) document for your group.* What is this thing? It's a compilation of the typical basic questions that a newsgroup tends to get from new users. The point is, they'd rather not see the same questions every time someone new comes along, so they compile the most common ones into a text document, as shown in figure 14.6.

Fig. 14.6

Here's a typical FAQ document, where often-asked questions are posted so that new users don't irritate veterans with common questions.

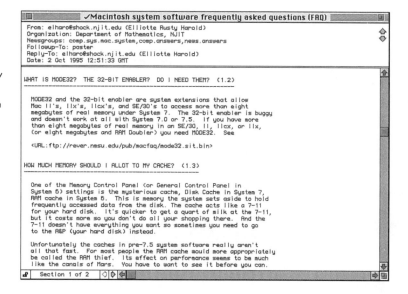

```
             ✓Macintosh system software frequently asked questions (FAQ)

From: elharo@shock.njit.edu (Elliotte Rusty Harold)
Organization: Department of Mathematics, NJIT
Newsgroups: comp.sys.mac.system,comp.answers,news.answers
Followup-To: poster
Reply-To: elharo@shock.njit.edu (Elliotte Harold)
Date: 2 Oct 1995 12:51:33 GMT


WHAT IS MODE32?  THE 32-BIT ENABLER?  DO I NEED THEM?  (1.2)
----------------------------------------------------------------

   MODE32 and the 32-bit enabler are system extensions that allow
   Mac II's, IIx's, IIcx's, and SE/30's to access more than eight
   megabytes of real memory under System 7.  The 32-bit enabler is buggy
   and doesn't work at all with System 7.0 or 7.5.  If you have more
   than eight megabytes of real memory in an SE/30, II, IIcx, or IIx,
   (or eight megabytes and RAM Doubler) you need MODE32.  See

   <URL:ftp://rever.nmsu.edu/pub/macfaq/mode32.sit.bin>


HOW MUCH MEMORY SHOULD I ALLOT TO MY CACHE?  (1.3)
----------------------------------------------------------------

   One of the Memory Control Panel (or General Control Panel in
   System 6) settings is the mysterious cache, Disk Cache in System 7,
   RAM cache in System 6.  This is memory the system sets aside to hold
   frequently accessed data from the disk.  The cache acts like a 7-11
   for your hard disk.  It's quicker to get a quart of milk at the 7-11,
   but it costs more so you don't do all your shopping there.  And the
   7-11 doesn't have everything you want so sometimes you need to go
   to the A&P (your hard disk) instead.

   Unfortunately the caches in pre-7.5 system software really aren't
   all that fast.  For most people the RAM cache would more appropriately
   be called the RAM thief.  Its effect on performance seems to be much
   like the canals of Mars.  You have to want to see it before you can.

Section 1 of 2
```

How do you get these? Most of them are available (or instructions for getting them are available) in the newsgroup **news.answers**. FAQs can also be downloaded via FTP from **rtfm.mit.edu**. Start in the directory /pub/usenet/.

15

Reading Newsgroups with NewsWatcher

● **In this chapter:**

- **Finding and setting up NewsWatcher**

- **How do I read messages?**

- **Adding your thoughts to a UseNet conversation**

- **Cleaning up the list of long subjects**

- **Can I create my own message threads?**

- **Saving messages in NewsWatcher**

- **Getting files from UseNet**

NewsWatcher is more than a great newsreader for Macs—it's easily among the best newsreader programs for any computer! . . . .

In the last chapter, we talked a lot about the differences between mailing lists and UseNet. Probably the most overwhelming difference is the tools available for reading UseNet. While mailing lists rely on your e-mail program, UseNet has many types of programs available for reading these messages. And, as is often the case, some of the best programs are available for the Macintosh! Spend a little time with NewsWatcher and you'll be thrilled with the power of UseNet.

NewsWatcher is great for reading, posting, and organizing UseNet articles, and it tries to conform to the Macintosh way of life. It makes it easy to read threads, respond to others, and start your own discussions.

Installing and setting up NewsWatcher

Before you can take advantage of the ease and power of NewsWatcher, you must set it up. Specifically, you need to get a copy of the software, install it, configure it for your Internet account, and subscribe to its newsgroups.

Getting the software

The latest version of NewsWatcher can be retrieved via FTP from **ftp.acns.nwu.edu** in the directory /pub/newswatcher/. You may also want to download the file user-doc.msword.sea.hqx which is a Microsoft Word file that includes complete documentation for the program.

 CAUTION **You can also find copies of NewsWatcher on national online** services like America Online, although it's difficult to know whether you're getting the most recent version. Be aware that there are other versions of NewsWatcher because the source code (the programmer's C-language code) is freely distributed and can be modified and recompiled legally by others.

Gathering news server information

To configure NewsWatcher, you'll need to know two different addresses for servers used by your site or Internet provider: the news server and the mail server. Examples might be **news.provider.net** or **mail.harvard.edu**. Ask your System Administrator for the specific addresses for your site.

Q&A *Why does NewsWatcher want to know my mail server?*

Because, aside from posting messages to UseNet groups, you can also choose to reply to an article author in a private e-mail message if you'd like to discuss something not pertinent or appropriate for the entire group. You can also send messages to yourself for later use.

Installing the NewsWatcher software

To install the software, double-click the NewsWatcher.sea file. A new NewsWatcher folder is created and a number of files are extracted into that folder. In that new folder is the program icon for NewsWatcher, which you'll use to start your first session.

CAUTION **If your file still has an .hqx extension to its name, you'll need to** drop the file on StuffIt Expander first.

Starting NewsWatcher

Double-click the NewsWatcher icon to automatically call MacTCP, which, in turn, makes any PPP or SLIP connections it needs to get started (assuming that you require PPP/SLIP and you've correctly configured MacTCP). Once connected, NewsWatcher brings up a dialog box, similar to the one in figure 15.1, asking for setup information.

Fig. 15.1
Tell the Welcome to NewsWatcher dialog box how you plan to use NewsWatcher.

Q&A *I'm not seeing any of this configuration stuff in NewsWatcher. What's wrong?*

You probably installed Internet Config when we were setting up Anarchie (or at some other time). With Internet Config active, NewsWatcher already knows just about everything it needs to about your system. You can skip to the "Connecting to the news server and subscribing" section of this chapter.

If you plan to use NewsWatcher on your personal Macintosh (or a Macintosh in the office that only you use), click the Private button. If you plan to share the same Macintosh and copy of NewsWatcher with other users, click the Shared button. You will then be asked to create a folder on the Mac's hard drive for storing your personal NewsWatcher information.

The final choice is the Lab button. Rather than creating a personal folder on the hard drive, you can create an individual NewsWatcher disk on which your personal information is stored. Using NewsWatcher this way enables you to use different Macintosh computers in a computer lab environment to access UseNet, but still maintain your personal preferences and configuration.

Configuring NewsWatcher

Next, a dialog box appears that asks you to enter the news server and mail server addresses for your particular site (see fig. 15.2). Enter the appropriate addresses in each field, and click OK when you're done.

Fig. 15.2
The Server Addresses dialog box requires addresses for your news server and mail server. These addresses tell NewsWatcher how to connect to your site's UseNet and e-mail services.

```
┌──────────────────── Server Addresses ─────────────────────┐
│                                                            │
│  Please enter the addresses of your news and mail servers. │
│                                                            │
│  You may enter either domain names ("host.sub.domain") or IP│
│  addresses ("128.1.2.3"). Domain names are preferred. Get this│
│  information from your network administrator.              │
│                                                            │
│  News Server:  [news.connect.net                    ]      │
│                                                            │
│  Mail Server:  [mail.connect.net                    ]      │
│                                                            │
│                            ( Cancel )  (( OK ))            │
└────────────────────────────────────────────────────────────┘
```

Entering personal information

The last setup dialog box asks for your personal information; this is the return address information that NewsWatcher sends with your posts. You are only required to enter an e-mail address, although it's a good idea to include a full name, too. On UseNet, this information lets others know who you are and how to send you e-mail messages if they want to discuss something with you personally.

TIP   **Your e-mail address can be any valid Internet address—it doesn't** necessarily have to be related to your mail server (although it often is). If you prefer to receive mail at a different address, enter that in the e-mail address field.

Connecting to the news server and subscribing

After you click OK in the Personal Information dialog box, NewsWatcher connects to the news server and begins to read the list of all the UseNet groups your server offers. This can take awhile, as your site may offer thousands of groups. When the list is compiled, two new windows appear (see fig. 15.3). The Full Group List window contains the list of all available UseNet groups. The Untitled window is for your personal list of groups—the groups to which you subscribe.

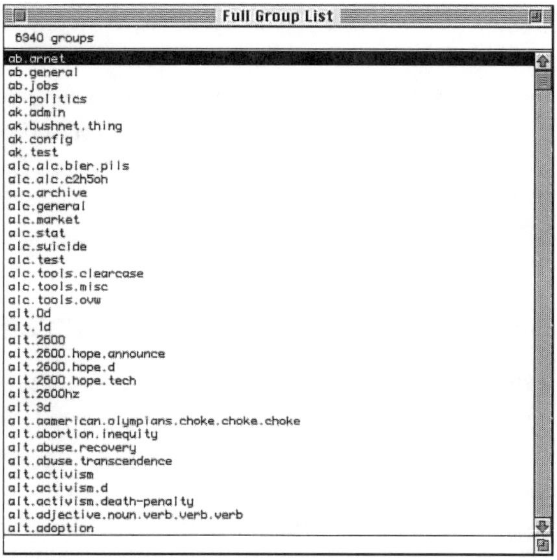

Fig. 15.3
The Full Group List and Untitled windows. Drag and drop a newsgroup name on the Untitled window, and you've subscribed!

Full Group List
6940 groups

```
ab.arnet
ab.general
ab.jobs
ab.politics
ak.admin
ak.bushnet.thing
ak.config
ak.test
alc.alc.bier.pils
alc.alc.c2h5oh
alc.archive
alc.general
alc.market
alc.stat
alc.suicide
alc.test
alc.tools.clearcase
alc.tools.misc
alc.tools.ovm
alt.0d
alt.1d
alt.2600
alt.2600.hope.announce
alt.2600.hope.d
alt.2600.hope.tech
alt.2600hz
alt.3d
alt.aamerican.olympians.choke.choke.choke
alt.abortion.inequity
alt.abuse.recovery
alt.abuse.transcendence
alt.activism
alt.activism.d
alt.activism.death-penalty
alt.adjective.noun.verb.verb.verb
alt.adoption
```

You can use the Full Group List to browse any group that looks interesting—in fact, you may want to use this list for awhile to make sure you're interested in what the group has to say. When you do find a group you want to keep track of, you can subscribe to the group by dragging the group's name from the Full Group List to the Untitled window (if you have System 7.5 or the Drag Manager extension installed!).

 TIP In NewsWatcher's Edit menu, you find a Find command that can be used to search for words in the Full Group List. Just enter a word for something you're interested in, like **mac**. You can use the Find Again command to continue your search.

After you've subscribed to the groups that interest you, save your group list. With the Untitled window selected, head up to the File menu and select the Save command. By default, this creates a new icon in the NewsWatcher folder. In the future, whenever you want to open NewsWatcher, double-click your saved groups icon. NewsWatcher will open automatically and check the server for new messages in your subscribed groups.

Q&A   ***NewsWatcher doesn't show my personal group list when it starts and/or all my preferences are wrong. What's going on?***

Depending on how you've set up NewsWatcher, you may need to be careful how you save your personal list. On a private Mac, you can put your saved groups icon anywhere on the hard drive. On a shared or lab Mac, you'll need to save it in the same folder as your NewsWatcher Prefs file. On a lab Mac, the NewsWatcher Prefs file and your personal group list will need to be on your personal NewsWatcher floppy disk. In all cases, remember to double-click your personal group icon—not NewsWatcher's icon—to start with your personal list open and ready for reading.

Unsubscribing groups in NewsWatcher

If you decide that you've lost interest in a particular group and no longer want to track it in your personal group list, you can unsubscribe the group to remove it from your list. Remember, **unsubscribing** means NewsWatcher will no longer track which messages have been marked as being read/unread or keep other statistics related to a newsgroup. You can still re-subscribe or read messages in the group by selecting it in the Full Group List.

To unsubscribe, select the group's name in your personal list, and choose Unsubscribe from the Special menu.

TIP   **You can also unsubscribe a group by selecting it and clicking the** Delete key, using the Cut command, or, in System 7.5, dragging the group name to Mac's Trash.

Reading articles

Reading articles is probably what you'll do about 90 percent of the time with NewsWatcher. Even the name of the program lends itself to that idea. You probably won't post too many articles at first, especially if you're just getting acquainted with UseNet.

TIP **To read a group regularly but never post an article is known as** *lurking.* Despite its unflattering name, lurking is actively encouraged. Posting for the sake of posting is considered very rude.

Opening a group's subject window

Before you read an article, you must open that group's subject window. The subject window displays all the articles that are currently in that list, enabling you to pick the articles you're interested in reading.

To open a subject window for a particular newsgroup, double-click the name of the newsgroup in the Full Group List window. If you've already subscribed to the group, you can double-click its name in your personal list window (see fig. 15.4).

The number of articles in the group.

The author of the article.

Fig. 15.4
Opening a group's subject window is as simple as double-clicking the group's name in the personal or Full Group list window.

The thread information.

The article subject.

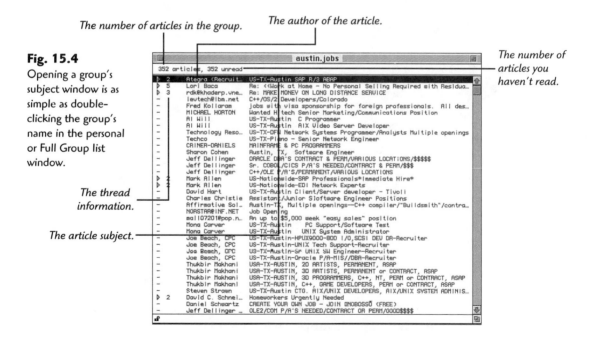

The number of articles you haven't read.

Following threads of conversation

Although UseNet groups are generally dedicated to a single topic, a number of different conversations occur within each group. Even if a group is dedicated to something as specific as Dallas Cowboys football, there will be a number of different conversations within those boundaries. People might discuss the referee's behavior at the last game, the most recent injury report, the 1970 Super Bowl, and who's the best Cowboys' receiver of all time—all in the same newsgroup.

NewsWatcher automatically threads articles by using the familiar Macintosh triangle control to indicate when an article has follow-up posts in its thread, as shown in figure 15.5.

A triangle control indicates that there are replies.

Fig. 15.5
In NewsWatcher's subject window, article threads are indicated by a triangle control. Clicking once on the control shows the follow-up messages to the original article.

An article with- — *out replies.*

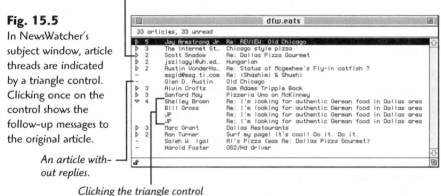

Clicking the triangle control reveals a threaded conversation.

From here, reading articles and following threads is a pretty easy process.

1 Scan the subject window for an article or thread that looks interesting.

2 Double-click the name of the article you want to read. A window pops up with that article's text (see fig. 15.6).

3 After reading the article, you can move on to the next article in the thread by pulling down the News menu and choosing Next Article. If you reach the end of the thread, NewsWatcher returns you to the subject window.

4 To select another subject or thread, double-click the name of a new article or press Return to continue with the next thread in the subject window.

Fig. 15.6
A standard article window displaying the text of the article.

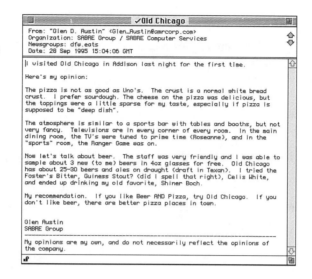

> ✓Old Chicago
>
> From: "Glen D. Austin" <Glen_Austin@amrcorp.com>
> Organization: SABRE Group / SABRE Computer Services
> Newsgroups: dfw.eats
> Date: 28 Sep 1995 15:04:06 GMT
>
> I visited Old Chicago in Addison last night for the first time.
>
> Here's my opinion:
>
> The pizza is not as good as Uno's. The crust is a normal white bread crust. I prefer sourdough. The cheese on the pizza was delicious, but the toppings were a little sparse for my taste, especially if pizza is supposed to be "deep dish".
>
> The atmosphere is similar to a sports bar with tables and booths, but not very fancy. Televisions are in every corner of every room. In the main dining room, the TV's were tuned to prime time (Roseanne), and in the "sports" room, the Ranger Game was on.
>
> Now let's talk about beer. The staff was very friendly and I was able to sample about 3 new (to me) beers in 4oz glasses for free. Old Chicago has about 25-30 beers and ales on draught (draft in Texan). I tried the Foster's Bitter, Guiness Stout? (did I spell that right), Celis White, and ended up drinking my old favorite, Shiner Boch.
>
> My recommendation. If you like Beer AND Pizza, try Old Chicago. If you don't like beer, there are better pizza places in town.
>
>
> Glen Austin
> SABRE Group
> ---
> My opinions are my own, and do not necessarily reflect the opinions of the company.

TIP While you're reading a message, you can use ⌘+I to read the next article in the thread, and press **Command+T** to move to the next thread in the subject window.

Marking articles "as read"

One of the advantages of subscribing to newsgroups is that NewsWatcher keeps track of the messages you've read in subscribed groups—and doesn't show you those articles again the next time you open that group's subject window.

Whenever you view the text of an article, NewsWatcher automatically marks the article as read. Recently read articles show a check mark in the subject window. And the next time you access the same group, previously read articles won't show up at all.

But what if you just want to get rid of the message without being forced to read it? You can mark it "as read" from the News menu with the Mark Read command. The next time you open the group, this article will not appear. To mark all articles "as read," pull down the Edit menu and choose the Select All command. Then, use the Mark Read command. In UseNet lingo this is called **catching up**. The next time you open this group, all articles and threads will be new.

Plain English, please!

Catching up a newsgroup is when you select all messages in a group and mark them "as read." Now only new messages will appear the next time you open the group's subject window. You've got a clean slate to get up to speed with the conversations in this newsgroup. "

Replying to an article with NewsWatcher

The most common type of article you'll probably post is a **follow-up article**, or in NewsWatcher-speak, a **reply**. A follow-up article adds to the thread created by the original article, so the idea behind your message should be similar to that of the original post.

Searching for articles with NewsWatcher

Is it possible to find the one message you need to read among the millions of messages on UseNet? If you're looking for messages with certain words in the subject, written by certain people, or coming from certain organizations, you can open the Special menu and choose the Search command to find these articles on your ISP's UseNet server.

To use the Search command, follow these steps:

1 Select a newsgroup or newsgroups (Command+click for more than one group) in your personal list or the Full Group List; then pull down the Special menu and choose the Search command.

2 Choose the type of information you want to search for (for example, Subject, From, Organization, and so on).

3 In the resulting dialog box, enter the text you want to search for in the Containing field.

4 Finally, click Search to begin.

Remember to pick the correct Header for your search in step 2. Subject is best if you know you're looking for discussion of something in particular. Author or Organization can be useful if you want to hear what a particular person or company has to say. Keyword and Summary searches will dig deeper, but can take a long time.

After NewsWatcher completes its search, a new group, Search Groups, is created (if at least one matching article is found). Click an article in this group to read as normal.

While the article you want to reply to is open, pull down the News menu and choose Reply. NewsWatcher will open a message window in which you can create your reply (see fig. 15.7).

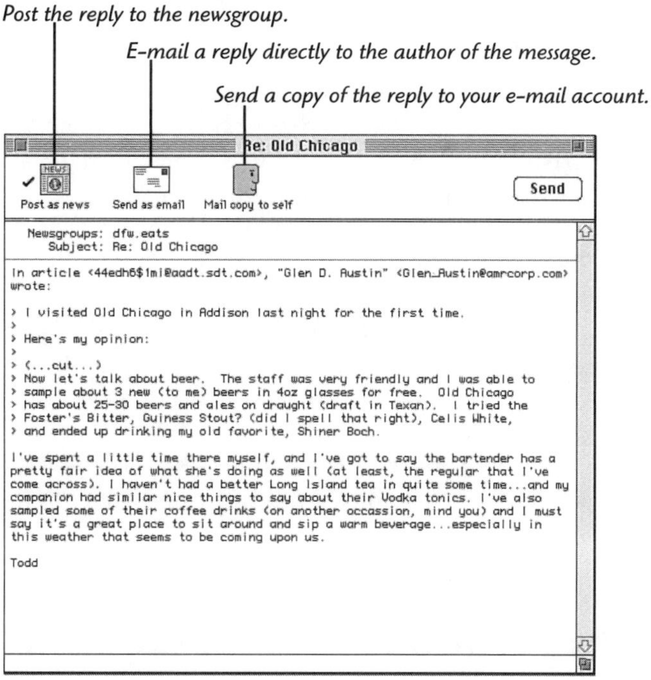

Post the reply to the newsgroup.

E-mail a reply directly to the author of the message.

Send a copy of the reply to your e-mail account.

Fig. 15.7

NewsWatcher's Reply window. Here you decide how to send your message, what you'll quote, and what you'll say.

```
                                   Re: Old Chicago
 ✓ [NEWS]          [=]          [ ]                              [ Send ]
  Post as news   Send as email  Mail copy to self

 Newsgroups: dfw.eats
    Subject: Re: Old Chicago

 In article <44edh6$1mi@aadt.sdt.com>, "Glen D. Austin" <Glen_Austin@amrcorp.com>
 wrote:

 > I visited Old Chicago in Addison last night for the first time.
 >
 > Here's my opinion:
 >
 > (...cut...)
 > Now let's talk about beer.  The staff was very friendly and I was able to
 > sample about 3 new (to me) beers in 4oz glasses for free.  Old Chicago
 > has about 25-30 beers and ales on draught (draft in Texan).  I tried the
 > Foster's Bitter, Guiness Stout? (did I spell that right), Celis White,
 > and ended up drinking my old favorite, Shiner Boch.

 I've spent a little time there myself, and I've got to say the bartender has a
 pretty fair idea of what she's doing as well (at least, the regular that I've
 come across).  I haven't had a better Long Island tea in quite some time...and my
 companion had similar nice things to say about their Vodka tonics. I've also
 sampled some of their coffee drinks (on another occassion, mind you) and I must
 say it's a great place to sit around and sip a warm beverage...especially in
 this weather that seems to be coming upon us.

 Todd
```

At the top of the window are three icons. These icons determine how your reply will be sent.

- **News Icon**. If checked, the reply is posted as a follow-up article.

- **Mail Icon**. If checked, the reply is sent directly to the e-mail account of the original article's author.

- **Self Icon**. If checked, a copy of the reply is sent to your e-mail account.

When selected, these icons will have a check mark next to them. To check or uncheck an icon, just click it. Any combination of the icons can be checked, so you can send a reply as a follow-up message, an e-mail to the author, *and* an e-mail to yourself.

TIP **Why e-mail yourself a copy? If you want a record of e-mail or** articles you send while in NewsWatcher, send copies to your e-mail account and file them. If you file your correspondence in different folders using Eudora or a similar e-mail program, it might be a good idea to keep track of your UseNet posts there, too.

In the text window, you may notice that NewsWatcher has added the full text of the message to which you're replying. This is the "quoting" that we discussed earlier in the e-mail chapters. Each quoted line is preceded by a ">" character to indicate that these are someone else's comments.

In the message window, you can now enter the text of your reply. Be sure to edit the previous author's quote liberally. In general, quote only argument points or questions to which you are directly responding. Quoting the entire message is considered bad netiquette on UseNet because it forces others to read the text of an entire message they just read.

Click the Send button when your message is complete. NewsWatcher will make sure you want to post the message—just its way of making you think twice. If you decide to go ahead, click OK and the message is off to UseNet!

Posting a new article—creating a thread

It doesn't happen as much as you might expect, but occasionally you'll need to create a new message thread to see discussion on a topic that you want talked about. As a general rule, be sure you lurk a little bit before jumping in with a new article. A dumb article (that is, an article that the members of the group feel is inappropriate) will probably draw considerably more flack than a dumb response.

To post a new article, follow these steps:

1 Select a newsgroup in either your personal list or in the Full Group List.

2 Pull down the News menu and select New Message.

3 Type the subject of your article in the subject field of the message window (see fig. 15.8).

4 Type the body of your message and click the Send button.

Fig. 15.8
Posting a new article to a UseNet group with NewsWatcher.

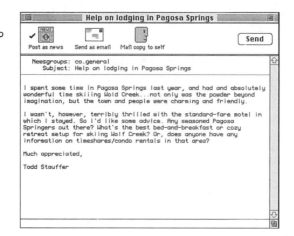

 TIP **Remember that your subject line needs to clearly state the nature** of your message so that readers can decide instantly if it interests them. Also, make sure you add **(long)** to the subject if your message is more than a page or so in length.

Storing articles for later reading

UseNet isn't just about discussion and entertainment…often, you'll get answers to technical questions or be able to research issues in the UseNet groups. And, at some point, you'll probably want to save some of these messages to read at a later time.

To save any article you are currently reading, open the File menu and choose the Save or Save As command. You can also save multiple articles at one time. Select each article with the mouse while holding down the Command key, then use the Save command. You are presented with the Save dialog box shown in figure 15.9.

If you select multiple articles, NewsWatcher will save all articles to a single text file, which you can name in the dialog box. In fact, entire threads are also saved to the same file.

Fig. 15.9
NewsWatcher's Save
dialog box lets you
rename an article and
decide how to save it.

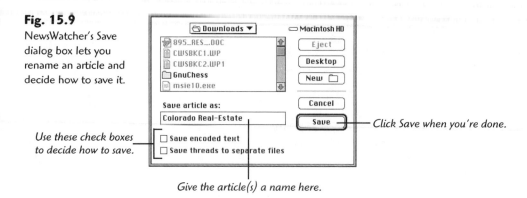

*Use these check boxes
to decide how to save.*

Click Save when you're done.

Give the article(s) a name here.

The dialog box also offers the following check boxes:

- **Save encoded text**. By default, NewsWatcher will not save binary files
  that have been UUEncoded or BinHexed. Choosing this option enables
  you to save this text with your article for later extraction.

- **Save threads to separate files**. NewsWatcher usually saves all
  selected articles and threads to the same file. To save different threads
  to different files, select this box. Now the first thread will be saved to
  your named file; all other threads will be saved to individual files using
  the thread's subject as a file name.

Getting files from UseNet messages

You have two ways to send and receive files through UseNet and Internet
e-mail posts. The first, **Mac BinHex**, is less common—but it is the most
important for Macintosh users.

The second, **UUEncode/UUDecode** (see fig. 15.10), is much more common,
especially for transfers between different computer types and for multi-
platform file types (like the common graphics formats GIF and JPG). We
haven't talked much about it because most Macintosh-specific binaries are in
BinHex format. But you will still encounter the UUEncode/UUDecode
method for graphics files and other documents (Word for Windows, for
example) that you can use on your Mac.

Plain English, please!

UUEncode and **UUDecode** were originally UNIX-based protocols for turning binary files into ASCII for sending across the Internet. The "UU" stands for "UNIX-to-UNIX", and the rest of each word suggests what's being done to the file. A UUEncoded file, then, is a binary file (on any computer type) that's been translated into ASCII text using the UUEncoding format.

Fig. 15.10
Example of a UUEncoded file, as it appears when read in SimpleText.

For the most part, NewsWatcher can automatically detect multiple-part binary posts and rebuild them. After you tell NewsWatcher to receive a binary, it tries to find all related posts and writes the binary to a temporary file. It then runs a helper program to decode the binary.

Getting and installing the helper programs

For BinHex files, the default helper file is StuffIt Expander. For UUEncoded files, the default helper file is uuUndo. The most recent versions of each of these files is available for download from **ftp.acns.nwu.edu** in the directory /pub/newswatcher/helpers/.

NewsWatcher requires only that StuffIt Expander and uuUndo be somewhere on your Mac's hard drive for decoding and decompression to work properly.

Download them using Anarchie or a similar program, and extract their archives. StuffIt Expander will extract automatically when double-clicked. Do this first, then double-click the uuUndo archive.

Receiving binary files with NewsWatcher

There is a fairly standard naming convention for articles with attached binary files. Because UseNet requires that every individual article be relatively short, binary files sometimes require more than one post (usually an article and multiple replies) to store the entire upload. Generally, a subject line that says part X of Y or part X/Y indicates a binary posting with one or more replies.

The first article in the post (generally numbered 1 of X) usually contains a short description of the file and the beginning of the coded binary. If you're already viewing that article, it's easy to extract the binary (see fig. 15.11).

Fig. 15.11
This article has an attached binary that can be extracted with a single click of the file icon.

In the top right corner of the window, a small file icon appears. Click this icon (in System 7.5, you can also drag the icon to the Desktop), and NewsWatcher extracts all parts of the binary and writes them to a temporary file. It then feeds this temporary file to the helper program, which decodes the file into a useful program or document.

Extracting binaries from the subject window

You can also extract binaries from the subject window. To do this, click once on the article thread that contains the binary you'd like to extract, pull down the Special menu, and choose Extract Binaries (see fig. 15.12).

Fig. 15.12
Extracting binaries from the subject window in NewsWatcher.

To extract multiple binaries, hold down the Command key while clicking subject names with the mouse. With multiple subjects selected, you can then pull down the Special menu and select Extract Binaries to receive all binaries.

TIP **You can even use the Edit, Select All command and then Extract** Binaries to receive all binaries in a given group. NewsWatcher automatically skips articles without attachments and incomplete uploads.

16

Chatting on the Internet: IRC

● **In this chapter:**

• **What is IRC? How do I chat on the Internet?**

• **How does IRC work?**

• **Some of the best IRC channels for Mac users**

• **Saying hello to (and with) Homer!**

Heard those stories about people falling in love on the Internet? Well, they probably talked about it first—and, if so, they used Internet Relay Chat (IRC) . . . .

f the Internet is a "virtual community," then we've seen the virtual mail service, virtual newsletters, and virtual bulletin boards. What's next? How about virtual coffee shops?

Internet Relay Chat (IRC) is the protocol that lets Internet users get together and chat, "live," with other users around the world. Once again, all it takes is a MacTCP and a special application. And, of course, the Mac has some great programs for just this task.

How do you chat on the Internet?

Well, you're not chatting as much as you are typing, but you are doing so in real-time with other human beings. It's a little like a conference call with your keyboard and Mac screen (see fig. 16.1).

66 *Plain English, please!*

Real-time is technobabble for "live." It just means that something happens without delay. Chatting on IRC is almost as instant as a phone call or a conversation in your local diner. 99

The IRC "channel" I've joined.   The "topic" for this discussion.

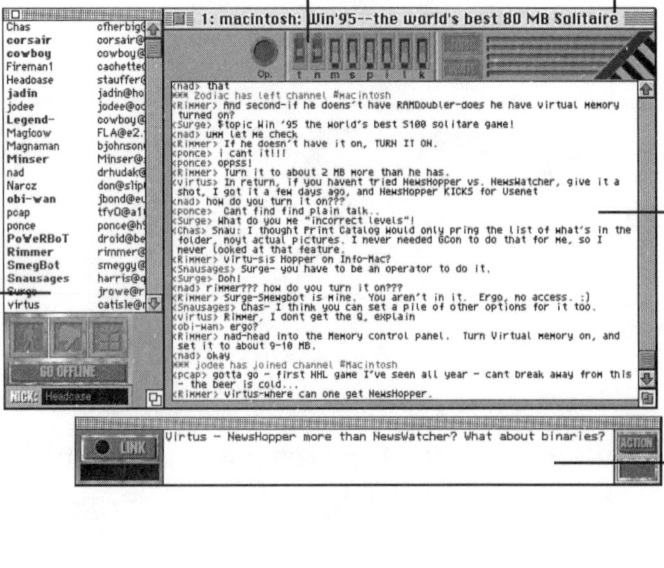

Fig. 16.1
IRC in action. I'm using a Mac program called Homer to talk to others around the world.

I can see who the people are in this window.

Others in the group are chatting away.

I type my contribution here.

Fire up your IRC program, sign on to a special IRC server, and you're ready to join an IRC group. These groups are called **channels** in IRC lingo. Pick a channel and a nickname for yourself—then enjoy a good conversation.

What channel is the good stuff on?

In e-mail, it's the address for UseNet, it's the newsgroup's name. So what's the common demoninator in IRC chatting? The **channel**. There are hundreds of discussion channels available at any given time, and picking one that meets your needs can be something of a chore. Of course, you're free to change channels at any time, and enter a completely different conversation.

CAUTION IRC can be as lewd and (im-)mature as UseNet—perhaps more so. Many channels are flirt and cybersex rooms where the language, content, and fantasy can send the old mercury through the top of the thermometer. Indeed, four-letter words can show up in nearly any channel—the only rules being whatever the channel operator decides to put up with. PG-13 to NC-17 ratings abound.

So what are these channels like? Well, here are a few examples. Popular channels include:

#macintosh. Discussion of Mac-related issues, including news, tech help, and Internet and Mac applications.

#hottub. Topic of the day. The group can get a little rowdy, but the point is to be an atmosphere similar to what you'd find in a hot tub at a local club or resort. Fun, light coversation.

#chat—More light-hearted chat. Just a get-to-know-you group where you'll come across a lot of people in different states of mind.

#talk—Generally a little more serious, but not far removed from the two above.

(By the way, the "#" sign is just a way to point out that something is an IRC channel.) There are, of course, literally hundreds of others—some regional channels like #Dallas, others that are professional/hobby-oriented like #writers, and others that are age-group oriented or social like #35Plus. And, since anyone can create a channel, there's an amazing number of possibilities.

Conversation tends to flow just like it would in a bar or at a good party...so the name of the channel won't always relate to the topic. You could walk in on a "Hi"-fest where people are just greeting one another; or you might run across political debate in a computer forum. You never know.

Who are these people?

For the most part, these people are just like you: tired, worn-out, reclusive, wretched souls sitting in a darkened room with their Macs as their only lifeline to humanity. Okay, so maybe that's just me. Man. I didn't expect that joke to be so depressing.

 TIP Most folks use a nickname (or "nick") on IRC, which acts something like a CB radio handle. Ideally, it's a clever way to represent your interests or personality to others on IRC—in nine letters or fewer.

Some of the folks on a channel will be a little more special than you or me, though. They're called channel operators, and they have special abilities (see fig. 16.2). Like what? **Channel operators** can change the topic of the group, kick users off the channel, ban them from any future discussions, and they can give operator status to other users in the channel.

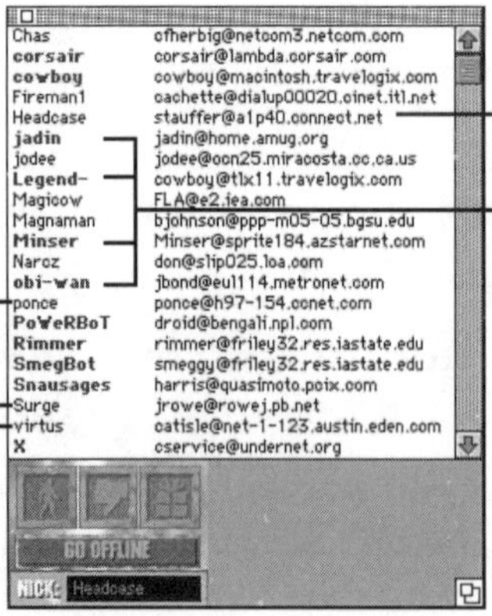

Fig. 16.2
Using Homer, the popular Mac IRC program, you can check the user list to see who's logged into the channel...and who has channel operator status.

These are normal folks.

Here are e-mail addresses.

Channel operators are highlighted.

In some programs, channel operators will be highlighted in the user list. In others, their names in the chat window will begin with an "at" symbol (@).

 TIP Want to be a channel operator? There are two ways. First, you can ask someone who's already an operator to give you that status (get to know them first, though). Or, you can start your own channel (more later).

Of course, I've gotta say something about chatting netiquette

You just can't get away from the netiquette stuff. As always, you just need a little common sense. But this is especially important with IRC, since it is instantaneous by nature. On UseNet, everyone is once removed from the discussion, so it's easier to forgive mistakes or step back and be less heated in your replies.

But IRC is here, now, and confrontational. Depending on the channel you join, you're very likely to run up against people who've been using IRC for months or years—and they often know one another. So it's important to approach a new channel like an open party at someone else's house—politely and with respect.

 TIP **Want to be well accepted by the group? Just show up often and** contribute to the conversation. In most channels, you'll get to know the regulars quickly...and they'll know you, too, if you act like a regular.

IRC netiquette tips

There are a couple of standard hints and tips for getting used to and comfortable with the way IRC works. In no particular order:

- *Understand your IRC program.* The most embarrassing thing you can do in an IRC chat is accidentally send commands or private messages to the group in general. You'll be instantly recognized as a "newbie" and, depending on the group, you may be chastised as such.

- *Be patient and spend some time on a channel.* If you're just getting your feet wet, jump around on a few different channels until you find one you like. Then spend some time with it. Get to know folks, watch for regular users and regular topics. Get comfortable and contribute when you feel confident.

- *Don't "flood the channel."* Changing your nickname often or sending "actions" in a channel often can annoy users who are trying to have a conversation. Contribute only when it's appropriate and when you really have something to add.

- *Follow conventions.* Generally, people say "Hi all" or something similar when they sign on to a channel, but it's bad form to try to say "Hi" to everybody in a group. It just wastes screen space and gets in the way of conversation.

- *No commercials.* Blatant wares-hocking is frowned upon everywhere on the Internet…including IRC. You can mention products in passing, or even endorse things every once in a while, but be guarded. Oh, and just one line of "*Insert your favorite Seattle-based Grunge band here* Rules!" is plenty.

- *Know the channel.* With as many "flirt" and "love" channels as there are with IRC, it's considered pretty rude to start making passes at someone in a current-events or profession-oriented channel. And, while it's probably okay to discuss the presidential race in #politics, don't expect to get far trying to find holes in the Republican platform with users in #car_audio.

Using Homer for IRC chat

As has been my guiding principle throughout this book, I'm going to suggest that you use *only* what is generally held to be the best program for IRC chatting with a Mac. Homer is an exceptional program that really makes a lot of the arcane commands and settings for IRC easy to grasp. Even for me.

TIP **Homer is shareware…the author requests $25 after continued use.** If you'd rather not pay, there is a freeware program called **Ircle** available for a slightly less sophisticated connection to IRC. Look for Ircle on Info-Mac mirror sites.

The first step is to get your hands (figuratively) on Homer. According to the author, Toby Smith, you can download the latest version from **zaphod.ee.pitt.edu** in the directory /pub/. Frankly, I haven't had much success with this site. If you need to, use Anarchie to perform an Archie search. If you use the phrase **Homer*.hqx** and select the Pattern Search radio button, you should easily find an FTP site featuring Homer.

TIP **This Archie search is also a good way to find the Homer manual,** which is generally distributed separately from the program. If you become a serious IRC nut, you'll need the Homer manual because I'm only hitting the basics here.

Starting up Homer

After you have Homer safely tucked away in a folder on your Macintosh's hard drive, double-click its icon to get things started. You'll be presented with an introductory screen telling you about Homer and its status as shareware. When you're through that, click Will Do, Chief to move on. The next screen you come across is shown in figure 16.3.

Fig. 16.3

Setting up Homer for the first time. You'll want to change all this information, just so people don't instantly know you're a newbie.

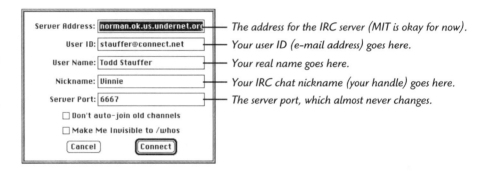

Server Address: `norman.ok.us.undernet.org` —— *The address for the IRC server (MIT is okay for now).*

User ID: `stauffer@connect.net` —— *Your user ID (e-mail address) goes here.*

User Name: `Todd Stauffer` —— *Your real name goes here.*

Nickname: `Vinnie` —— *Your IRC chat nickname (your handle) goes here.*

Server Port: `6667` —— *The server port, which almost never changes.*

☐ Don't auto-join old channels
☐ Make Me Invisible to /whos
[Cancel]   (Connect)

I've got to warn you here. Mr. Smith is setting you up here for a fall. Log on to nearly any IRC channel with a user name like newbie and a nickname like KickMe, and you're likely to get roughed-up. Pay attention here and we'll keep your newbie status a secret. Okay?

• *Server address.* It's in this field that you decide which IRC server you're going use for your connection. Since you don't really know any others, it's okay to use the default for right now. Eventually, you'll want to use one that's easier to connect to—and preferably closer to your part of the world.

Q&A *How do I find another IRC server to use with Homer?*

The best way is the IRC Server Guide file (using the Apple Guide system), which helps you find the IRC server closest to you. The Server Guide has been included on the MacNet disk that came with this book. You can download the file from **ftp.mcp.com** in the directory /pub/que/inetapps/ mac/. Then, put the IRC Server Guide file in your Homer folder. Now, when Homer is active, you can select the Server Guide from the Help ("?") menu, and follow on-screen instructions to find a close IRC server.

- *User ID.* Ideally, you would put your e-mail address here. But that's up to you—IRC is all about anonymity. If you want to fake something, I guess you can. (Some servers don't like it.)

- *User Name.* This is what appears in parentheses after your e-mail address. If this example were real, then my address and name would appear to other IRC users as: **stauffer@connect.net (Todd Stauffer)**. But, again, you don't really have to put your real name—you could put a short quote or fake name if desired.

- *Nickname.* To old-hand IRC users, this is your **nick**. It's what will precede anything you say on IRC—like CB radio, it's your handle. Come up with something clever, and stick to it if you want to get known.

- *Server Port.* This is a number that Homer needs to connect to your IRC server correctly. It is almost always 6667 (as unfortunate a number as that may seem) and you probably won't have to change it.

By the way, this is also the screen that appears whenever you want to *change* these settings, which explains the checkbox labeled Don't auto-join old channels. Since you haven't accessed any channels, you don't have any old channels yet. But you will. Clicking once on this option will disallow Homer from automatically connecting you to any channels that were open when you last ended a session. You'll probably want to decide this after you know a little more about IRC.

Q&A **Homer is always automatically connecting to a server! How do I change Homer's configuration??**

After your initial Homer session, things will act a little differently. Generally, you shouldn't have to change your settings often, so Homer was designed to be a bit more efficient.

The next time you start up Homer, you see a dialog box that tells you that Homer plans, after waiting three seconds, to connect to the IRC server using your default settings. If you want to change these settings click once on the Click Me to Change the Connection Settings button. Now Homer shows you the startup screen that you just went through in figure 16.3. You can change anything that needs changing and click Connect to start up again.

If you don't need to make any changes, just wait the three seconds. Homer will connect automatically, using the same server choice, name and nickname you entered initially.

Connecting to the IRC server

Once you have everything set up correctly, you're ready to connect to the IRC server. Click Connect in the setup window. Now Homer will look for the IRC server and start your connection. When it's connected, you're shown something like figure 16.4.

Fig. 16.4
IRC is deeply routed in UNIX, so when you first connect to your server, you'll get an all-text response.

The Homer Control Panel window.

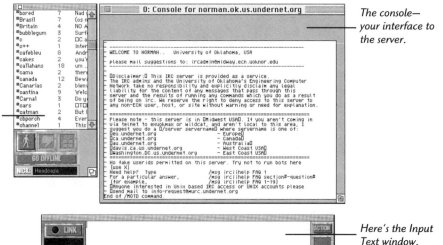

The console— your interface to the server.

Here's the Input Text window.

You're up-and-running when the Homer Console window appears, giving you the welcome message from your IRC server. If everything goes well, you're ready to get a list of all the available channels and start chatting. Incidentally, as you go through this, you'll notice that the Homer Control Panel window is used for both the channel list and the user list, depending on whether or not a channel window is currently the "active" window. To make the channel list active, just click once on the Console window (the one that has the server's welcome message in it).

CAUTION **Read your server's welcome message carefully. Some servers won't** allow fake user IDs or certain types of connections; or they may ask you to connect only at certain times. Just check and make sure you're doing everything according to their wishes.

Finding a channel and entering a discussion

You're connected, but there's not much chatting going on. That's because you need to find a channel you want to join and jump into the conversation. But how can you tell what channels are available? You need a **channel list**.

Pull down the Options menu and select the Channel List command. That brings up the dialog box in figure 16.5.

Fig. 16.5
You've got to know what channels are out there before you can join. Setting this option gives you a channel list every time you connect.

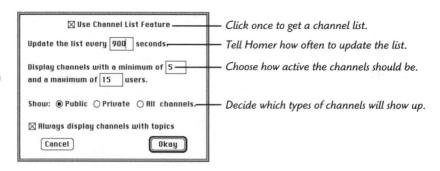

The channel list is strictly optional—if you happen to know what channel you want to join, you don't necessarily need this list. But I like to have it handy every time I access a new server. Channels come and go, and it's nice to see what's been created recently, and how active things are out there.

In the dialog box, make sure you've got Use Channel List Feature checked (click once on the little box). Then, tell Homer how often you want to update this list. If you have a modem connection, you should probably enter something between 600 and 900 seconds (10 to 15 minutes). The time it takes to download a channel list can be very long and it will disrupt your chat sessions if it's set to download frequently.

Next, choose a range for the number of users in the channels that will be displayed. You may want to eliminate channels that have only a few users—there's probably not much worth chatting about with just one or two folks.

 TIP   **You may also want to set a maximum number of 15 or 20 users** in this dialog box when you're first getting started with IRC. Get more than 20 users in a channel and the conversation can be difficult to follow.

Then, select whether you'll see public or private channels. Public is best, for now. You can click once to check the box labeled Always Display Channels with Topics if you want Homer to ignore your other rules when a channel sends a specific "topic" line with its channel name (not all do). Finally, click Okay to make these settings active.

Where is the channel list?

Now you've got to find the list. You should see it beginning to build in the Homer Control Panel window to the left of your Console window. It may take a minute or two, but eventually you'll have a long list of available channels to scroll through and examine (see fig. 16.6).

Fig. 16.6
Here's the channel list for this IRC server. There are many choices, but at least now you have some good hints.

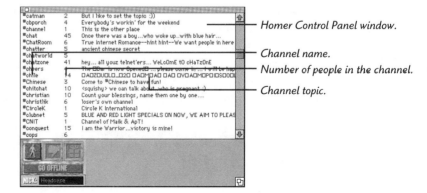

Homer Control Panel window.

Channel name.

Number of people in the channel.

Channel topic.

Entering a channel

The easiest way to start the chat experience is from the channel list. When you find a channel that looks interesting, just double-click its name in the list.

You can also join a channel by pulling down the File menu and selecting New Channel. In the resulting dialog box, enter the name of the channel (don't forget the # before the name), and click Join. Soon, a new window will open and the discussion will unfold.

 TIP **If you enter a channel that doesn't exist in the New Channel** dialog box (by typing a name for it in the Channel to Join field), IRC will create that channel for you. And, guess what? You're the channel operator!

Chatting and getting around in the channel window

Regardless of how you get there, once you have a channel window open, you're ready to start interacting. This is where the Homer interface is very powerful—most folks using other programs or platforms have to use some pretty cryptic commands to get things done. But not us, by gum. We're Mac people!

Chatting is the easy part. All you really need to do is type your message in the Input Text window (the long, horizontal window at the bottom of the screen), and hit Return to send it into the channel. Everyone will see what you have to say and can react accordingly (see fig. 16.7).

You should take some time to sit back and notice *how* things appear in the channel window. Clearly, there's the text of people chatting. But there are some other things, too, like people entering and exiting the channel (Homer shows this automatically), and people's status being changed (usually by the channel operator). All of these different notices and lines of dialog appear in different colors to make it easier to know what each is.

 TIP **Is all the noise driving you nuts? You can decide when Homer** should play sounds by pulling down the Options menu and selecting Sounds.

Fig. 16.7
Here's Homer with an
open channel. You're
ready to chat.

*The Homer Control
Panel window
changes from a list
of channels to a list
of users in this
channel.*

*A new
channel
window
opens to
show the
discussion.*

*The Input
Text window—
type what you
want to say
here and
press Return
to send your
message to
the channel.*

Sending an IRC action

Chatting isn't the only way that you can communicate in the channel. You can
also send something called an **Action**. To send an IRC Action, type it as you
would a normal line of talk. But instead of pressing Return to send it, click
once on the Action button in the Input Text window. It will be sent to the rest
of the channel as an Action (in a different format and color) instead of as a
line of dialog.

 Plain English, please!

> Since other folks in the channel can't see you, IRC lets you send **Actions**,
> which are formatted differently to tell folks what you're *doing* while you're
> chatting. (Like you're laughing or crying, etc.) "

Notice that Actions are generally different from dialog…like the description
lines in a screenplay, they're intended to *show* something that you couldn't
normally communicate through dialog. Hi Candy! is a bad Action; Todd fell
off his chair holding his stomach is a little better.

TIP   **Homer automatically puts your nickname at the beginning of any**
Action, so start with a verb. If I type **eats his cake** and click Action, other
users will see Action: Todd eats his cake automatically.

Getting to know the other folks

Let's get back to that Homer Control Panel window for a second. Remember that it has changed to show the users in this particular channel instead of the whole channel list (see fig. 16.8). But what good does that do us?

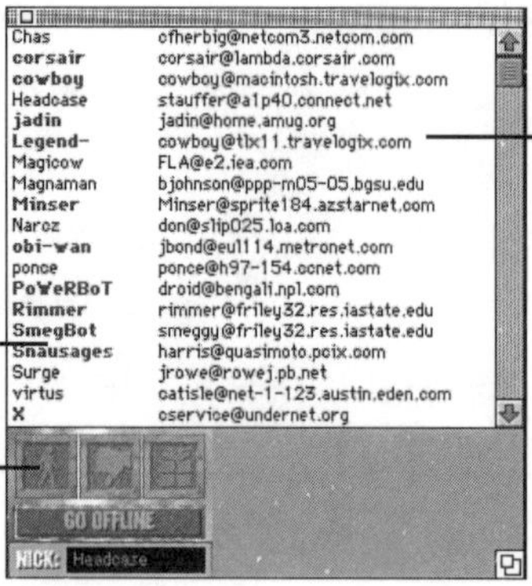

Fig. 16.8
Homer gives you a little information on the other users in the channel.

User e-mail addresses.

User nicknames.

User Info button.

Aside from a convenient list of who's present, you can figure out two things from the user list. First, notice that some names (at least one or two) are highlighted in red. These are users with Channel Operator status—they can throw you off the channel if they feel like it. Just so you know.

The other thing you can do is select a user with a single click in the list, then click once on the User Info (sometimes called Finger) button in the Homer Control Panel window. That results in a short paragraph of information about the user, which shows up back in the channel window (see fig. 16.9).

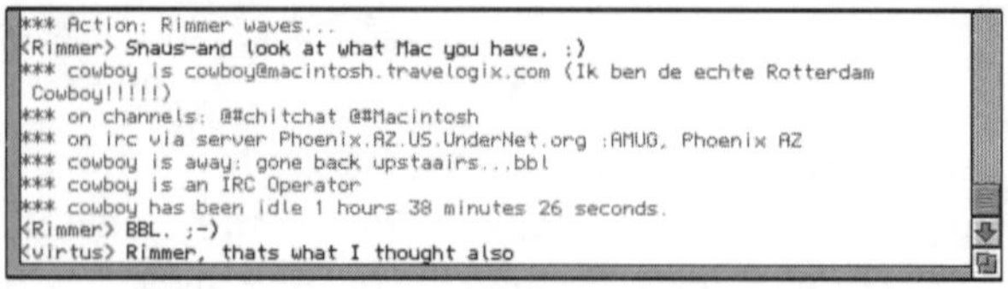

Fig. 16.9
User information that results from clicking the User Info button in the Homer Control Panel window (the user info starts with ***).

This info sometimes tells you the person's real name, where her connection orginates, and how long she's been idle (how long it's been since she last sent text or an Action to the channel). Occasionally, you'll even get a message letting you know that the user is away from her computer.

I need to...uh...stretch my legs...

There are a couple of other things that you can do with the controls in these windows. The first is: walk away from your computer. Sounds simple, right? Well, if you're going to do it right, then you need to hit the Go Offline button in the Homer Control Panel window. Click it once, and you'll be given an opportunity to enter your "While I'm away" message (see fig. 16.10).

Fig. 16.10
The right way to walk away. Now other users won't wonder if you've fallen and can't...you know.

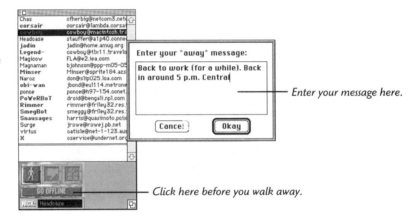

Enter your message here.

Click here before you walk away.

Change your nickname "on-the-fly"

Of course you decide what your nickname will be before you begin your IRC session in the Homer, but you can also change your nickname from the Homer Control Panel window anytime you want. See it at the bottom there? Just click once in the nickname field and edit to your heart's content. Press Return when your inner artist is satisfied with the improvements.

 CAUTION The entire channel is notified every time you change your nickname. Doing so often is a breach of netiquette—it will annoy people.

Closing a channel

Said it all? Had it out with another user? Decided that your vow of sleep-deprivation and fasting was a bit hasty? There are a number of different ways to get out of a channel:

- *Simply close the window.* Clicking once in the close box in the top left corner of the channel window not only closes the window, but ends your session in that channel. All other users will be notified that you have left.

- *Pull down the File menu and select Close Channel.* This will close the channel associated with the currently active window. (Channels in the background are unaffected.)

 TIP   **If you've been chatting at all, good IRC netiquette suggests that** you say **Bye** to everyone (although not necessarily *individually*) before leaving the channel.

- *For an even more dramatic exit, pull down the Action menu and choose Close IRC Connection, or choose Quit from the File menu.* Doing this closes all of your open channels, and gives you an elegant chance to get in one last line of dialog before returning to the Land of Actual Human Beings (see fig. 16.11).

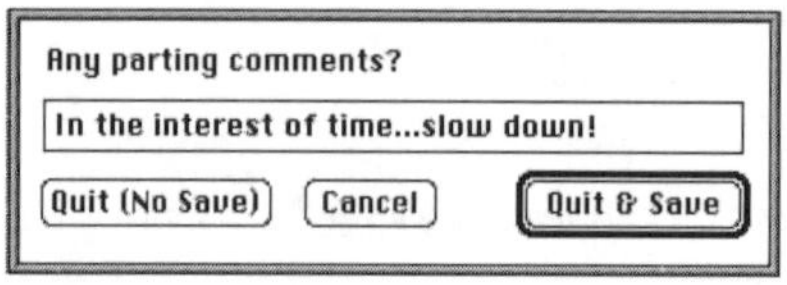

Fig. 16.11
You get the last word when you close channels by quitting Homer.

Any parting comments?

In the interest of time...slow down!

[Quit (No Save)]   [Cancel]   [Quit & Save]

You have two choices for quitting: you can Quit & Save or Quit (No Save). What you're saving is any preferences you've changed during this Homer session (text colors, sounds, etc.), so it's up to you.

17

Surfing the Net: the World Wide Web

● **In this chapter:**

- The truth behind the World Wide Web

- How do you get around on the Web?

- The multimedia explosion...and how to be a part of it

- Web addresses: understanding URLs

- Why would I use any of the other Internet services if I can use the Web?

Did you happen to spend most of last year on this planet? If so, you've probably heard of the most explosive, exciting service on the Internet—the World Wide Web . . . .

t's called the World Wide Web, WWW, W3, or the Web, for short. (It's very rarely called "the Wu-Wu-Wu," and insisting on calling it that will definitely not win favor in board meetings.) Often enough, when people talk about the excitement of the expanding Internet, they're actually talking about the Web.

The Web is the fastest growing service on the Internet, due basically to its discovery by the business community as a medium for advertising and customer service. It's the only truly multimedia Internet service—it can transfer graphics, sounds, and movies as well as text—and that glitz and glamor has definitely contributed to its overwhelming popularity.

What makes the Web so interesting?

There are two things, really. If it weren't for the multimedia capabilities that the Web offers, it would be a lot like the Gopher service that we discussed earlier in this book. At its essence, the Web is just another way to distribute information on the Internet—electronic pages of text that are offered on the Web by individuals around the world.

 Plain English, please!

The electronic documents available on the Web are always referred to as **pages** or **Web pages**. Figure 17.1 is an example of a Web page.

It just so happens that, on the Web, these pages can also be sent with magazine-like graphics, digital sounds, and even little electronic animations and movies (see fig. 17.1).

 Plain English, please!

The word **multimedia** is highly overused in the computer industry and is often a source of confusion. In this case, multimedia refers to the ability to use more than plain text—graphics, page layout, sounds, and digital movies—to communicate ideas.

Formatted text for communicating information.

Fig. 17.1
Multimedia elements, like sound, graphics, and formatted text (bold, italics, etc.), allow a Web page to communicate well while keeping the reader's attention.

Graphical elements spice up the presentation.

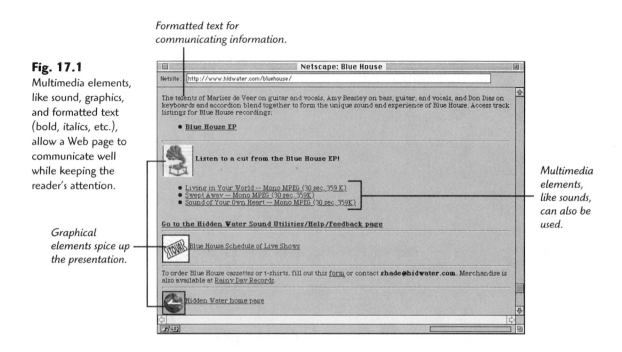

Multimedia elements, like sounds, can also be used.

The other feature that differentiates the Web from Gopher and other similar services is the way pages are organized. (Or aren't organized.) In fact, the reason it's called a "Web" is because it's not hierarchical like Gopher—it's basically a tangle of interconnected points woven together, like a spider's web, by electronic links.

Remember the odd way that a Roget's thesaurus used to be organized? It wasn't an alphabetical listing like a standard dictionary—it was a jumble of cross-references based on some sort of esoteric index. Well, that's a little like the Web compared to Gopher. A Gopher system is menu-based—you choose a menu item to dig deeper into a subject, then choose another and another to find the information you want.

At the heart of the Web concept, though, is the cross-reference. On any given Web page, you will find cross-references to other information—perhaps by that same author or organization, but more likely by someone else, in a completely different part of the world. The Web was designed initially for academics around the planet to share ideas, and building electronic cross-references into one another's work to share concepts was a brilliant move. This concept of cross-referencing, at least in the computer world, is known as **hypertext**.

Fig. 17.2
While Gopher relies on
a hierarchical menu
system to organize
information, the Web
allows you to move
more freely by cross-
referencing informa-
tion on a page with
other information,
anywhere in the world.

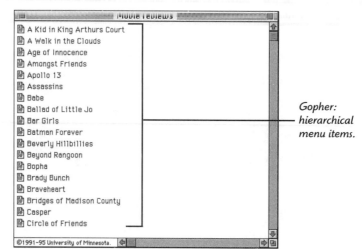

*Gopher:
hierarchical
menu items.*

*Web: graphical
cross-references.*

*Textual cross-
references.*

Hypertext: prose or Prozac?

I happen to think it's a pretty silly word. **Hypertext**. Sounds like some sort of
season-ending injury for professional librarians, doesn't it? But it's a simple
concept, really.

Assume that this page you're reading now is actually text on your computer
screen, and you're viewing a page on the World Wide Web. You're reading
about the Internet and the Web, and everything is going along fine. Suddenly,
I mention that the Web is a little like `Chicago Cubs baseball` in some
hopeless attempt at a metaphor.

If this actually were a Web page, then that underlined, bold text—Chicago Cubs baseball—would represent a hypertext link. Clicking on it with your mouse pointer would then erase the page that you're currently reading, and present you with another page…hopefully one that had a whole lot to do with Chicago Cubs baseball. Get it? (See fig. 17.3.)

Fig. 17.3
See the hypertext link? If this were a color picture, you'd notice that it's also a different color from the surrounding text. Click once with your mouse pointer on that link, and you'll move to the second Web page.

A hypertext link.

Standard text, just for reading.

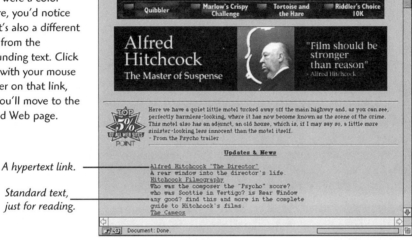

This page results from clicking that link.

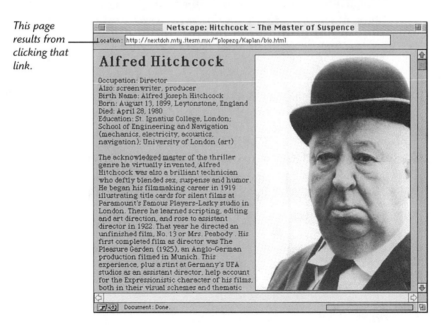

Plain English, please!

A **hypertext link** is the computer version of a cross-reference. Clicking on a hypertext link with your mouse pointer will take you to another part of the document, or a completely different Web page, that offers information related to the linked text.

When you click a hypertext link, it sends a special address to the Web program, or browser, that you're using. The Web browser then takes that address and looks for it on the Internet. When it finds it, it downloads the new Web page to your computer, and presents you with the results.

TIP **The Mac program that you use to access the World Wide Web is** generally called a **browser** or **Web browser** program. The pictures in this chapter show Netscape, currently the most popular Web browser for the Mac.

For example, let's say you're reading your local university's Web page about space travel—using your Web browser. You come across a link that refers to the `space shuttle`. You click that and you're transported to NASA's Web pages, where, after a little reading, you find a link to `government job listings`. So you click that, and while you're reading about openings at NASA, you also come across listings for mail carriers. In those, you notice a hypertext link to the `US Postal Service`. After reading about the USPS's offices in Washington, you come across a link that will let you send `e-mail to the Postmaster General`. You click that link and your browser is sent an e-mail address, which automatically loads your e-mail program. Now, finally, you can complain directly to the "big boss" about how slowly your alimony checks seem to travel from Florida to Montana.

Maybe that feels like a backwards way to get at your goal. But because each of those pages had more than one link, you had to decide where to go next—which wave to catch to get closer to the information you wanted. That's why Web experts often call it **surfing**. Sometimes it's indirect—and you've got to pick the right waves—but most of the time it will get you where you want to go. Uh...dude.

Hypermedia...the next step

We've talked about hypertext and we've talked about multimedia—the two major advantages of the Web. Well, here's the term that throws those two together: **hypermedia**. Don't let that mouthful scare you. You already know what hypermedia is.

On a Web page, we move around by clicking the mouse pointer on hypertext links. Well, we also need to click the mouse to access multimedia features on a Web page. The only difference is, we call a link to a multimedia feature a **hypermedia link** (see fig. 17.4).

Fig. 17.4
A hypermedia link doesn't send you to another page; instead, it downloads pictures, sounds, and digital movies to your computer for you to experience.

The browser automatically loads a viewer to show you the movie.

Click this hypermedia link.

When you click on a hypermedia link, a graphics, sound, or digital movie file is sent to your browser, which can then be shown or played in another program. When you're done, you're still at that same Web page, so you can keep reading, click another hypermedia link, or use a hypertext link to move to another Web page.

How do I get on the Web?

As was mentioned earlier, you need a special program, called a Web browser, to view hypertext pages on the Web. Popular browsers for the Mac include Mosaic, MacWeb, and Netscape. Chapter 18 will discuss the best browser for your Mac, Netscape. For most of us, Netscape is the perfect choice, and that's why you also see it in the figures for this chapter.

Once you've installed your browser software, you simply need to initiate your Internet connection. (See Chapter 5.) If you connect to the Internet through your office's LAN, of course, you can skip this procedure. Then, you just start up your browser program by double-clicking its icon. As it begins, it will check to make sure you're properly connected to the Internet and present you with your **home page**, which is your starting point on the Web.

Starting from home

Okay…watch out for this one. As with any jargon, World Wide Web jargon can be a bit confusing. And, even more often, it can be *confused*.

When your Web browser is first started, it automatically loads your **home page**. Depending on the browser, this is generally a site maintained by the organization that created the browser. Once you're more familiar with the Web, you can decide that the browser should load a different Web page as your home page—or you can even create a "home page" document that you save on your own computer (as opposed to a server) and use as a starting point to your favorite places on the Web.

Figure 17.5 shows the standard home pages for Netscape and Mosaic. When you first load these programs, these pages are provided to you as your home page—they're designed to help you explore the Web. Notice that each is maintained by its respective company—the Netscape's browser's home page is the Netscape, Inc. Web page and the Mosaic browser's home page is the NSCA Web site.

 Plain English, please!
A group of Web pages produced by one person or organization is generally called a **Web site**. For instance, Netscape and NSCA maintain many, many Web pages, organized together into "sites." 99

Fig. 17.5
Top: Netscape's
default home page;
Bottom: NSCA
Mosaic's home page.

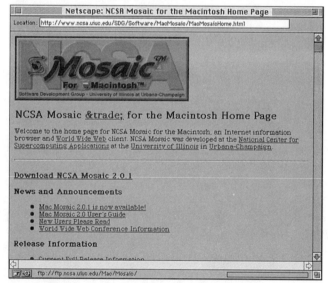

Now, here's the confusing part. Many people refer to their own Web sites as home pages. People will come up to you and say, "Hey, check out my new home page at **http://www.dunce.com/**." Even if this is their home page—and it actually loads when they fire up their browser—it's not necessarily yours. It's the default page for their Web site.

Plain English, please!

A **default page** for a Web site is the Web page that introduces you to a Web site. For instance, when you first reach Apple's Web site, you are presented with their default page. On it you'll find the Apple logo, some text about Apple's Web site, and a number of hypertext links to different services It offers on the Web.

The home page revealed

Now we know what a home page is. (We'll talk about how to change your home page in Chapter 20.) Now we can talk about why the home page is interesting.

For the most part, a browser's standard home page, as shown in figure 17.5, is designed with the Web newcomer in mind. It offers hypertext links to a wide variety of other Web sites that you may find interesting. It also offers links to Web pages that let you search the Web for interesting subjects, cool sites you might like to visit, and new sites that have just popped up on the Web (see fig. 17.6).

Fig. 17.6
The typical browser's home page gives you many different jumping off points for exploring the Web.

Here's a link to cool sites.

This link takes you to Search pages.

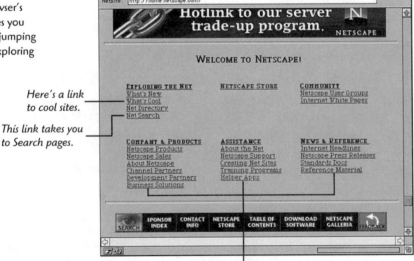

Click here to find sites for downloading files.

You can see why we might want to call this "home." It's a comfortable place to click around until you get the hang of the Web. Then, like an ideal child-hood home, it gives you suggestions for jumping off into the real world to get your feet wet. Of course, in the Web world, you can always come back home when you feel the urge. And you don't even have to memorize the address. With nearly any browser, you just click a button marked Home or select Go, Home from its menu.

URLs: if you take a cab, know the address

If you think about it, the way we've discussed getting around on the Web is a little like trying to get across town on a city bus. You've got to make a couple of stops, jump on a cross-town bus, then stop again, look for the blue line bus and head east. Then you walk a few blocks to get the green line bus heading further south.

With Universal Resource Locators, or URLs, you can take the Web version of a taxicab. You just have to know the code: the addresses for individual Web pages, Gopher sites, and other places on the Internet. Since they're used primarily for Web browsers, though, we'll concentrate on them now.

 Plain English, please!
A URL, or **Universal Resource Locator**, is simply the address for a specific Internet resource. It can be a Web page: **http://www.technology.com/ default.html**; a Gopher site: **gopher://gopher.university.edu/**; or even an FTP site: **ftp://ftp.cdrom.com/**. URLs are direct paths to a particular site or resource.

When you click on a hypertext link on a Web page, it's actually a URL that is sent to your browser—giving it the exact address for the Internet resource that's associated with that link. Click a link called `Chevrolet Cars` and your browser might take you to a Web page with the address **http://www.gm.com/ cars/chevy.html,** or something similar.

At the top of most Web browsers is a field designed specifically to show the URL for the current Web page or Internet resource (see fig. 17.7). On most browsers, you can also enter a URL in this field yourself, press Return, and be taken directly to that resource.

Fig. 17.7
Using Netscape, you can move directly to nearly any Internet resource—if you know its URL.

This is the URL field.

Here's the URL for the Web page that's being displayed.

URLs all follow a particular formula, and while they may not have been designed to make sense to the average human, they will often give you some clue as to where you are. Here's the formula:

resource://Internet address of server/path/filename.ext

For the benefit of your Web browser (and you), a URL starts with the type of resource it represents. These can be nearly any type of Internet resource, such as:

http—Web page

gopher—Gopher site

ftp—FTP (download) site

mail—Internet e-mail message

news—UseNet newsgroup

And so on. As you can see just from this short list, your Web browser can access many different Internet services. So, a URL needs to identify the resource to let your browser know what type of information to expect.

Next, as we discussed in Chapter 2, all Internet services have server computers that send information over the Internet to you, so a URL must include the name of that server. For example:

http://www.tamu.edu/classnotes/100795.html

The example address tells you that you are going to be accessing a Web page that's on a server named www at Texas A&M University. After the server name is a /, then you see the directory path on that server to get to the actual Web page document. It's in a directory called classnotes, and the name of the Web document is 100795.html. If you enter this address in the URL field of our Web browser and press Return, you should go directly to this server and be able to view this document.

TIP   **Although it's not always the case, many server computers are** named for their function, as in **www.tamu.edu**. So, if you didn't know the full URL for this server, you could guess that it's an http resource (a Web server) since its name starts with www (for World Wide Web).

Using URLs and Web hypertext links, you can actually connect to nearly any Internet resource. And, once you know the URL address of something, you can connect directly to it, instead of "surfing" all the time.

Q&A   ***I entered a URL in my browser, but the document couldn't be found. I got an error. Why?***

It could be one of three things. First, you may have entered the resource name incorrectly. Don't forget the colon and two forward slashes (://) after you enter the resource type. Second, you may not have given the correct server or document name. Because this is an *exact* address, you'll need the complete name for the server and the exact file path. Third, that document (for example, 100795.html) may no longer exist at that location.

Why not just use the Web all the time?

Actually, you might just want to. Even as recently as a few months ago, I might have suggested that you learn other Internet applications just as vigorously as you learn your Web browsers. But, given only one factor, I might be willing to let you just use your Web browser.

That factor is a high-speed Internet connection. How fast is high speed? At least a 14.4Kbps—and preferably a 28.8Kbps—modem connection to an Internet provider. If you connect to the Internet through your office LAN, your connection is probably even faster than this. If you have that kind of speed, then I'm willing to let you get rid of all your other Internet programs.

The need for speed

Why this need for speed? We've discussed in early chapters how most Internet services—mail, Gopher, UseNet—are text-based. And text generally doesn't take very long to transfer. But the Web is a different story. Consider figure 17.8.

Fig. 17.8
Here's a very attractive graphical Web page that really uses the capabilities of the Web to its advantage.

Pretty, isn't it? Here's the rub…I have a high-speed 28.8Kbps connection to my Internet provider. And this page still took nearly two minutes to download and view on my computer. Doesn't sound so bad? Consider the fact that two minutes is about your standard commercial break on network television, and then figure you'll spend maybe an hour or two tonight surfing the Web.

If every page takes this long—or even half this time—how many minutes are you losing to download time? How many commercial breaks are you willing to sit through?

TIP If you plan to use the Web, you'll definitely need a high-speed connection to the Internet. Consider getting a 14.4Kbps modem connection or faster before spending much time on the Web.

The more graphically intense an Internet resource is, the longer it will take to download and view with your browser. Every time I click a link to a graphical Web site, I'm losing valuable time while it downloads to my computer. That's a trade-off, sure, but it means less information that I might otherwise be able to come across in a UseNet newsgroup or Gopher server.

The Web advantage

The Web is still the fastest growing Internet service out there, and there are more and more diverse types of information available on the Web than anywhere else.

Interested in doing research for school or business? Want to contact a particular company or organization? Want to shop on the Internet? Looking for travel information, hotel guides or vacation planning?

If somebody has a service, product, or idea he wants to share with the Internet community, chances are he'll put it on the Web. And *that*, above all else, is why you'll want to be on the Web, too. It's where all the action is!

18

Using Netscape to Browse the Web

● **In this chapter:**

- **Where to find the latest version of the popular Netscape browser**

- **Learn to navigate the Web...quickly**

- **What are all these Netscape buttons?**

- **I know the URL! What do I do?**

- **Is there any way to "save my place" with Netscape?**

Is Netscape the killer application of the 1990s? It definitely is if you bought stock in the company when it went public!. . ❯

Did you skip directly to this chapter? Have you even read *any* other part of this book?! Actually, I wouldn't be too surprised. With all the excitement the Web has generated, some folks figure the Web is the only thing that's worth playing with on the Internet. And they might be right.

We're going to talk specifically about the Netscape Web browser from Netscape Communications, Inc. because it's the best Web browser for any platform, and easily the handiest browser to keep on your Mac. There are others out there, but I'd be hard pressed to come up with a good reason to recommend them over Netscape.

Finding and installing Netscape

To get Netscape, FTP the latest version from **ftp.netscape.com** in the directory/netscape/mac/. It's a pretty big download, so it could take a couple of minutes, even with a high-speed connection.

TIP **Netscape is shareware, unless you use it in an educational or** non-profit environment (then it's free). Netscape, Inc. has different pricing plans, so check their corporate Web site (**http://www.netscape.com/**) for information on how (and how much) you should pay for your copy.

What results from your download is the Netscape Installer program, which you double-click to start. You're shown something like figure 18.1, which is the standard Installer screen you may have encountered before with other Mac programs.

With the Installer, you can determine where on your Mac's hard drive you want Netscape stored. You can also decide whether or not Netscape will be a "fat binary," which can run on either type of Mac (Custom Install), or if it will install only the appropriate type of computer code for your particular Mac (Easy Install). Then the installer will decompress the Netscape program and create its icon in the folder you chose.

TIP **Additional installation instructions and information about** Netscape are available when you click the Read Me button in the top right corner of the Installer dialog box.

Fig. 18.1
Installing Netscape.
Choose the type of
installation (fat binary
or machine-specific)
from the pop-up menu
in the left-hand
corner.

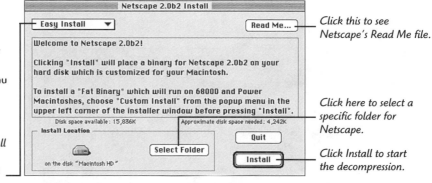

*Click this to see
Netscape's Read Me file.*

*Click here to select a
specific folder for
Netscape.*

*Choose Custom Install
to install a "fat
binary" that can run
on either a 680x0
or Power Mac.*

*Click Install to start
the decompression.*

Your first time out with Netscape

After you have it properly installed, you start Netscape by double-clicking its
icon. Netscape will take a little time to make sure your MacTCP connection is
running, connect via MacPPP if necessary, then look for its home page. If it
finds the Netscape WWW server, it will load the home page for a few seconds, eventually showing you a screen similar to figure 18.2.

What's so special about Netscape?

Aside from being one of the most feature-
complete browsers (if not the most complete) on
the market, there are a couple of other interesting things about Netscape that make it worth
using.

For the most part, Netscape sets the standards on
the Web. Many Web sites use Netscape-specific
commands when they build their Web pages—
commands that other browsers can't handle. That
means that pages always look their best when
viewed through Netscape.

Even more important, however, is Netscape's
built-in security. Netscape has one of the most
complete answers for electronic transactions over
the Internet. When you're hooked up with a
Netscape-brand Web server, you can safely pass
credit card and other personal information with
little fear of it being stolen.

That's a big step toward turning the Web into
what it's destined to be—a new electronic
medium for communication and commerce. Why
is Netscape the most impressive browser? Because
there's money involved, of course!

Fig. 18.2
The Netscape home page. From here you can springboard off into the wonders of the World Wide Web.

TIP   **I'll show you how to change your home page in Chapter 19.**

It's a little like Netscape is signalling the mother ship, huh? But it really is a great place to start. If you have some idea of how this works, feel free to click around on the Netscape Web site and get a feel for how everything looks. If you're still a little lost, stick with me. You'll see exactly what you have to do to get your little alien friend to behave.

Moving around on the Web with Netscape

In the last chapter, I mentioned that there are really two different ways to get around on the Web: one is like taking a city bus, and the other is more direct—like a taxi cab. Well, let's start out with the city bus method—clicking the Web links. Then we'll move directly to some interesting Web sites.

Clicking links: basic Web transportation

When you don't know exactly where you want to go with Netscape, your best bet is to start clicking links and see where they take you. In Netscape, a **link** is text on the page that appears in a different color and underlined on the screen. Click once, and you're off to another page.

TIP **Links are often pictures or other small graphics, too. In figure** 18.3, for instance, each item has both a text link and a graphic link—clicking either will take you to the same new page.

Fig. 18.3
Links can be either graphics or text—and sometimes both.

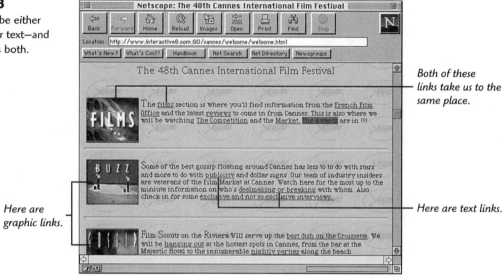

Both of these links take us to the same place.

Here are text links.

Here are graphic links.

Clickable maps and command bars

Actually, there's one other type of link that we haven't talked much about. As the Web gets more and more graphical, more clickable area maps are being used as an alternative to text and individual graphics links. Generally, these are used to make the links more easily recognizable—and to make Web sites more attractive. You may notice that Netscape's Web site features an area map that acts as a "command bar" at the bottom of each Web page to help you get to frequently accessed pages (see fig. 18.4).

Different areas are "mapped."

Fig. 18.4
With area maps, exciting graphical interfaces can be created for the World Wide Web.

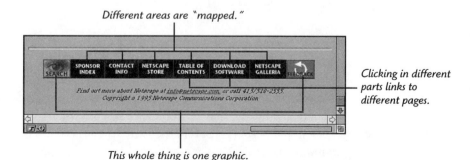

Clicking in different parts links to different pages.

This whole thing is one graphic.

Plain English, please!

A Web-based **area map** is a graphic file that has been divided into different (invisible) sections. This allows a Web user to click a section of the graphic (say, the top right corner) and be linked to a different page from a user who clicked another part (the bottom left corner) of the same graphic.

What if I want to go back?

Links don't do everthing you want them to do. Sure, they're fun for surfing around on the Web and finding interesting things, but what if you make a mistake, or if your trail starts getting cold? Can you go back? Sure!

At the top of the Netscape window, there is a series of buttons that lets you make different decisions about moving around on the Web. If you've gotten to a page that seems like something of a dead end, click once on the Back button at the top of Netscape's window (see fig. 18.5). Netscape moves you back to the previous page.

 TIP   **Notice how quickly it moves back? Netscape creates a "cache" on** your Mac's hard drive where it saves your most recent pages. Instead of reconnecting to the remote server, it just loads the old page from your hard drive. We'll talk more about the cache in Chapter 19.

Fig. 18.5
Netscape's toolbar lets you perform certain standard commands with a simple click of the mouse.

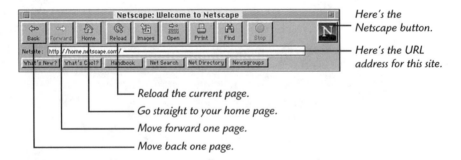

Here's the Netscape button.

Here's the URL address for this site.

Reload the current page.
Go straight to your home page.
Move forward one page.
Move back one page.

Now, once you've moved back, you can also click the Forward button to move one page forward. Clicking once on the Home button will take you to Netscape's home pages, where you started when you first launched Netscape. Finally, the Reload button won't take you anywhere…it just reloads the current page. This is useful especially when there has been some problem with the transmission—for instance, when not all of the graphics show up.

TIP **If you've changed your home page from the Netscape pages to** another URL...well, you've gotten ahead of me. But you should know that clicking the Netscape button in the top-right corner will always take you directly to Netscape's Web site.

Stopping a transmission

For various reasons, you'll sometimes want to stop a page from coming across the Internet. It may be that you've already realized you're headed off in the wrong direction. Or maybe it's just a waste of time; you don't feel like wasting precious seconds or minutes watching this whole page transfer. Can you stop it? Yup.

On the toolbar is the Stop button. This stops the current page from loading, leaving whatever has already been transferred over the Internet. This is especially useful if you've already seen the next link you want to choose— you don't have to wait for everything to download (see fig. 18.6).

Fig. 18.6
Cut down in mid-flight. *Since Netscape shows you the page as it downloads, you can still access any links that appeared before you hit Stop.*

Click once on Stop to cancel the transfer.

Jumping straight to a specific URL

Now let's take that taxicab. At the top of the Netscape window, just under the toolbar, is the Netsite field where current URLs are displayed. But, guess what? You can also click once in the field to place the cursor and enter a URL yourself (see fig. 18.7). Enter the complete URL and press Return. Your Netscape button should start animating, as Netscape looks for the address you've requested.

Fig. 18.7
Forget all this clicking
and hail a cab. Gives a
whole new computer-
nerd-sorta feel to the
word "hackie".

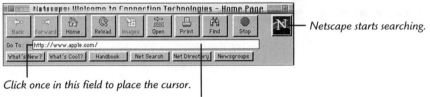

Netscape starts searching.

Click once in this field to place the cursor.

Enter a new address and press Return.

Once you're there, all of your choices are still available: you can start clicking links again, use the Back button or enter another URL. It's up to you.

Q&A   **What's up? I entered a URL, but Netscape couldn't find it.**

Did you enter it correctly? Netscape doesn't necessarily *require* the **http://** part, but it does need a good server address and path to the Web page. These addresses are long—double check everything. Also realize that the Web changes quickly. If everything seems in order, it could be that the particular page is no longer available.

Did I ever catch a wave! Uh, oh...how far downshore am I?

In one sense, the Web is brilliant. It works the way people think: threads of logic weave themselves beautifully from link to link until you stumble onto an idea and everything suddenly makes sense.

But the Web diverts your attention in the same way. There are many evil roads you can take—bad decisions, illogical choices, and hard lessons to learn. Well, maybe it's not that awful...but it is very easy to get lost or waste time on the Web. Those other links—the bad ones—sure are tempting.

Playing hit-or-miss with corporate Web sites

While you're entering URLs, here's a fun little thing to try. Think of a company that you want to get information on (computer companies are best, but try anything). Then, take the company name and put www. in front of it and .com in back of it. Now set it up like a URL, type it in, and see what happens. Here's your first one:

http://www.apple.com/

I'm making this part up...

Oh, sure, you're diligently searching for information on a story you're writing concerning your personal literary hero, Mark Twain. Link after link of academic studies, critical reviews, and contemporary sources are all there for the picking.

Then, innocently mired in the depths of a serious investigation, you stumble across a link to some inside dope on *Star Trek: The Next Generation*. After all, Mark Twain was a major character in the cliffhanger episode in Season Five. Why not just click that link quickly, scan briefly for a few seconds and jump back into your research?

 TIP There is a Web-based solution for just such an occasion...and many others like it. Memorize this URL: **http://www.800flowers.com/**.

Your history

Luckily, Netscape keeps a "history" of all of the sites you've visited in your current session. To head back to the point where you made a bad decision or a wrong turn, just pull down the Go menu.

See all those addresses (see fig. 18.8)? That's the history of your current session. Select one of those titles and you're sent scuttling back through time. Here's your second chance—choose a different link on the old page, and you start a new path. Make this one the right one, if possible.

 CAUTION This actually works a lot like time travel. When you go back to a page in your history and start down a new path (by choosing a different link) it's a little like you are changing the past by creating a new Netscape "history" from this point. All your other "wrong path" links will disappear.

Fig. 18.8
Sure you wavered from
your path. You're
human! But you can
always go back.

Your history is under the Go menu.

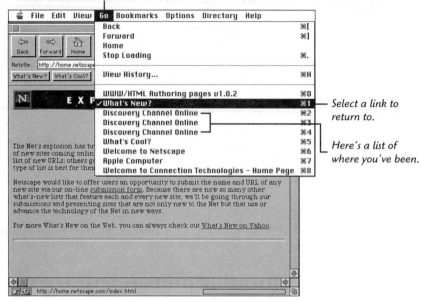

Select a link to
return to.

Here's a list of
where you've been.

I keep finding great pages! Do I have to write them all down?

Your other aces-in-the-hole for instantaneous connections to interesting
pages are called **bookmarks**, and they let you save any page you come
across for access at a later date.

Creating and using bookmarks

With Netscape showing a particularly useful or interesting page, pull down
the Bookmarks menu and select Add Bookmark. Now, the next time you
access the Bookmarks menu, you'll see that this site has been added to that
listing (see fig. 18.9).

It's important to make a distinction here. When Netscape creates a bookmark, it actually just saves the title of the page (for your convenience) and
the URL for the page (for its own use). It does not save the entire page to
your hard drive.

Fig. 18.9
Adding a bookmark in Netscape. The next time you need to access this page, just select its title in the Bookmark menu.

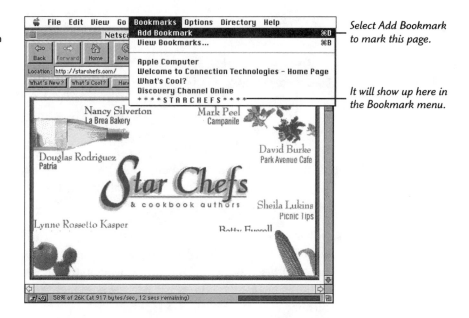

Select Add Bookmark to mark this page.

It will show up here in the Bookmark menu.

When you go back and select the bookmark, Netscape will attempt to load the page from the saved URL. But you can run into the same problems as with other pages—the server could be down or the page may no longer exist.

TIP **You can also create a bookmark from your history. In the Go** menu, select View History. In the dialog box, click once on the page's title, then click the Add to Bookmarks button.

Managing bookmarks

If you spend any amount of time on the Web, you'll soon come to find that using bookmarks is an amazing timesaver. But you'll also find that, after you've got twenty or so bookmarks, the system begins to lose some of its luster. You're spending a lot of time sifting through all those titles of pages in your Bookmarks menu.

To combat this eyestrain, Netscape allows you to create **hierarchical menus** within the Bookmarks menu. That means you can create topics (headers) under which you can store your bookmarks. This lets you store many more bookmarks than would be otherwise possible, and you can construct a logical system for getting at them (see fig. 18.10).

Fig. 18.10
A hierarchical bookmarks menu. Now you can store tons of bookmarks and find them easily.

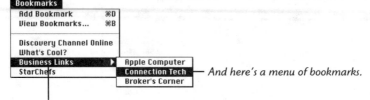

And here's a menu of bookmarks.

This is a header (on the first level).

To create your hierarchical menu, pull down the Window menu and select Bookmarks. This starts Netscape's Bookmark Editor. You'll see a window appear with all of your current bookmarks, as in figure 18.11.

Look familiar? This works exactly like Mac's Finder when you're viewing a folder "By Name" or "By Type". If you can't see the items that are under a particular header, for instance, click once on the little triangle control to the left of the header's folder icon. Then the bookmarks in that header's folder will appear.

Fig. 18.11
Creating your menu system. Notice that menu items are indented a bit under their respective headers.

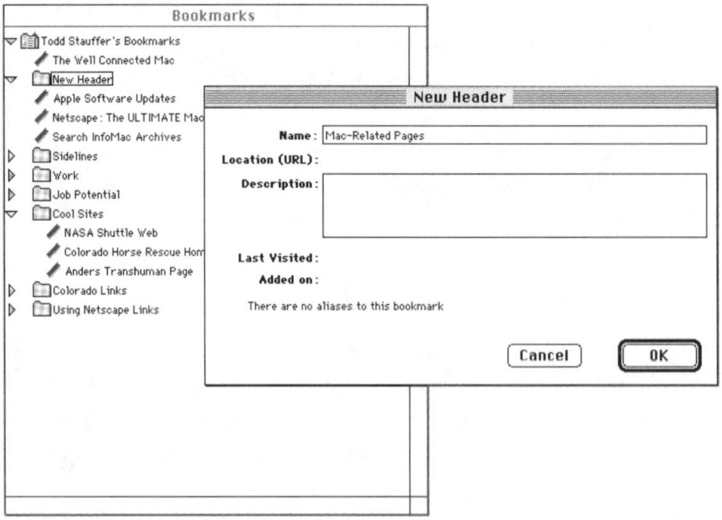

To create a new header, pull down the Item menu and select New Header (this item may also be called New Folder in your version of Netscape). An untitled folder will appear in your Bookmarks window, and a dialog box pops up so you can name the header. Enter a name for it and click OK.

To place a bookmark in that header's menu, drag the bookmark's name and drop it on the header's folder icon. You'll notice that the bookmark is not only under the header, but also indented.

Now, when you pull down the Bookmarks menu, you'll have a hierarchical listing to deal with. (You can test this by pulling down the Bookmarks menu while you're still in the Bookmark Editor.) If you put all of your bookmarks into a menu system, you'll easily be able to deal with hundreds of bookmarks!

 TIP Use this dialog box for many other tasks, too. To delete a bookmark, select its name in the list and click Remove Item. Or, search for a bookmark by entering text in the field below the list and clicking Find.

Keeping Web pages for your very own

Eventually, you may just come across a Web page that's important enough to keep forever, squirreled away on your hard drive somewhere. Or maybe you need a printout. Easily done! Just select the appropriate command from the File menu.

Printing Web pages

To print a Web page, start by loading that page in your Web browser (by entering its URL or clicking links until you get there). Then, just pull down the File menu and select the Print command. Up jumps your standard print dialog box, just like in all your other applications.

But Netscape is a little different. If you pull down the File menu and choose Page Setup, you'll notice something a bit odd (see fig. 18.12). By default, Netscape will automatically resize windows so they are the appropriate width for printing on your printer. That's nice, but if you want it the way *you* set up the page, you'll need the change this option.

Of course, since Web pages can be more than a few screens *long*, you may get more than one page when you print.

Fig. 18.12
Page Setup with
Netscape. By default,
Netscape will resize to
print every line of text
on a Web page.

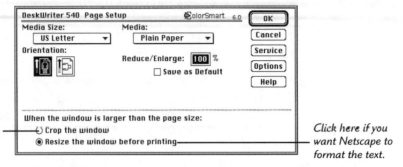

Click here if you want
it to leave the window ———
the way you've got it.

Click here if you
——— *want Netscape to*
format the text.

Saving Web pages to your Mac's hard drive

If you'd rather store a page electronically, you can do that too. With the page in the browser window, pull down the File menu and select the Save As command. Again, you have a choice in this dialog box (see fig. 18.13). You can use the pop-up menu below the file's name to save it as either text or source.

Fig. 18.13
Netscape lets you save
Web pages in two
different formats.
Unfortunately, neither
is as pretty as the real
thing.

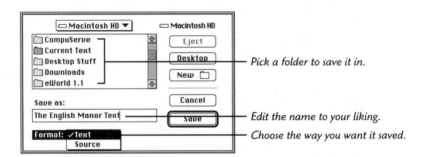

——— *Pick a folder to save it in.*

——— *Edit the name to your liking.*
——— *Choose the way you want it saved.*

Choose to save the page as text; Netscape will create a file that includes all of the text on the page but none of the other elements. Instead, it will substitute [image] for all the graphics on the page. It's pretty plain-looking, but it gets the job done (see fig. 18.14).

Choose Source and you're in for a treat. Netscape still creates a text file, but in this one it stores the original HTML codes used to create the page. This is what Web page designers use to create the look and feel of their pages. We'll talk a whole lot about HTML in Chapter 20.

Fig. 18.14

On the top: Netscape's default page in text. On the bottom: the HTML source for that same page.

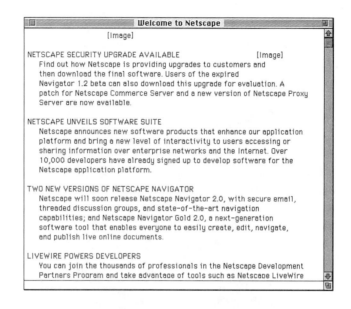

19

Advanced Netscape Topics

● **In this chapter:**

- **How do I see and hear all of this multimedia stuff?**

- **Getting your hands on Netscape's Helper applications**

- **How do I set up Netscape to recognize incoming files?**

- **Customizing and setting your preferences for Netscape**

- **Reading UseNet news with Netscape's built-in reader**

- **Can I access FTP and Gopher?**

You'll probably spend a lot of time with Netscape—maybe even all your time. Let's tune it up to make your experience as perfect as possible! . . . . ▸

Spend a little time with Netscape and the Web and you'll come to see that it really isn't that difficult to grasp. You've got your pages, your links, and your URLs. Suddenly, you're surfing around like a champ—landing on entertaining sites, informative sites, and a few useless sites. You're not sleeping so much any more and you've stopped working—but the bill collectors can't get through now that you're always busy on the phone line.

Now let's concentrate on optimizing Netscape for the total experience. In order to deal with multimedia on the Web, you'll need a few additional programs. Plus, you can use Netscape to access nearly all other Internet services—like Gopher, UseNet, and FTP.

Helper applications: accessing hypermedia

If you've come across a few hypermedia links and tried them out, you may have noticed that some are easier to get working for you than others. Why is that? Well, some graphics, for instance, can be shown directly in Netscape—it was written to deal with them. But other multimedia types, especially digital movies and sounds, require what Netscape calls **helper applications**.

When you click on a hypermedia link, a file is transmitted over the Internet to your computer. Depending on the type of file (sound file, graphics file, movie file, and so on) Netscape can either present the file's contents to you on its own, or it may require an outside application to do the showing for you—a helper application.

These multimedia files are as different from one another as, say, a Microsoft Word document and a FileMaker Pro database file. You need a separate program for each document in order to load, display, and print them. Same for multimedia files. For sound, you need a sound-player application. For movies, you need a movie player. For some types of graphics files, you need a graphics application. Even compressed or archived files need a helper application to help Netscape expand them into a useful form.

Where do I get helper applications?

Netscape automatically recognizes certain helper applications after you've installed them on your Mac. Using these recommended programs is really the best way to go—the default applications are very good and readily available on the Internet. You should be able to find them in a number of places.

A good starting point is on the Netscape home pages themselves. On Netscape's default page, scroll the screen down until you see the Welcome to Netscape section. Under Assistance is a link to Helper Apps. Click that link, and, on the next page, choose the link to Macintosh archive sites. You get a screen that looks something like figure 19.1.

Fig. 19.1
Here are some of Netscape's recommendations for helper applications.

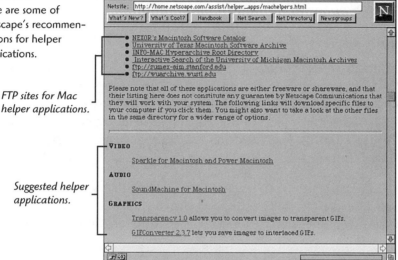

FTP sites for Mac helper applications.

Suggested helper applications.

My personal favorite is the University of Texas archive because it's well-organized with good descriptions of the files. The URL for the University of Texas archive is:

http://wwwhost.ots.utexas.edu/mac/main.html

TIP **Probably the single most useful helper application is StuffIt** Expander, which you may already have installed. Netscape will use it automatically if it's on your Mac's hard drive.

Sound apps

There are two good choices for sound helper apps: SoundApp and SoundMachine.

Both of these are useful for basic sounds (.au extension) and high-end Macintosh sound (.aiff extension files). When you download one of these sounds by clicking a hypermedia link on the Web, SoundApp or SoundMachine will automatically be launched and the sound file fed to the program (see fig. 19.2).

Fig. 19.2
SoundMachine's
sound-playing dialog
box.

SoundMachine seems to be the more common of the two, although SoundApp has the added advantage of being able to play the popular Windows Wave (.wav) sound files.

Movie apps

There are two basic movie types you'll encounter: QuickTime (.mov) and MPEG (.mpg). QuickTime is an Apple-created technology for movie playing; if you have System 7.5, you probably have the QuickTime extension installed. Any QuickTime movie player will work fine, including Apple's Movie Player. Even SimpleText, the Mac's text editor, is capable of displaying QuickTime movies.

For MPEG movies, the recommended choice is Sparkle, a program by Maynard Handley. Actually, Sparkle can handle QuickTime movies, too; it can convert between the two formats.

Graphic viewers

I mentioned before that Netscape is capable of viewing both JPG and GIF files. At different places on the Web, though, you can download graphics files, and you can pull any graphic off of a page and save it as a graphics file if you desire. To view these, you'll need a special program.

JPEGView is an excellent program for viewing, cropping, and resizing JPG (.jpg) and GIF (.gif) graphics. It's also available on the University of Texas site in the Graphics section.

 TIP To pull *any* graphic element off of a Web page, just click and hold your mouse on the graphic. After a second, a menu will pop up, allowing you to copy the graphic to the Clipboard or save it as a file.

Setting up helper applications

Once you've downloaded all of the helper applications you need—and decompressed or otherwise installed them on your hard drive—you should be ready to go. If you've chosen the recommended programs, Netscape should automatically recognize that they are available on your hard drive.

Just to make sure—or if you've chosen helper apps that *aren't* the defaults—you can look at how Netscape plans to deal with multimedia by pulling down the Options menu and selecting General Preferences. In the General Preferences dialog box, use the tabbed menu at the top to select Helpers (see fig. 19.3).

Fig. 19.3

Setting up your helper applications. Here you can decide how Netscape will react to each type of file it receives.

Here are the different file types.

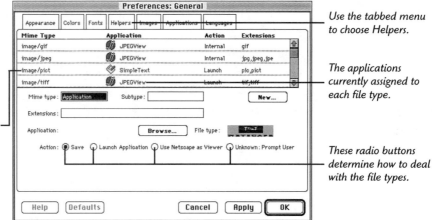

Use the tabbed menu to choose Helpers.

The applications currently assigned to each file type.

These radio buttons determine how to deal with the file types.

Notice that every file type has an application associated with it. If you come across a file type that has the wrong application (or you want to use a different one), click once on that file type's row in the table, then click Browse. Now you can search your hard drive for the program you'd rather use.

You can also decide that, instead of using an application, Netscape itself will deal with the file, or it will download the file directly to your Mac's hard drive. How? With the radio buttons that run across the bottom of the dialog box. With these, you can decide that when a particular file type is encountered, Netscape will automatically Save the file, Launch the file with a helper, View it in Netscape, or Prompt you for a decision at that time. Click once on an option to make it active for the file type that's currently selected in the table.

With everything the way you like it, click OK. You might also want to pull down the Options menu and select Save Options. (Netscape won't automatically save your options until you quit the program.) Now, you're ready for just about anything the Web can throw at you!

TIP What helper apps do you *need*? You should definitely have helper apps for QuickTime and MPEG movies, .au and .aiff sound files, StuffIt archives, and Mac BinHex files. It's not a bad idea to have JPEGView or a similar program around to deal with downloaded graphics, too.

Other Netscape options and preferences

Aside from helper apps, there are a couple of other things you can do to customize Netscape. These fall into basically two categories: Options and Preferences. Under the Options menu, you can decide how the Netscape window will appear and how certain Web elements will be displayed. An item with a checkmark next to it is currently active.

You can also decide whether or not images on Web pages will be shown automatically. To check or uncheck an item, just pull down the Options menu and select the item.

TIP If your connection is particularly slow, you may want to uncheck Auto Load Images. Now, only the text of Web pages will be transferred. If you want to see the images for a particular page, Netscape will reload with images when you select the Images button in the toolbar.

The preferences dialog boxes

You've already seen the General Preferences dialog box when you were setting up helper apps for Netscape. Well, there are other preferences you can set here, too. Here's a quick run-down:

- **Appearance**. Allows you to give a new address for your home page (if you want to use one other than Netscape's); decide whether to launch the Browser, Mail or News readers at startup; and tell Netscape how you want the toolbar icons to appear. You can also decide whether links should appear underlined and how often they should be assumed to have expired.

Q&A *How do I change my home page in Netscape?*

In Netscape's General Preferences dialog box, choose Appearance from the tabbed menu. You should see a field called Home Page Location. Click in that field, and type the URL for your new home page. Notice that you can also choose a blank page with the radio buttons to the left of the field. Click OK when you're done.

- **Colors**. Here, you can decide what colors Netscape should use for links, text, and the background. Notice that choosing Always Use Mine will override the Netscape background graphics commands on other people's Web pages.

- **Fonts**. With this option, you choose the default proportional and monospaced fonts for Netscape to use.

The next dialog box is the Network Preferences dialog box. Pull down the Options menu, select Network Preferences, and you're presented with these tabbed options:

- **Cache**. Netscape keeps recently accessed pages in a "cache" on your hard disk. Select the size of cache you want and denote how often Netscape should check to make sure pages haven't been updated.

 TIP   **A big cache is nice, but setting it too high will sometimes cause** Netscape to pause quite awhile after you've quit the program. If you notice that Netscape is moving slowly, try lowering the cache a bit. Five megabytes is generally plenty.

- **Connections**. Here, you can set the maximum number of browser windows that can be open simultaneously. (Notice that the more browser windows you have open, the slower each will react.)

- **Proxies**. These are used in corporate LAN setups when "firewalls" are necessary to access the Internet. If you connect over a PPP connection, you won't have to worry about these.

In order to use the e-mail and newsreader capabilities built into the latest verion of Netscape, you need to set certain preferences, including the addresses for the news and mail servers. You can do that through the Mail and News preferences:

- **Appearance**. Select the type of font to use for e-mail and news messages, and how you would like quoted text to stand out in the message.

- **Composition**. Here, you decide the default behavior for creating mail and news messages. You can choose the standard for mail (MIME is the default)—whether or not to mail copies to yourself or save copies of outgoing messages to a file. You can also choose to have Netscape automatically "quote" messages to which you are replying.

- **Servers**. This one is very important. You'll need to fill in the NMTP, POP, and News server fields to use the Netscape e-mail and newsreader programs. You may also need to fill in the POP username field (with your username—usually the first part of your e-mail address). Aside from that, you can also determine how long mail messages should be and the maximum number of UseNet messages to download in a given session.

- **Identity**. Here, you decide what information Netscape will include in your e-mail and news message headers. You can also choose a small text file to use as your signature.

- **Organization**. Netscape's mail and news housekeeping options are here. You can decide when Netscape mail will throw out deleted e-mail messages, whether or not messages will appear as threads in mail and news, and how you want messages sorted.

The last preferences dialog box is the Security preferences dialog. Again, pull down the Options menu and select Security preferences to change these:

- **General**. Netscape can be set to let you know whenever you're accessing a secure document and when you're sending information over an unsecure connection. Click these check boxes to decide exactly *when* it will alert you.

- **Passwords**. If more than one person uses this copy of Netscape, it's important to create a password for each. This keeps you from using one another's personal electronic addresses and certificates (see sidebar) while online.

CAUTION **Never send passwords, credit card numbers, or other personal** information over the Web unless you are certain that your connection is secure and the receiver is legitimate. You can tell when a connection is secure from the Key icon at the bottom of the Netscape window. When it is whole (not broken), you're connected to a secure server.

Using Netscape for other Internet services

Netscape has the built-in capability to deal with most of the Internet services that we've discussed throughout this book. And, with URLs you can move directly to almost any type of server on the Internet—including Gopher, FTP, and news servers. How does it work?

Accessing UseNet newsgroups

First, you need to make sure you've entered a mail server in the Main and News Preferences dialog box (discussed in the previous section). This is the same mail server address used for NewsWatcher and other newsreaders (see Chapters 14 and 15).

With that set, you can access UseNet by clicking once on the directory button marked Newsgroups, or you can pull down the Window menu and choose Netscape News. Netscape will create a newsgroups file for you, then present

Certificates of authenticity

Not yet in widespread use, **certificates** are among the latest security measures to be added by Netscape, Inc. to its Web technology. They offer an advanced method for sending secure, encrypted documents over the Web and through the mail.

A **certificate** is a little like a car's "valet key"—it makes certain things public and keeps others private. Your car's valet key starts the engine and unlock the doors, but it won't let you into the glove box or trunk.

A certificate has both a public and a private element. The *public* key is for folks who want to send a secure message to you. They create the message, then use your public key to encrypt it.

When you receive your message, you use your *private* key to decrypt the message and make it, once again, readable. Once a message is encrypted with your public key, no one but you (with your private key) can decrypt and read it. Not even the person who *sent* it to you (although, of course, he can make a copy before encrypting).

So, how do you use these certificates? Well...you don't. Not yet, at least. Currently the only common use for certificates is Netscape's Commerce Servers, and these certificates are used automatically for transactions between you and the commerce server. Soon, however, we may all be distributing our public certificates—just to keep things a little more private.

you with the Netscape newsreader, as shown in figure 19.4. Now, in the left window of the browser program you'll see an icon or two: these are your active newsgroup servers.

Fig. 19.4
The latest version of Netscape includes this full-function newsreader that in some ways rivals the ease of use of NewsWatcher.

Click here to see a list of your subscribed newsgroups.

Click here to access the group.

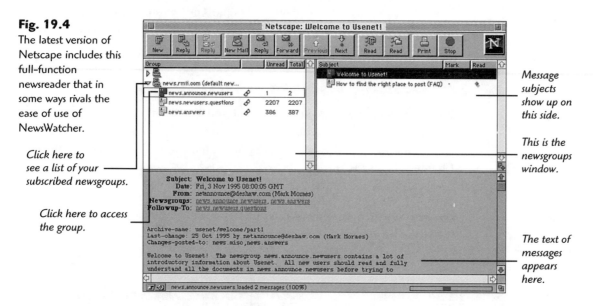

Message subjects show up on this side.

This is the newsgroups window.

The text of messages appears here.

To see a listing of all available newsgroups, pull down the Options menu and select Show All Newsgroups. After it gathers the newsgroup information for a few minutes, a listing of the newsgroups that are available to you will appear in the newsgroups window (see fig. 19.5).

On this first level, most of the group names include an asterisk (*) at the end to indicate that there is another level of groups available to choose from. Click once on one of these links to expand the group list. (For example, click on alt.* to see all of the alternative groups.)

Netscape allows you to subscribe to any number of groups at one time—just click once on the small box next to a group name. When you're done subscribing, return to the Options menu and select Show Subscribed Groups. Now, all that will appear in the newsgroups window are the groups you've chosen to subscribe to.

Fig. 19.5
Show All Newsgroups.
From here you can
sample individual
newsgroups or check
them for subscribing.

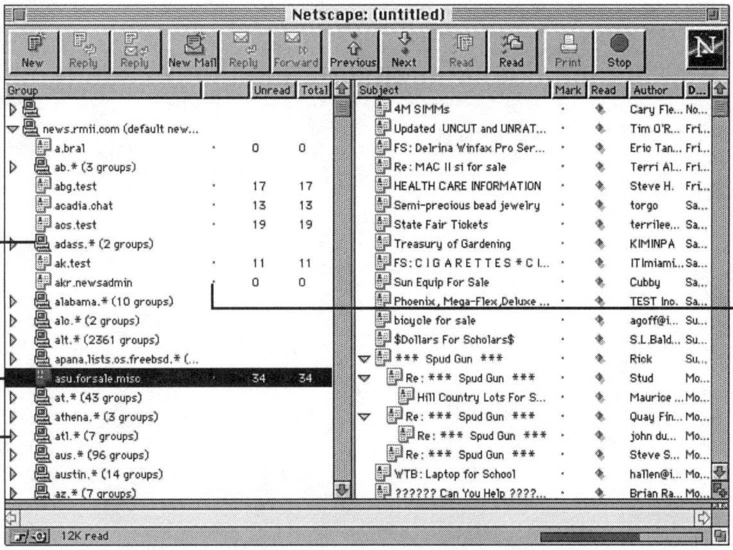

Links with an * *in
their name indicate
another level.*

*Click a name to
access the newsgroup
(without subscribing).*

*Click the triangle
control to see
the next level.*

*Click the
field next to
that group to
subscribe.*

[Screenshot: Netscape: (untitled) window showing Group list on left and Subject list on right]

TIP   **As with NewsWatcher, Netscape will keep track of what you have**
and haven't read only when you subscribe to a group. If you access a
newsgroup that doesn't have the little "eyeglasses" icon next to its name, it
will not mark articles as "Read."

To access a particular newsgroup, click its name in the newsgroups window.
Now, on the right side of the screen, you'll get a listing of the message
subjects (see fig. 19.6). You're ready to read.

TIP   **If you have the Show Subscribed Newsgroups option selected, it's**
easy to unsubscribe a group. Just click once in the box next to that group's
name, and the little eyeglasses will disappear. The next time you Show
Subscribed Groups, this group will not show up.

To read an article, just click its title. The text shows up in the lower portion
of the Netscape newsreader window. To reply to an article, simply move to
the bar at the top of the newsreader window and click the button marked
Reply with the picture of a message listing. (The Reply button with a picture
of an envelope is for replying via e-mail.) This opens a window for you to
type in your reply and send it off to the group. (See fig. 19.7.)

*Reply to a message
by clicking here.*

*Use this button to reply
to e-mail messages.*

Fig. 19.6
Netscape's UseNet
interface lets you do
most of the things a
good newsreader does.
It even has a nice,
visual way of showing
message threads!

*Click here
to mark this
message as
Read.*

*Click once
on a subject
to read the
article.*

*Message subjects
appear here.*

*This is an
original
post.*

*These are
replies.*

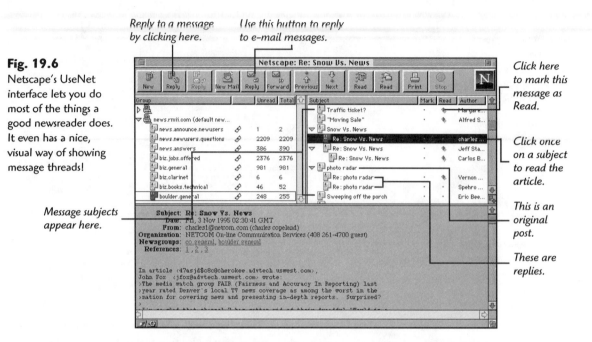

Fig. 19.7
It's easy enough to
reply with Netscape
newsreader...just click
the right button!

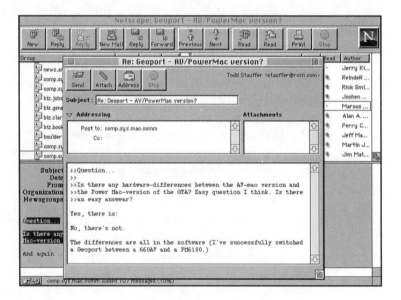

You follow the same procedure for posting a new message to the group—just click the New button in the left corner of the bar. Then enter your message in the resulting window, and click Send.

From here, I'll just let you explore. Netscape's UseNet interface is very straightforward, thankfully, and you should be able to get around your newsgroups with little trouble. (For more on UseNet, check out Chapters 14 and 15.)

Accessing Gopher and FTP sites

There's a little less you need to go through to access Gopher and FTP sites—all you really need is a link to one or a URL for a particular site. Then, Netscape does its own little magic to display Gopher and FTP directories (see fig. 19.8).

Fig. 19.8
Gopher à la Netscape. Notice that the icons , like those in TurboGopher, suggest what's behind those links.

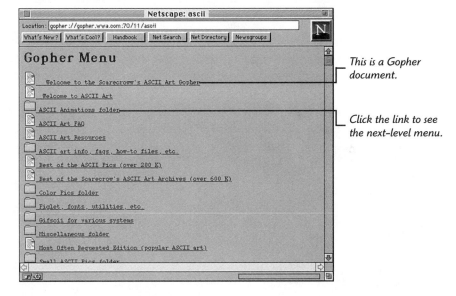

This is a Gopher document.

Click the link to see the next-level menu.

In fact, the only real difference between using TurboGopher or Anarchie and using Netscape is that you only have to click once on Netscape links instead of double-clicking on files and directories in those other programs. And you can only see one menu or directory at a time in Netscape (see fig. 19.9).

Fig. 19.9
FTP, as seen with
Netscape. Again, icons
let you know if you're
seeing a directory or a
file to download.

*Click this link to see
a subdirectory*

Here's a directory.

This is a file.

*Click here to
download the file.*

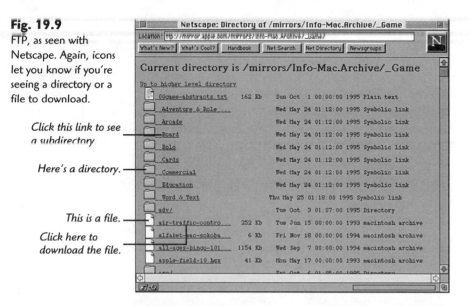

Once you've chosen to download a file, Netscape will open a dialog box and
ask you where you want to save that file. Netscape will then open a small
status box to let you know that it's currently downloading and saving that file
to your hard drive. Netscape still has access to all of its helper applications
while accessing Gopher and FTP sites, so for the most part, archives will be
processed by StuffIt Expander and any multimedia file you encounter will be
automatically played.

20

HTML: Building Your Own Web Pages

● In this chapter:

- **What is HTML?**

- **What you need to create your own Web pages**

- **Behind the scenes of your Web browser**

- **How do I get graphics on my Web page?**

- **How much should this cost me?**

- **Great tips for first-time Web designers**

Sick of hearing, "No Web site? Where ya been?!" in the employee cafeteria? Get your personal Web site up and running fast with this chapter! . . . .

Why would you create your own Web page? You might want to put your resumé online, create a page for your business, or place some interesting tidbits about your favorite hobby on the Web. You're probably starting to see a lot of Web URLs on brochures and business cards. Professionally speaking, this is a good time to get started on the Web.

At this moment, though, building a Web page is still a little tricky. You do need to know a couple of new things to create your page, and you might want to be at least *familiar* with a program like Adobe Photoshop for graphics. That said, however, it's definitely not impossible to do. By the time you get through this chapter, you could easily have your personal Web pages available for the world to see.

What is HTML?

The HyperText Markup Language, or **HTML**, is the coding standard that the World Wide Web uses to display documents. Any Web browser, like Netscape or Mosaic, is designed to interpret these commands, displaying your text and pictures in a standard way.

If you've ever seriously used an older text-based word processing program, like WordPerfect for DOS, then you may see some similarities between HTML and Reveal Codes in those programs. Basically, an HTML document must have directions built into its text to tell a browser what should be highlighted, how big the text should be, and whether or not it should be bold or italic.

And, of course, you've got to decide which words will be used as hypertext links to other documents (see fig. 20.1).

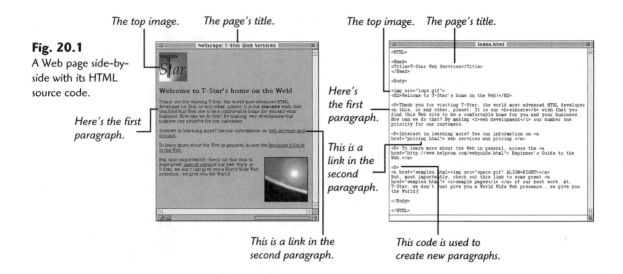

Fig. 20.1
A Web page side-by-side with its HTML source code.

The top image. *The page's title.* *The top image.* *The page's title.*

Here's the first paragraph.

Here's the first paragraph.

This is a link in the second paragraph.

This is a link in the second paragraph.

This code is used to create new paragraphs.

Doesn't look so tough, does it? It's not really. If you've ever used a word processor or desktop publishing program to create something as complicated as, say, a newsletter, then you're in good shape for learning HTML.

HTML editors and getting started

Let me say this right off…you already have the tools needed for creating HTML pages. Everything you need, in fact, came with your Mac. It's called SimpleText.

Because it has to be transmitted across the Internet, HTML is ASCII text by its very nature. Since you enter all the codes into the text manually, you don't necessarily need a special program to help you out.

Most of the shareware programs available to help you edit HTML pages are simply designed to make it less important that you remember the actual HTML codes—freeing you to spend more time worrying about how the page looks, and what you're going to say. In figure 20.2 you see Arachnid, a popular HTML editor.

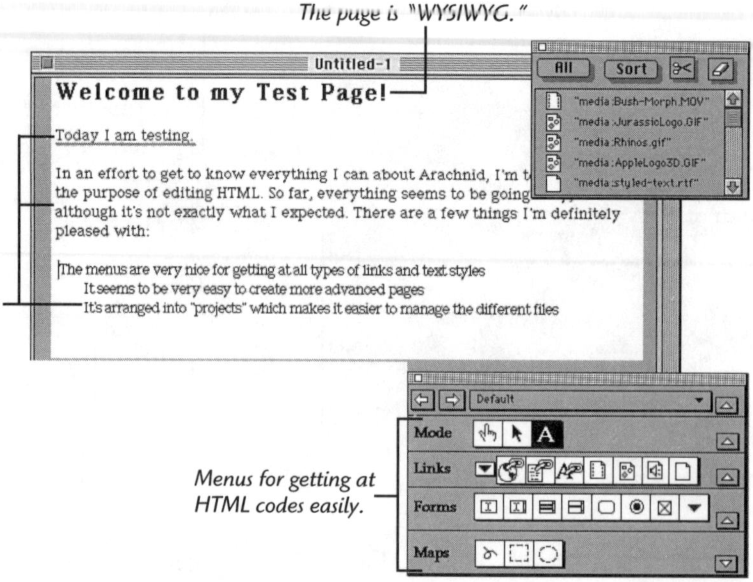

Fig. 20.2
Arachnid, an advanced
HTML editor. It hides
the HTML codes, and
makes Web creation
more like word
processing.

The page is "WYSIWYG."

*Notice, no
HTML codes.*

Untitled-1

Welcome to my Test Page!

Today I am testing.

In an effort to get to know everything I can about Arachnid, I'm t
the purpose of editing HTML. So far, everything seems to be going
although it's not exactly what I expected. There are a few things I'm definitely
pleased with:

The menus are very nice for getting at all types of links and text styles
    It seems to be very easy to create more advanced pages
    It's arranged into "projects" which makes it easier to manage the different files

All   Sort

"media :Bush-Morph.MOV"
"media :JurassicLogo.GIF"
"media :Rhinos.gif"
"media :AppleLogo3D.GIF"
"media :styled-text.rtf"

*Menus for getting at
HTML codes easily.*

Default

Mode
Links
Forms
Maps

Probably the most sought-after feature in an advanced HTML editor is
WYSIWYG (pronounced "wizzy-wig") which means What-You-See-Is-What-
You-Get. When you create an HTML page in SimpleText, you have to imagine
what it will look like—or test it in Netscape—based on the codes you've
chosen. With a program like Arachnid, you'll see it right there in its window.

 TIP   **Arachnid will even let you test its links without using Netscape or**
another browser to test your Web site.

What you need to begin

I'll use SimpleText to show you HTML, so that you can see how it really
works. Once you understand the ideas behind HTML, then feel free to move
on to a WYSIWYG editor.

Aside from SimpleText, you'll want to create a folder on your Mac to use for
your Web page. If you have any graphics you've created or scanned, put those
in that same folder.

CAUTION Because HTML links are *static*, it's important to keep graphics files and HTML pages in the same directory. If you move them around, you'll have to edit your HTML page to account for that.

Basic HTML: playing tag with words on the page

At the heart of HTML is text. That's basically the point—communicating something. Sure, the graphics and forms and links and all are great. But the key to your Web pages is your text. Everything else is secondary.

And that's why much of HTML is focused on text. As you're typing in the text that will eventually become part of your Web page, you can add HTML tags to the text in order to format it. Want it bold or italic? Want a new paragraph? Want some of your text to stand out as a header or be arranged in a list? Use a tag (see fig. 20.3).

🦆 *Plain English, please!*

A **tag** is simply any HTML command. Tags are designed to communicate directly with the Web browser, telling it to do something special to text or to display an image in a certain way. 🦆🦆

This is a header tag.

Fig. 20.3
Tags are the building blocks of HTML code. Most tags concentrate on the document's text.

Here's a paragraph tag.

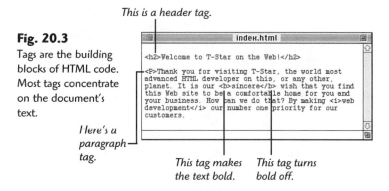

```
index.html

<h2>Welcome to T-Star on the Web!</h2>

<P>Thank you for visiting T-Star, the world most
advanced HTML developer on this, or any other,
planet. It is our <b>sincere</b> wish that you find
this Web site to be a comfortable home for you and
your business. How can we do that? By making <i>web
development</i> our number one priority for our
customers.
```

This tag makes the text bold. *This tag turns bold off.*

Notice in figure 20.3 that these tags are the "commands" we were talking about earlier in this chapter. Some of the commands can be turned on and off, like the bold tag. Others are given once, and they don't even have to be near text (like the paragraph tag).

Enclosing tags

When you have a pair of on and off tags, we call them **enclosing tags**. These operate specifically on the text that's inside of them. For instance:

`<b> This text is boldface </b>`

The <b> tag tells the browser that all subsequent text will be bold until the </b> command is received. This is a very typical tag—most on and off tags are the same except for the / in the end tag.

Table 20.1 shows you some of the more common enclosing tags and their functions. For the most part, these tags act on text to change its appearance in some way.

Table 20.1 Common HTML enclosing tags and their functions

On tag	Off tag	What they do
<A>	</A>	An anchor: creates a hypertext link
<B>	</B>	Boldfaces text
<Body>	</Body>	Defines the body of the page
<Center>	</Center>	Centers text on the page
<EM>	</EM>	Emphasizes text
<H1>	</H1>	Marks text as a level-one header (biggest)
<H6>	</H6>	Marks text as a level-six header (smallest)
<Head>	</Head>	Defines the head of the page
<I>	</I>	Italicizes text
<OL>	</OL>	Makes a numbered list
<Pre>	</Pre>	Leaves text as preformatted (with spaces)
<Title>	</Title>	Sets enclosed text as the title of the page
<UL>	</UL>	Makes an unnumbered list

TIP I didn't list them all, but header tags actually go from 1-6, as in <H3>, <H4>, and so on. They simply define different levels, or sizes, of header text.

All of these tags require both the on and off tags to work properly. In between the tags, type the text that you want affected.

Empty tags

The other type of tags we come across are **empty tags**, meaning they do something all by themselves; they require no text to work on. They also have no off tag; they act once and then are ignored. Table 20.2 lists some common empty tags.

Table 20.2 Common HTML empty tags and their functions

Empty tag	What it does
 	Line break (enters a Return)
<HR>	Horizontal rule (draws a line)
<IMG SRC="filename">	Displays a file as an image
<LI>	A bullet (UL lists) or a number (OL lists)
<P>	Creates a new paragraph

You can see that these tags aren't really designed to directly affect text—they stand alone.

Creating an HTML page

There are certain elements that nearly every HTML page should have. These include a title, header, and body section. Every time you create a new HTML page, you'll need to include these enclosing tags, and some text to go along with them. So why not set up a template (see fig. 20.4)?

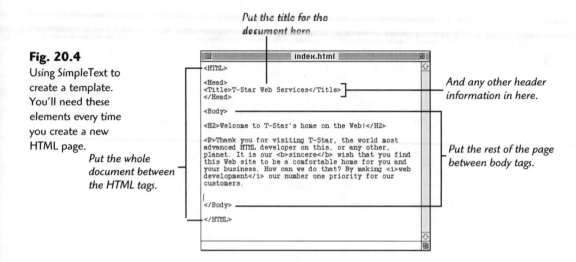

Fig. 20.4
Using SimpleText to create a template. You'll need these elements every time you create a new HTML page.

Put the title for the document here.

And any other header information in here.

Put the whole document between the HTML tags.

Put the rest of the page between body tags.

In your HTML editor, create a template like the one shown in figure 20.4. Then choose File, Save As, and save this page as template.html, or something similar. Now, whenever you go to create a new page, you can load this template and use the Save As command to give it a new name.

TIP **The <title> tag tells most Web browsers the name of your page—** it's what the browser puts at the top of its window. It's also what is used to name Bookmarks in Netscape. So make it as descriptive as possible.

Entering text for your page

From the template, you use the Save As command to create a page called **index.html**. This is the default for your Web site. (Don't forget to save the file in the folder you'll be using for all of your Web work.) Then, you start by giving your HTML page an appropriate title in the head of the HTML page.

Now, in the body section of your sample HTML page, start by entering a paragraph of text. Of course, every page will be different, but most new HTML writers start with a lot of text and fewer images. This is the most basic HTML coding—it's just text with a few enclosing tags for emphasis (see fig. 20.5).

Pick a good title for your page.

Fig. 20.5
The start of a sample
page. It's just text, so
far, but it still requires
some HTML codes.

*Here's a
(level 2)
header.*

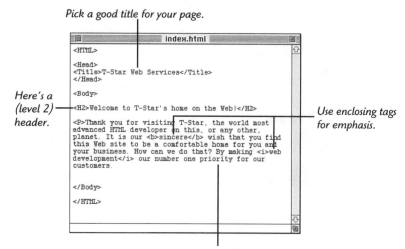

```
                    index.html
<HTML>

<Head>
<Title>T-Star Web Services</Title>
</Head>

<Body>

<H2>Welcome to T-Star's home on the Web!</H2>

<P>Thank you for visiting T-Star, the world most
advanced HTML developer on this, or any other,
planet. It is our <b>sincere</b> wish that you find
this Web site to be a comfortable home for you and
your business. How can we do that? By making <i>web
development</i> our number one priority for our
customers.

</Body>

</HTML>
```

*Use enclosing tags
for emphasis.*

Type text in the body section.

Notice that you start with a <P> paragraph symbol. HTML doesn't recognize any additional spaces or Returns you type in the text editor. All the words will flow together like a continuous paragraph, regardless of how many times you hit the space bar or Return key. In order to create a new paragraph, you need to use the paragraph tag.

 TIP You really need paragraph tags only in basic text. HTML assumes you want a Return after header tags, list tags, horizontal line tags, and some others.

URL links revealed

Our next step will be to create some hypertext links in the sample page. Like other enclosing tags, you use the <A>,</A> anchor tags by wrapping them around text on your page. But to create the link, there's something else you need to do with these tags.

 Plain English, please!

These are called **anchor tags** because they connect this page with another one somewhere on the Internet. Anchor tags simply help you create hypertext links on your page. **99**

For a hypertext link to another document or file, you need to at least know the name of the document (if it's a "local file" in the current folder). If you're linking to a document that's out on the Web, you need to know the full URL, including the complete name of the HTML document. Then you need to form the link correctly. Here's a sample link:

<A HREF="document.html">Click here to move on</A>

The HREF parameter is used to tell the anchor tag what sort of link this is: it's a link to another document. With this particular link, there should be a file named document.html in your Web folder on Mac's hard drive. If it were a link to a document at another Web site, you'd need the complete URL (see fig. 20.6).

Fig. 20.6

Different types of anchor tags for different hypertext links. Notice that you can wrap an anchor tag around another enclosing tag.

A link to a "local" HTML page.

An anchor tag pointing to a remote site.

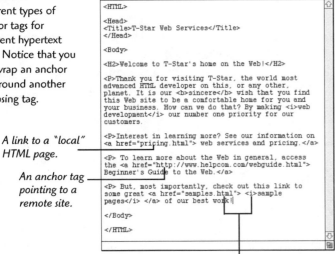

```
                    index.html
<HTML>

<Head>
<Title>T-Star Web Services</Title>
</Head>

<Body>

<H2>Welcome to T-Star's home on the Web!</H2>

<P>Thank you for visiting T-Star, the world most
advanced HTML developer on this, or any other,
planet. It is our <b>sincere</b> wish that you find
this Web site to be a comfortable home for you and
your business. How can we do that? By making <i>web
development</i> our number one priority for our
customers.

<P>Interest in learning more? See our information on
<a href="pricing.html"> web services and pricing.</a>

<P> To learn more about the Web in general, access
the <a href="http://www.helpcom.com/webguide.html">
Beginner's Guide to the Web.</a>

<P> But, most importantly, check out this link to
some great <a href="samples.html"> <i>sample
pages</i> </a> of our best work.

</Body>

</HTML>
```

An anchor around italic text.

Aside from local and remote links, there's a third type of anchor tag you can create: label links. These allow you to create a link to somewhere else on the same page. You do this by creating two separate anchor tags. For the first one, type something like:

<A HREF="#keyword">Click here to go elsewhere on this page.</A>

The keyword can be anything, but you need the # sign to tell it that this is a label link. Now you need to put the actual label somewhere in your document, like this:

<A NAME="keyword">Welcome to a new section!</A>

The NAME parameter tells the anchor command that you're just creating a name for this section of the document. Unlike any other anchor tags so far, the text Welcome to a new section! would not be clickable or highlighted in any particular way. The NAME anchor is only for internal reference.

 Q&A *I've created some hypertext links in my HTML document, but they're not working. Why?*

Remember that most links require an outside filename or URL to access the new document with a link. If your filename is bad, the URL is incorrect, or your Internet connection isn't active then you'll have some trouble.

With label links, make sure that you include the # symbol with your keyword in the HREF tag, but put just the keyword in the NAME tag. Also, label links are case-sensitive. Make sure both keywords are the exact same in spelling and capitalization.

Creating lists and other nested tags

Now that you've seen how some of the HTML tags can work separately, let's put them together. Tags, working in concert, can create some pretty spiffy Web-style layouts. Don't get too carried away, but realize that you can apply more than one tag at a time.

Oh, by the way…I'm going to talk about algebra here really soon. It's just a metaphor for nesting tags—a simple example. Nothing to get all worked up about. It's just algebra. I thought you might like to know it was coming.

Lists: nesting tags on purpose

To create a list, all you need to do is use either the enclosing tags <UL>, </UL> (for an unnumbered list) or <OL>,</OL> (for a numbered list). Here's a simple list (both <UL> and <OL> work the same in this example):

```
<UL>
This text is indented one column<BR>
So is this text<BR>
</UL>
```

You can see where this particular tag already has some nesting going on. While the <UL> tag is still in effect, I've thrown some <BR> tags in there to get line breaks. It's very similar to adding bulleted points to your list:

```
This is a bullet listing<BR>
<UL>
<LI> Here's the first bulleted point
<LI> Here's the second
</UL>
```

And, for a numbered list, an example would be:

```
This is a numbered listing<BR>
<OL>
<LI> Here's the first numbered point
<LI> Here's the second
</OL>
```

What does that look like with a browser? Check it out in figure 20.7.

Fig. 20.7
Creating lists in HTML.
Notice that you nest
the <LI> tag within the
<UL> and <OL> tags.

*This is the
bulleted list.*

*This is the
numbered list.*

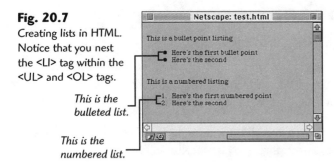

So, creating a list is one good reason to nest tags within one another, but it was designed for that, wasn't it? What happens when you start nesting tags *more or less* at random?

Nesting other tags

Let's start with *less* at random. We'll also start with a quick algebra refresher course. Here goes.

Remember in algebra how you get a different answer according to how you place parentheses in a problem? For example, (x * y + z) is completely different from x * (y + z).

You do need to watch how you nest your tags, or things can get really confusing. The best rule of thumb is: *start first, finish last.* You need to finish the tags that are nested in other tags first, then finish the outside tag. Like this:

<A HREF="filename.html"><I>Italicized link!</I></A>

In the example, I've decided that I want the text to not only be a hypertext link, but I also want it to appear in italic. I need to finish the italic tag first, though. Then I can move on to the </A> to close out the anchor tag.

Q&A ***Everything looks like you explained, but my nested tags still aren't working. What did I do?***

Not all nested tags will work as you hoped. For instance, many browsers won't show text as both bold and italic, so <b><i> text </i></b>, although formatted correctly, will often only return italic text. Also, multiple <P> and <BR> tags are often ignored by browsers. Use the <PRE>,</PRE> tags (with a few Returns in between the two) to add space on a page.

Adding images to your sample page

You've got a decent-looking page so far and, believe it or not, it's doing most of what any good page needs to do on the Web. It's communicating information and using hypertext links to connect to itself to other pages in your Web site or out on the Internet somewhere. Just look at it in figure 20.8. I mean, you're just about done!

Fig. 20.8
Your sample Web page
through the eyes of
Netscape. Formatted
text, links...what else
can there be?

Okay so it's a little bland. There's text, and it's good. But maybe it's not enough. Let's add some images.

Where to get the images for your page

Ever heard of a Mac program called Adobe PhotoShop? That's where the *real* pros get their images. Before that, they get them from flatbed scanners, digital cameras, or art-studio programs like Adobe Illustrator. So where can you get yours? In the same places, if you have them. If not, any program that creates GIF or JPEG graphics will do.

CAUTION **Even though many, many graphics are available for downloading** on the Internet, they may not all be public domain. It's against the law to use copyrighted material for publication—even on a personal Web page. Do so at your own risk.

I guess I'll use PhotoShop, but I'm just going to create a logo—I don't have the time or talent to go shoot some digital photographs. I'll just create a quick graphic in PhotoShop, then save it to my Web site folder as a GIF or JPEG (see fig. 20.9).

Fig. 20.9

Some of the best graphics for Web pages are graphics you create. (Graphics I create are another story completely.)

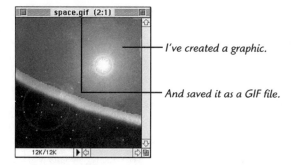

— I've created a graphic.

— And saved it as a GIF file.

Once you have the graphic stored correctly in your Web folder, you can create a tag for that image file in the text of your HTML page, following the format:

<img src="*filename.ext*">

"*filename*" is the name of the graphic file and "*ext*" is a three-letter extension (either .gif or .jpg). This extension business is really for the benefit of folks using non-Mac computers out there—the tag will work without it. By the way, **img** stands for image and **src** stands for source.

Notice, too, that <img src> is an empty tag. It doesn't require on and off tags or any other information. Like text, however, an image *can* be enclosed by an anchor tag. That's how you get clickable graphics on your page (see fig. 20.10).

Fig. 20.10

Including images in your sample HTML page. Now things are starting to get jazzed.

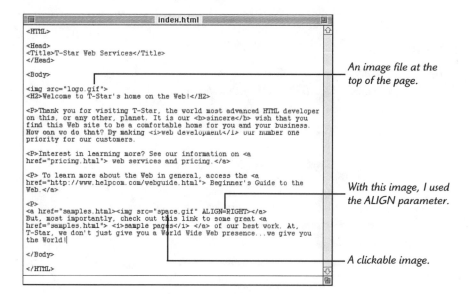

— An image file at the top of the page.

— With this image, I used the ALIGN parameter.

— A clickable image.

The <img src> tag, like some others, can take a few different parameters to change the way it appears on the screen. Most often used with this tag is the ALIGN parameter, as follows:

<img src="*filename.ext*" ALIGN=TOP>

The HTML standard allows you to set ALIGN to TOP, MIDDLE, or BOTTOM. It's aligning in reference to the text that surrounds it—not the page itself. Netscape extends the ALIGN to include RIGHT and CENTER, which are in reference to the page, but won't necessarily work with browsers other than Netscape.

Q&A   ***How can I view my HTML pages in Netscape?***

If you're ready to test your HTML page, first save it in SimpleText (you don't have to close it). Then, with Netscape active, pull down the File menu and Choose Open, File. In the dialog box, find the HTML file you want to test and click Load. If it's properly formatted, it should appear in the browser window.

Web images: bigger is not always best

There's one thing that's more important than anything else you can say about graphic images on the Web. It's more important than color. More important than light. More important than composition.

It's file size. With so many 14.4Kbps or slower modems out there trying to chug along the Web (surfing their little hearts out!) you've got to keep the file size of your graphics to an absolute minimum. Even at 28.8Kbps, a 30-kilobyte graphic (by no means large) takes ten to fifteen seconds of transfer time.

So how do you make images smaller? If you're using a program like Photoshop, you'll probably need to learn a whole lot about it before you're

competing against the experts. But, here are a few tips.

- *Use the JPEG format.* It compresses tighter than GIF, although GIFs tend to look better.

- *Use lower color-depth.* Use an 8-bit or lower color palette. 16- or 24-bit color is too much for small graphics anyway—that color information just wastes download time.

- *Crop the image.* Communicate *only* what you need to with the image. Cut it to the bare minimum and leave the beautiful background for your print advertising.

Getting your Web page on the WWW

After you've designed your Web pages and created all of the graphics to go along with them, you'll probably want your work of art displayed in front of the Internet community as a whole. Right? You're ready for primetime.

But how do you get your Web pages on the Web? You need a server. And you get *that* from the people who bring you all your other servers—your Internet Service Provider.

What is this going to cost?

I've seen many creative ways to charge for Web server space, some more in favor of the customer and others a big help to the ISP. What's reasonable? Kinda depends. There are two important considerations from the ISP's point of view:

- *How much disk space do you need?* The typical user's Web page will probably only be a few pages of text and a few graphics. Maybe 100 kilobytes total. That's not so bad. But a large corporate online catalog could run in the tens of megabytes. So, many ISPs charge based on the amount of disk space used.

- *How popular will the site be?* If your dream Web site is entitled, "The Capitalization of e.e. cummings," you probably won't get enough visitors a month to tie up a pair of shoes—much less an Internet connection. But that same corporate online catalog (if it's the next Lands' End) could make monkeys out of the ISP technicians. So, ISPs often charge based on the number of **hits**, or visits, that the site receives each week or month.

For a typical, run-of-the-mill personal Web site, it's reasonable to pay between $5 and $25 per month for your ISP to display the page. (If they design the page or update it, they'll definitely charge you more.) Business and corporate sites can expect to pay more. But they can expect more service, too.

 TIP **Some ISPs offer Web server space as an incentive to get you as a** customer. Look for Web server promotions for little or no charge in addition to your Internet account—especially if you live in a large city.

How do I get my files from here to there?

You usually create and update your Web site using FTP, although I've come across some providers who prefer that you use a shell account (Telnet, for example) to access the file system. Let's assume you're using FTP.

If you've set up your Web folder as recommended, then you should have no problem simply transferring the contents of your Web folder to the directory that's been set aside for you on the Web server (see fig. 20.11). Where is this directory? You'll have to ask your ISP. Some of them will create a directory called /users/*username* for every customer who has a Web page.

Fig. 20.11
My Web site's files, all in one nice, neat folder. Now it'll be a snap to upload to my provider.

However they do it, your ISP should provide a standard way for you to access and save your pages on the Web server. Some may even make you learn some UNIX. Yuck.

The last word: design tips

Honestly, we haven't covered half of what's possible with HTML. But you have seen the basics, and that's really all you need to get started. If you have a reasonably priced opportunity to get yourself up on the Web with your own page, I'd definitely recommend it. It can be a lot of fun, a great way to make contacts, and it definitely shows some Internet savvy.

With what we do know, however, it's still possible to create some truly hideous Web pages. Here are a few recommendations:

- *Concentrate on your text.* So maybe I'm a writer, but I can't stand to see typos, poor grammar, and misspellings on Web pages. Yes, it's an electronic medium, but it's still text. Keep it clean and snappy.

- *Be creative but stingy with graphics.* Keep your graphics simple and small but cleverly pepper them throughout the text. Never include graphics *just* for the heck of it. Be considerate of your modem-based browsers.

- *Do you need a front door?* While there really aren't many rules on the Web, it's a good idea to create a **front door page** if the material you're presenting may be offensive to someone (see fig. 20.12). Even if it's only strong language, let users know with a disclaimer and a link to your index page. If they click the link, apparently they want in.

Fig. 20.12
A sample "front door" page.

- *Consider creating a text-only alternative.* Another reason for a front door page is to let your browsers choose whether or not to see your graphics. You can easily duplicate all of the links and text of your site without the graphics, and make it available to users with a link from the front door.

- *Keep a solid text-to-link ratio.* If everything on your page is a link, then arrange it in a bulleted or numbered list. Otherwise, make sure there's some useful text in between links. A paragraph of underlined color is not only difficult to read, it's ugly.

- *Shop for ideas.* Look at some Web pages before you create your own. You'll quickly get a feeling for what sells and what doesn't. Learn from the mistakes of others, and you'll have a great site to show off your new HTML talents!

21

Finding Cool Sites (or Anything Else) on the Internet

● **In this chapter:**

● **Choosing the best Internet service for the job**

● **How do I search for stuff on the Web?**

● **Is there any way to search the entire Internet?**

● **I'm not sure what I'm looking for— the Internet should have a table of contents!**

Surfing the Internet is fun when you're playing around, but unbearable when you're on a deadline. Isn't there a faster way to find stuff?. . . . . ➤

Now that we've seen all of the different services that the Internet has to offer, we're left with two dilemmas. The first one is that *we still like to watch television.* Sorry, but there's nothing I can do. You might as well give it up now…you'll never again see another episode of *Mad About You.*

The other dilemma is, *which service do I use for what?* Some of the best fun you'll ever have on the Internet is when you've got absolutely nothing better to do, and you're ready to kill some time. But some of the worst headaches you'll experience will come when you're trying to quickly find some specific *something* on the Internet.

Trying to find a particular answer in those billions of pages and files of digital information is a little like trying to find food in a modern supermarket. It may be out there somewhere, but you'll have to wade through a lot of gardening equipment and auto supplies to find it.

Type of information = Internet service

The first thing you need to consider is the type of information you are looking for. That can go a long way toward helping you determine what Internet service is most appropriate for your search.

Most of the Internet services were initially conceived to answer a very specific problem. E-mail, for instance, was designed for personal communications. UseNet was created for collaborative discussion. The World Wide Web was created for electronic publication. Knowing that, and understanding how each service has evolved, will help you figure out which service is best for your particular search.

Let's look at all of the different Internet services and try to get a handle on which is designed for what. We'll follow the order that they were presented in this book:

- **Electronic mail.** For the most part, e-mail is designed for communicating with a specific person or group of people. If the best way to get information is to ask someone who knows—and you know that person's e-mail address—send an e-mail.

- **Mailing lists**. Mailing lists are designed to be read regularly. It's difficult to find a specific answer in one, since the conversations tend to move on from day to day. That said, however, you might find that a mailing list is the easiest place to find people with special knowledge concerning a particular topic—especially for hobbyists, enthusiasts, and professionals. If that's the case, then post your question and hope you get an answer relatively soon.

 TIP   **For both mailing lists and UseNet, sometimes the best place to** find an answer to a specific question is in the FAQ. Don't forget to look there first before asking in the group.

- **FTP**. While FTP is all about files, you can still often find answers to difficult questions as documents to download. What type of answers? Documentation and tips for computer applications, FAQs, scientific papers and studies, entertainment and book reviews, and electronic books.

- **Gopher**. Gopher holds somewhat unique status in the Internet world, if only because it's more static than many of the other services. The Web has taken over many of the duties formerly relegated to Gopher. A lot of what's left on Gopher is at universities, so you'll find that academic answers abound. If you're looking for dissertations, research results, position papers, and other studies, try Gopher. You'll have especially good luck if you're looking for info that's a few years old. You'll come across some hobby-related material too, but not nearly as much.

- **UseNet newsgroups**. Like mailing lists, UseNet newsgroups are designed for continuing conversations. But unlike mailing lists, UseNet threads are available anytime for you to peruse with your newsreader. That makes finding answers a little easier. UseNet covers an amazing breadth of topics, and groups tend to have folks with specialized knowledge. If it's not in the FAQ and no one else has asked it recently, post your question.

- **IRC channels**. More than any of the other services, IRC is designed more for diversion than dissemination. But that doesn't mean you can't find an answer. If your question is one that will fit in a particular group, like #macintosh, IRC is a great place to get an instant answer to your question.

- **The World Wide Web.** This should be your starting point for most types of answers. In my opinion, your "searching" options are among the best of Internet services, and the breadth of content is unparalleled. Many universities and goverment agencies have pushed their information to the Web; and thousands of corporations have begun their Internet presence here. Not to mention the number of hobbyists and enthusiasts who've created their own pages. Even if the information *is* on another service, it may have a link on the World Wide Web.

Searching on the World Wide Web

The Web should probably be the place where you start most of your searches—unless you're absolutely sure that another Internet service is a much better option. In fact, the only caveat to my recommendation is this: even though the Web is "interactive," it's still used primarily for one-way communication. Occasionally, you will be better off going directly to UseNet, mailing lists, or IRC for one-on-one discussions with experts.

But for nearly any other type of information, the Web is the way to go. And that's the crux of our paradox here. The Web is such a valuable resource, but its very nature makes it very difficult to find things on the Web. With no logical hierarchy (like Gopher), where do you go?

The Netscape search pages

The best place for those of us using Netscape is right under the URL field in Netscape's window, behind a button called Net Search. Click once on that button and you're whisked gently away to one of the most useful pages on the Web (see fig. 21.1).

 TIP **Most other browser home pages offer a similar link, but it's** up to you to find it. Look for links to Internet search pages, InfoSeek, WebCrawler, or any of the other specific sites we talk about in this section.

Fig. 21.1
The Netscape search pages. If you're looking for something on the Web (or even on UseNet), here's the place to start.

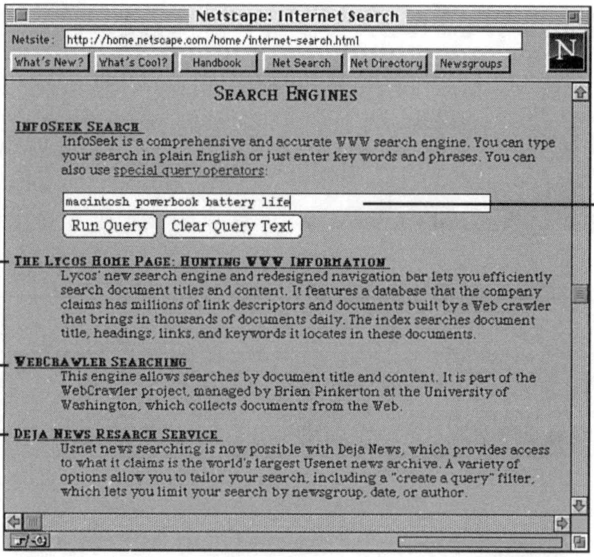

Link to Lycos Web Search.

Link to WebCrawler.

Search UseNet newsgroups.

The InfoSeek keyword field.

What are these **search engines**? Most of them are designed to poll the Web, gathering tidbits of information on every page they encounter, which is then used to try and match your search request. Others require that Web page creators **register** their pages with them, sending descriptions and keywords for the search. Depending on the search engine, you're probably searching millions of possible Web pages. Even if that's only a fraction of what's available, you're likely to find something that gets you closer to your goal.

 Plain English, please!

A **search engine** is a program designed to search a database for matches. Although the actual program is hidden from view, each of these Web search pages allows you to enter words you want to search for, then it accesses a program that searches a database of available Web pages for those that match your criteria. **99**

By way of an informal test, I'll try to search each of these engines for information on extending the battery life of the Macintosh Powerbook-series computers. It's probably not a scientific comparison of the capabilities of the engines, but it'll give you a good idea of how they work.

The InfoSeek search engine

Netscape makes it clear which engine you should try first—the InfoSeek search field is right there on the search page itself. How do you use this? Just type in a search phrase (with AND, OR, or NOT operators, if desired) and click once on Run Query. In a moment, InfoSeek will return a list of up to 100 different Web links for you to try (see fig. 21.2).

Fig. 21.2
A search with the InfoSeek Web search engine.

Click new search to try again.

Click the link to see the Web page.

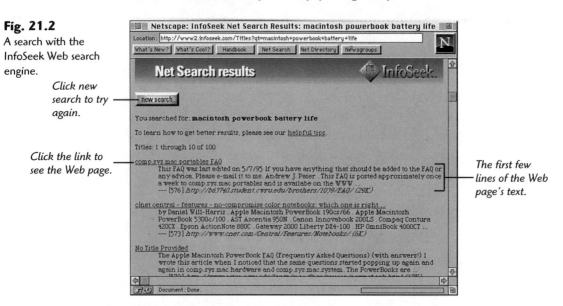

The first few lines of the Web page's text.

The result of the search generates up to 100 links to different pages, which may or may not meet our search criteria. It also shows the first few lines of text on the page, just so we can get a feel for what's being said. To follow any of them, just click once on the link. You can use the Back button or your Netscape History to return to the InfoSeek listing.

If this search doesn't yield decent results, you can try again with the New Search button. Click once and you're presented with the Web page in figure 21.3.

TIP **Notice that this is the actual InfoSeek search page. The previous** page was Netscape's interface to InfoSeek. I'd recommend creating a bookmark for the search page so you can go directly to it for searches. In fact, it's a good idea to create a separate bookmark for all of the Internet search engines discussed in this chapter.

Fig. 21.3
The actual InfoSeek search page. Here you can not only search, but follow links in a directory of cool sites.

These links lead you to pre-selected "Cool Sites."

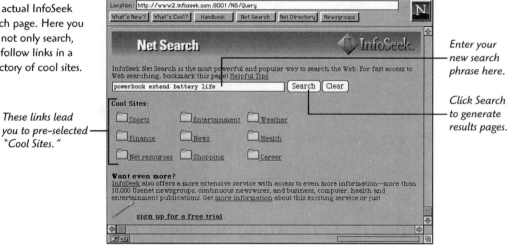

Enter your new search phrase here.

Click Search to generate results pages.

Enter a new search phrase (just try something a little different), and click once on Search to send the InfoSeek engine into motion. You'll get up to 100 more links to possible matches. Follow any links that seem promising!

The Lycos search engine

From the Netscape search page, click once on the link to Lycos. You're shown a single search field, where you can enter a search phrase and set Lycos in motion. If you're using Netscape, however, I recommend that you click once on the Search Options link. That gives you a Web form for entering your search phrase, as pictured in figure 21.4.

Fig. 21.4
This form uses pop-up menus to help you decide exactly how the Lycos search will work.

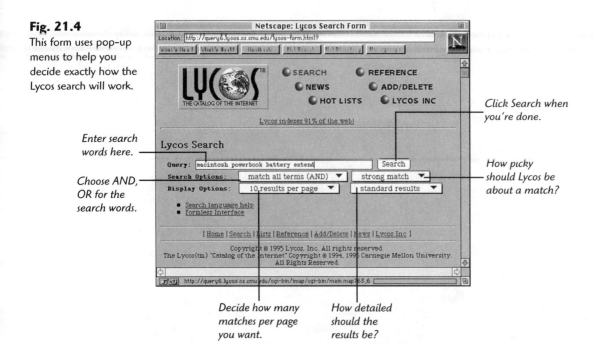

Enter search words here.

Choose AND, OR for the search words.

Click Search when you're done.

How picky should Lycos be about a match?

Decide how many matches per page you want.

How detailed should the results be?

Using this convenient format, you can easily set your preferences for a Lycos search. This is a great way to narrow the possibilities. If, for instance, I tell Lycos to match all of my search words, and I make it a strong match, then I'm not likely to get anything but an answer to my question.

If Lycos is having trouble finding something, I can set things to be a little more loosely matched and be given many more choices of Web sites. Then it's up to me to follow up links and see if any of those sites have the answers I'm looking for (see fig. 21.5).

The Loose Match search netted over 400 resulting links to look into, but that will take some time. It's probably a better idea to try another search phrase, or go for something in the middle (like a good match of three keywords). The links that Lycos does find are available by scrolling down the browser window.

Fig. 21.5
Left: a strong match search, matching all keywords. Right: a loose match search, matching only two keywords.

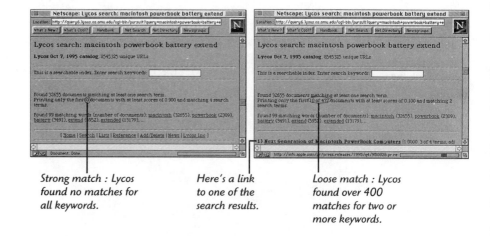

Strong match : Lycos found no matches for all keywords.

Here's a link to one of the search results.

Loose match : Lycos found over 400 matches for two or more keywords.

WebCrawler search engine

So far, it seems like I've thrown a tough one at these Web search engines. That's not terribly surprising, since Macintosh and PowerBook are commonly found words on the Web. Let's give it one more try with WebCrawler.

From the Netscape search page, scroll down to the WebCrawler link and click it once. On the WebCrawler search page, enter some keywords for your search and use the pop-up menus to decide how many keywords to match (either ALL or ANY) and how many results WebCrawler will show (10, 25, or 100).

Q&A *Every time I send a new search phrase, I get a message from Netscape that says I'm sending my information over an unsecure connection. Can I safely stop the message from appearing?*

Yes. If you click Don't show again, it will just turn off the message for this site. You'll still get the warning on new pages.

Click Search; WebCrawler will begin the search, giving you a results page, as shown in figure 21.6.

Fig. 21.6
WebCrawler only gives
you the titles of the
pages found, no
descriptions. But is
that so bad?

Here are the
first of 100
links.

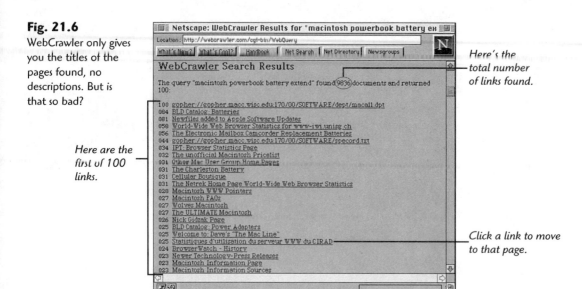

Here's the
total number
of links found.

Click a link to move
to that page.

I like this approach a whole lot. Most of the other search engines give you all
of that description along with the pages, and it takes a while to wade through.
Not here, though. Just click the title of a page and start searching.

By the way, when I used the ALL choice on the WebCrawler search page,
I got nothing. This listing (see fig. 21.6) is the result from an ANY search,
which means that most of these links are probably not helping much. I'd be
better off taking out really common words like Macintosh, and focusing on
Powerbook and battery in my next search phrase.

Searching UseNet: DejaNews

Our last try from the Netscape search page will be DejaNews, a search engine
for UseNet newsgroups. This is an interesting one to watch because we've
moved away from searching Web pages and onto UseNet. It's also where
we'll get our best results for this particular search.

Why do I say that? It goes back to considering the *type* of information we're
seeking. It's certainly plausible to believe that someone has set up a Web
page that talks about Powerbook battery life. But it's much more likely that
someone has asked that question, and a conversation has developed concerning it, on UseNet.

Click the DejaNews link to get to its Web site, then click the Search link at the top of the page (just under the advertisement). Now you've got the DejaNews search page, as shown in figure 21.7. This is a great page for a bookmark!

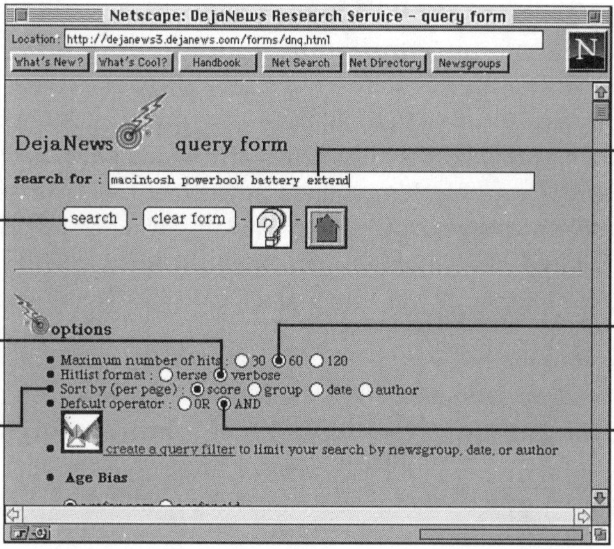

Fig. 21.7
The DejaNews search page. Any chance of finding the answer on UseNet?

Click here to search.

How much description?

Choose how to sort the results.

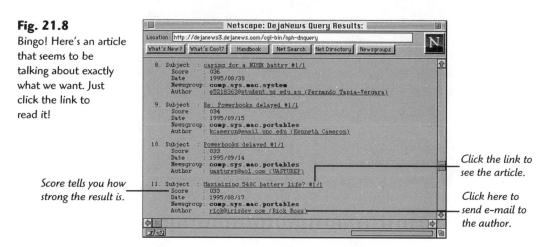

Enter keywords for the search.

Click the radio button for the maximum number of links.

Search for ALL keywords or ANY?

Here's the moment of truth. Once you've set all the parameters you're interested in for your search, click the Search button to send it to DejaNews. The result is a listing of UseNet articles (see fig. 21.8).

Fig. 21.8
Bingo! Here's an article that seems to be talking about exactly what we want. Just click the link to read it!

Score tells you how strong the result is.

Click the link to see the article.

Click here to send e-mail to the author.

See what I mean? This Powerbook battery thing was definitely a question for UseNet. But, without DejaNews, it would have taken quite some time to sift through all the articles in comp.sys.mac.portables to find an answer.

The Net directory: Yahoo!

We've discussed countless different ways to search for information on the Internet. And, true to form, I've saved the very best for last. It's called Yahoo, and it's probably the most exhaustive attempt at classifying Internet resources available. It's not quite a complete Table of Contents to the Internet, but it's a good start. This brainchild of David Filo and Dr. Jerry Yang (when grad students at Stanford) has exploded into the most sought-after Directory of the Internet. If your site is listed in Yahoo, you've arrived.

Next to the Net Search button on Netscape's interface, choose the Net Directory button to move to Netscape's directory resources, then click the Yahoo link (the direct URL for Yahoo is **http://www.yahoo.com/**). Set your Netscape bookmark for this page, if desired. Now you're at the index (default) page for Yahoo's Web site, ready to find some stuff (see fig. 21.9).

Fig. 21.9
You can search with Yahoo, but that's not the main point. Much more gratifying are the directory links.

Enter a search phrase here to search Yahoo.

Or click a link in the directory.

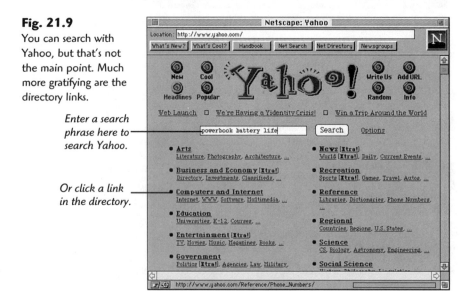

Yahoo can handle typical search keywords, separated by spaces, or you can click the Options link next to the search field for a more detailed search. But more often, you'll probably want to use the Yahoo directory to get at things in a more organized fashion. It's a little more like "shopping" for the best links, but chances are good that you'll find something interesting.

To move along to the next menu level, click its link. As you dig deeper into the directory, you'll begin to see links to actual sites around the world. This is part of the charm of using the Yahoo directory instead of searching. There's more of a chance you'll come across something you didn't think of before in these menus (see fig. 21.10).

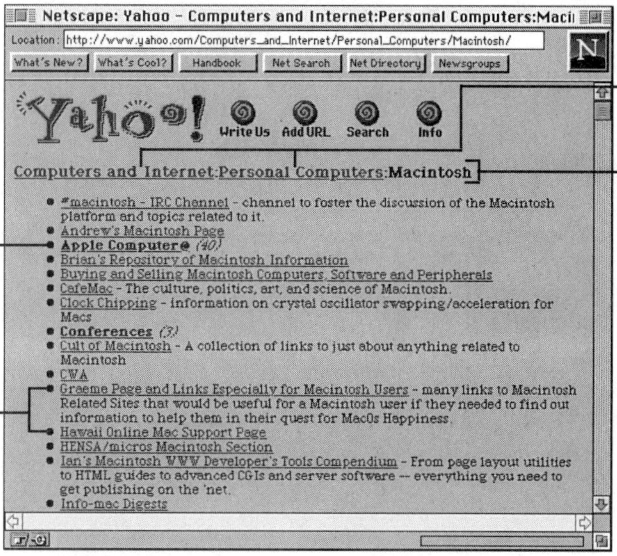

Fig. 21.10
Digging deeper into the Yahoo directory to find something interesting. Doesn't this feel a little like Gopher?

These links will take you back to previous menus.

Here's how far I've gone in the directory.

This one is another menu level.

And here are links to different Web sites.

Now I haven't come across anything specific about PowerBook battery life yet, but all of these links are interesting. It seems that there are a number of ways to get at information that I hadn't really considered before.

Was it covered in a back issue of a Mac-related magazine? Try that menu. Would there be any info on battery life in the Mac user group areas? Try that, too.

Get out there and have some fun!

Hopefully, you'll come up with some better reasons to search the Internet with these and other tools (as described in the chapters on e-mail, mailing lists, UseNet, and Gopher) than extending PowerBook's battery life. But whatever your reason for seeking something, I only hope that ye shall find it.

If you don't...create it yourself. Once you do find the answer, put it on your home page, e-mail it to people, chat about it on IRC, or send it through UseNet to some other lost soul. Ultimately, that's the point. If the Internet is to be the next great society—ignoring political boundaries, bringing together millions around the world, and making information as easy to access as oxygen—then we all need to work at it together.

Go then into cyberspace, turn the lights down, play some soft music, order a pizza, and step into your most comfortable slippers. Then fire up your Internet connection, unlock your imagination, and, by all means, *interact*!

Index

DejaNews
(newsgroups),
288-290
InfoSeek, 284-285
Lycos, 285-287
WebCrawler, 287-288
**search phrases,
NetFind (Internet
service directory), 93**
**searching Yahoo
directory, 290-291**
see also finding
**security, Netscape,
231**
**self-extracting
archives (files), 140**
**Send File command
(Mail menu), 82**
**sending e-mail
messages,** *see*
posting messages
**Serial Line Interface
Protocol (SLIP), 34,
40-41**
servers
Archie, 150-151
defined, 28
service providers,
41-42
**service providers
(ISPs)**
connections, 40-42
closing, 59-60
opening, 57-59
troubleshooting,
58-59
defined, 20, 40
fees, 44-45
avoiding, 45-46
local, 42-43
national, 43
selection criteria,
43-47
servers, 41-42
services, 16
see also online
services

**SET listname ACK
command (mailing
lists), 127**
**SET listname
command (mailing
lists), 127**
**SET listname DIGests
command (Mailing
lists), 127**
**SET listname INDex
command (Mailing
lists), 127**
**SET listname NOACK
command (mailing
lists), 127**
**SET listname NOMail
command (mailing
lists), 127**
**SET listname
NOREPro command
(mailing lists), 127**
**SET listname REPro
command (mailing
lists), 127**
shareware
Anarchie, 143
defined, 15
Homer (IRC), 202
shell accounts, 32-33
shopping, 13
**Show All Newsgroups
command (Options
menu), 254**
**signatures (e-mail
messages), 105-106**
**Signature command
(Window menu), 106**
SIGNOFF *
**(NETWIDE)
command (mailing
lists), 127**
**SIGNOFF * command
(mailing lists), 127**
**SIGNOFF listname
command (mailing
lists), 127**
SimpleText, 248

**singing, VOCALIST
(mailing list), 117**
.sit files, 139
sites
FTP
Apple Support
Archives, 134-135
defined, 132
finding, 133-136
INFO-MAC FTP
Sites, 134-135
University of
Michigan Mac
Archives, 134-135
University of Texas
Mac Archives,
134-135
University of
Washington Mac/
Internet Archives,
134-135
mirror sites, defined,
74
World Wide Web
default page, 222
defined, 220
fees, 275
hits, 275
**SLIP (Serial Line
Interface Protocol),
34, 40-41**
**Small Business
Resource Center, 10**
**.soc (social issues
newsgroup), 170**
software
freeware, Ircle (IRC),
202
front-end, defined, 70
NewsWatcher,
downloading, 180
shareware
Anarchie, 143
defined, 15
Homer (IRC), 202
**SoundApp (helper
application), 247-248**
setup, 248-250

PLUG YOURSELF INTO...

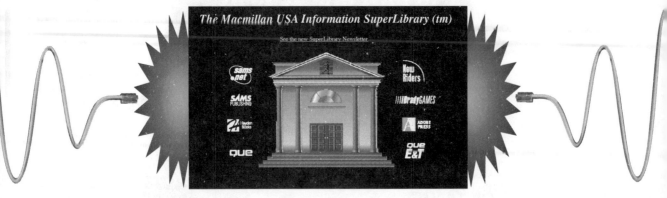

THE MACMILLAN
INFORMATION SUPERLIBRARY™

Free information and vast computer resources from the world's leading computer book publisher—online!

FIND THE BOOKS THAT ARE RIGHT FOR YOU!
A complete online catalog, plus sample chapters and tables of contents!

● **STAY INFORMED** with the latest computer industry news through our online newsletter, press releases, and customized Information SuperLibrary Reports.

● **GET FAST ANSWERS** to your questions about QUE books.

● **VISIT** our online bookstore for the latest information and editions!

● **COMMUNICATE** with our expert authors through e-mail and conferences.

● **DOWNLOAD SOFTWARE** from the immense Macmillan Computer Publishing library:
      - Source code, shareware, freeware, and demos

● **DISCOVER HOT SPOTS** on other parts of the Internet.

● **WIN BOOKS** in ongoing contests and giveaways!

TO PLUG INTO QUE:

WORLD WIDE WEB: **http://www.mcp.com/que**

FTP: ftp.mcp.com

User-Friendly References for All Your Computing Needs

Que's *USING* Series

For the fastest access to the one best way to get things done, check out other *Using* books from Que! These user-friendly references give you just what you need to know to be productive—plus no-nonsense tips and shortcuts in plain English. Whatever the topic, there's a *Using* book to ensure computer confidence!

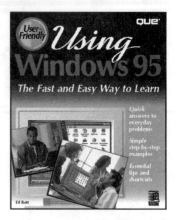

User Identification Level

New   Casual   Accomplished   Expert

Que's *SPECIAL EDITION USING* Series

For accomplished users who desire in-depth coverage, *Special Edition Using* books are the most comprehensive references. These books contain professional tips and advice—as well as valuable tools and software—to optimize results with all major hardware and software topics.

User Identification Level

New   Casual   Accomplished   Expert

Look for **Using** *books and* **Special Edition Using** *books at your favorite bookstore!*

How to Use the MacNet Disk

The programs on the disk are all compressed, or "stuffed" files. Simply load StuffIt Expander onto your hard drive, and you'll be able to extract the other files from the disk. StuffIt Expander is itself a compressed file, but is self-extracting (double-clicking on its icon begins its decompression and it walks you through its install procedure). It creates a folder for itself on your hard drive and an alias on your desktop.

Drag the "stuffed" files from the disk to a folder on your hard drive to copy them onto your hard drive. Drag the copied file onto the StuffIt Expander alias to start the decompression process; the program will be unstuffed into the folder where they were copied. Simply repeat the process with all the programs and files found on the disk.